Blues to Blessings
Moving from Fearful to Faithful

By Suzette Webb
Edited by Ashley Y. Ludgood

Blues to Blessings™

Blues to Blessings: Moving from Fearful to Faithful
Copyright © 2017 by Suzette Webb

SECOND EDITION

International Standard Book Number: 978-0-9961127-2-7
Library of Congress Control Number: 2017914182

Names: Webb, Suzette. | Ludgood, Ashley Y., editor.
Title: Blues to Blessings : Moving From Fearful to Faithful / by Suzette Webb ; edited
    by Ashley Y. Ludgood.
Description: Second edition. | Chicago, IL : Light of Mine Publishing, LLC, 2017. |
    Includes bibliographical references.
Identifiers: ISBN 978-0- 9961127-2- 7 (print) | ISBN 978-0- 9961127-3-4 (ebook)
Subjects: LCSH: Webb, Suzette— Religion. | Christian biography— United States. |
    Self-actualization (Psychology)— Religious aspects— Christianity. | Christian life.
    | LCGFT: Autobiographies.
Classification: LCC BR1725.W348 A3 2017 (print) | LCC BR1725.W348 (ebook) |
    DDC 277.3083092— dc23

Light of Mine Publishing is pleased to provide discounts for bulk orders. For more information, email customerservice@thelomgroup.com.

Scripture quotations marked (NLT) are taken from the Holy Bible, New Living Translation, copyright © 1996, 2004, 2007 by Tyndale House Foundation. Used by permission of Tyndale House Publishers, Inc., Carol Stream, Illinois 60188. All rights reserved.

Scripture quotations marked (NIV) are taken from the Holy Bible, New International Version', NIV'. Copyright © 1973, 1978, 1984, 2011 by Biblica, Inc. ™ Used by permission of Zondervan. All rights reserved worldwide. www.zondervan.com The "NIV" and "New International Version" are trademarks registered in the United States Patent and Trademark Office by Biblica, Inc.™

Scripture quotations marked (KJV) are taken from the King James Version of the Bible. Public domain.

Scripture quotations marked (ESV) are taken from the English Standard Version © 2001 by Crossway Bibles, a division of Good News Publishers.

LIGHT OF MINE PUBLISHING, LLC   *Produced in the United States of America*
401 N. Michigan Avenue   **First eBook edition:** April 2015
Suite 1200   **First print edition:** May 2015
Chicago, IL 60611   **Second print edition**: October 2017
Visit our website: www.bluestoblessings.com   **Second eBook edition:** October 2017

Dedication

This book is dedicated to those who think something is missing—may you discover that something in the arms of God.

This book is also dedicated to my mother, husband and children. Thank you for allowing me to tell your story so that I might tell my story, and fulfill what God has called me to do.

"And be not conformed to this world: but be ye transformed by the renewing of your mind, that ye may prove what is that good, and acceptable, and perfect, will of God."
Romans 12:2 KJV

Table of Contents

Acknowledgments

My Heavenly Father, I praise You and thank You for every moment of my life and for every person whom You have made an integral part of my life. I express my deepest thanks to the following people—*my angels*:

Jonathan Webb, my husband, who has supported my vision even when it seemed, at times, that I had no clear vision. My children, Joshua, Julian, Jonathan II and Leslie for their individual gestures of encouragement to pursue my life's calling, and for just being great children overall. Arnette Jones, my mother, for her tireless efforts to inspire my endeavors in countless ways and for her love. My grandmother, Mrs. Mildred Primm, whom I fondly call "Millie." Her love and character have not only paved the way for my mother and me but for generations to come. Myrna Webb, my mother-in-law, who has often sacrificed her own endeavors for the sake of our family's; and, for ensuring this independently published book was major publishing house quality. Toi Jones and Michael Moore for being the best extended family one could wish for. Mike Robinson, for being my brother both in business and in life. Bill Pickens, for always enlightening me with his spiritual wisdom and for treating me like his daughter. And, all my family in Heaven; especially, my grandfather, Bishop Howard Thomas Primm; my brother, Samuel Jones III, whom I miss and will forever love; and my two uncles, Harold Nash and George Nash, for their constancy and the indelible marks of love they left on my life.

I have learned through the years that God will never give you a vision without giving you the resources to execute that vision. My utmost thanks and gratitude to the resourceful Ashley Ludgood, my fearless and committed editor who has stood by my side, dried my tears and lifted me from the floor when necessary to press out of me this *assignment* that God placed on my belly many years ago. Special thanks to Amy Collins of New Shelves Books for her absolute professionalism, unstoppable passion and above all, un-wavering integrity, which were all imperative to the completion of this second edition. Thanks to Ann Foster and her Millennium Counseling Center team for their steadfast mission to help hurt-ing people recover their lives.

Michelle White, my dear friend whom God was working through nearly ten years ago when she gave me a crystal butterfly that still sits on my desk today. Elizabeth Labat, for your genu-ine friendship over the decades and for fiercely pushing me to-wards my dreams no matter the circumstance. Cheri Ausberry, for always knowing how to make my soul laugh when it needs it most. Joakima Blanc, for being that calming center for us all. Margie Cooper Stanton, my Sister in Christ for always expressing her truths, and giving of herself in so many ways. The one and only wicked smart Vicky Free, my friend and sister who will never be to too bright or too busy to share her time, talent and treasure with those in need. Geannine Harris, for being a true servant and impressing that upon me. Miah Leslie, for staying true to your calling. Kim Orr, for showing me resiliency through all seasons. Angelique Francis, my friend, my sister, my mirror. Even though our friendship stretches across the miles—Kim Bondy, Andrea Burleson, Carla Crawford, Carmella Haywood and Deb Jones—we are still connected.

Sheila Buralli, my friend, for forwarding me Bible verses and daily meditations for the last few years. Tom Kepler, the graphic designer, for his talent and relentless focus to please his clients. Ron Stodghill, a heavyweight among us writers, for his weighing in at those critical junctures. Gina Hilse, a special editor who always encouraged me to remain true to my voice. David Aretha, my copyeditor, whose constant pursuit of flawless copy ensured this work was ready for prime time. Elizabeth Marck, for taking the words from my heart and editing them in a way that resonates so beautifully. My son Julian, for editing certain parts of the book and giving me back my voice when I was still unsure of myself. Author and hairstylist Ehryck Gilmore, for whispering your words of wisdom to me while in your chair, and, of course, your assistant, Teri Manson. Other contributors to the **Blues to Blessings** project include: Patrick Brown, Dan Duverney, Marcus Geeter, Pamela Minter, Brett Newton, Spencer Porter, and Andre and Frances Guichard of the Guichard Gallery.

To give **Blues to Blessings** its final shape, my focus group participants gave of their time to read this book—Mi'chele Crump-Murphy, Frances Guichard, Geannine Harris, Elizabeth Labat, Leslie Lopez-Butscher, Jo Ludgood, Kim Orr, and Myrna Webb.

Finally, my debt of gratitude goes to those people and places where much of the manuscript was written and edited. Ms. Ina, of Ina's Restaurant, for creating a great space where projects of this nature could come to life. The very special Bernice and Lynn at Eppel's Restaurant, for treating me and my work with such great service, and for knowing my order better than I do. Annette Hubbard at the Golden Apple Grill for making each of my dining experiences feel like I was in your home. Wicker Park Starbucks, for having the best baristas on this side of the Mississippi. The East Bank Club, a staple in Chicago, where the final *I* was dotted, and *T* was crossed in the **Blues to Blessings** manuscript.

Author's Note

I recalled my own life experiences and consulted others who shared in some of those experiences to write this book. I also referred to previous years' personal journals. I changed the names of some individuals and omitted the names of others for anonymity purposes while maintaining the substance of my story.

Part One

Awareness

Overview

HOW AMAZING THE BUTTERFLY! The butterfly begins its life as a tiny egg on the green leaf of a plant. Eventually, this egg hatches and a caterpillar emerges. The larval stage is a stage of growth for the butterfly, and so the caterpillar spends most of its time eating and growing on the leaf of the plant on which it was hatched. What's fascinating is that certain caterpillars will only feed on certain plants; therefore, the mother butterfly must inherently sense which plant her caterpillar will want to eat. The caterpillar at this stage is too small to move to another plant, so either he's been laid on the right plant or his fate is doomed.

This soon-to-be butterfly is unconscious of the divine intelligence that has guided his mother to lay her eggs on the correct leaf. In this egg form, he is completely unaware of what potential his future holds—the endurance to fly thousands of miles and the fortitude to withstand inclement weather conditions. While the transformation process from egg to butterfly isn't an easy journey, it's a purposeful one.

Some of us are fragile and vulnerable just like the tiny egg protected by love, time, and fate. You may never know it. Picture that woman who seems to have it all together. You know this woman— Starbucks in one hand, keys to a luxury car in the other, a designer bag swung across her shoulder, and a phony smile plastered on her face that's perfectly timed to light up just as the elevator doors open in her office building. She's a master at conforming. Just as water takes on the shape of any vessel that holds it, she similarly conforms to most situations she's in—attempting to "fit in." She measures her value by what she has rather than by who she is. She allows her self-esteem to fluctuate depending on what she believes others have or have accomplished in comparison to herself. She's oblivious to the deeper meaning of what it really means to live a full and purposeful life.

Just as the butterfly egg lies in an unconscious state on the leaf that was created just for him, she too is unconscious of the divine love and intelligence that protects her, even as she *sleeps*.

Ultimately, the caterpillar becomes cramped and squeezed, and breaks through his shell to find himself surrounded by the nourishment he needs to sustain the rest of his journey. Suzette also feels cramped and squeezed by her life's circumstances and wants to break free so that she can assume the mantel of her life; however, she remains fearful of what may, or may not, lie ahead for her.

To My Readers:
A Beginner's Circle

"In the beginning God created the heavens and the earth. Now the earth was formless and empty, darkness was over the surface of the deep, and the Spirit of God was hovering over the waters." (Gen. 1:1-2 NIV)

What happens to the soul when our lives are stuck? Many seek purpose but see no progress.

These words are from my personal journal to God from March 20, 2006:

I have been praying to you daily for strength, and the last few days I haven't really prayed at all because I'm tired. I guess I'm tired of praying and not getting the results that I truly desire. My days don't even seem to be under my control or I am truly doing a poor job of managing. I know that the boys really need me now, and if I were off fulfilling my own dreams then I could not keep them on track to realizing theirs.

At the same time, a part of me wants to respect, and believe, that my life is unfolding exactly as it should. Deep down, I truly want to believe that my life has purpose, but more often, I find myself doubting if I will ever fulfill that purpose. I believe I was put on Earth to

help others, but sometimes I question if I am even qualified to do so. If I'm having so much difficulty staying on
top of the things in my own life, how in the world could
I expect to make a difference in another person's life?

My story begins a few years before I wrote this journal entry.
It was the beginning of a journey that led me to come full circle,
as my faith and trust in God was tested at each arch of the circle
through the various situations in my life. Come full circle with me
and be renewed.

May you always remember the beauty that God creates
from emptiness, darkness, and waste.

Chapter 1

Sleepwalking

IT HAS HAPPENED AGAIN: I hit the snooze button one time too many, and now it will be another morning of hustle and bustle. The boys both squirm a bit when they hear my voice, but no one is moving to get out of bed. So, I yell, "I need to see you both put your feet on the floor!"

We have three boys: Josh, Julian, and Jonathan II. When my husband, whom I frequently call by our last name, "Webb," and I met, we each had a two-year-old son. My son Julian is from my first marriage, and Webb has a son, Josh, from a previous relationship. Webb is my second husband, and after two years of marriage, we completed our family by having Jonathan II. Josh lives in upstate New York with his mother, Maria, and his stepfather, Donald, whom we are grateful to share a genuine relationship with, while Julian and Jonathan live with us. Josh is older than Julian by four months, and he never lets Julian forget it, although Julian is taller now, so he never lets Josh forget that either. I also recognize a daughter named Leslie from my first marriage. Although she is not my daughter through birth, I love her as if she were my own.

The boys have not responded to my first plea to get out of bed, so I head to their room, turn on the light, and nudge them gently to say, "Mom's in a rush this morning, so I need you to wake up now."

They both roll over.

They say, "Okay," but their bodies are still neatly tucked under the covers. I follow with, "I need to see you put your feet on the floor."

This little trick always works, because if I can get them to put their feet on the floor, it's highly unlikely they will go back to bed. Our youngest, Jonathan, responds (albeit in slow motion) like it's one of his preschool games, similar to "Simon says...put your feet on the floor," so his feet always land on the floor first.

Julian, who is in second grade, hates this tactic. He would rather I just believe his word that he won't go back to bed. While Julian is struggling to rise from his bed, I walk over to their dresser drawers and begin to coordinate their outfits for the day. If Julian is not up when I'm finished, my tone changes, and he swiftly gets his feet from underneath the covers and onto the floor. He hates it when I hover over him until I see him actually get up.

I picked the worst day to oversleep. I need extra time to figure out what to wear today, as I am presenting to one of the division heads, and my boss will be there. Furthermore, I still need to tweak the presentation deck before the meeting.

I am what some call the Diversity Police at my company. My job is to ensure that senior management hires and promotes more qualified women and people of color within the management ranks of their division. There is obviously more to the role than this, but at this time of the year, I will meet with each division head to help set their diversity goals for the number of women and people of color that they plan to hire or promote in their division.

This is my second meeting of this type with this particular executive, and I need to remember what I wore to the last meeting to make sure that I don't wear the same outfit today.

I think to myself, "I can't go wrong with navy, and this particular suit looks better when I pull my hair back anyway. Perfect. There will be no time to use the curling iron this morning."

I find a delicate set of pearl earrings and a necklace given to me by my grandmother, Millie. I carefully put them in the zipper pocket of my purse so I can put them on later in the car.

Webb is awake and beginning to prepare for his own day. He enters the bathroom, but something in his peripheral view stops him. I think he sees the look on my face that says, "Don't even think about getting in that shower first." He gazes at me and shakes his head slightly as he exits the bathroom, conceding to the fact that for approximately the next twenty minutes, the bathroom is off limits to him.

As I shower, I reflect on him shaking his head and interpret it as him really asking me, "When are you going to get your act together?" Sometimes my husband's head shaking pushes play on a self-reflective voice recording in my head. First, I admit that if I had not hit that snooze button multiple times, I could avoid giving him a reason to shake his head. This leads to the next nugget of truth—I chronically run late for things no matter how much I want to be punctual. This thought reminds me that as much as I have tried to hone my time management skills, I have never been able to sustain any improvement in this area. This realization guides me to my next pearl, which is that I'm always pledging to change something about myself but can never maintain the change.

I then switch to thinking about our marriage. Webb and I waver through periods of being connected, never seeming to remain on one accord for any significant period of time. I guess it's similar to my bad habits—improvement in spurts, but little sustainability.

I can genuinely say that we love each other, but we seldom see things the same way. We can both agree that there is a problem, but completely disagree on how to solve it. Then, we move into a space where each of us tries to justify our individual positions...

Shoot! I've spent too much time reflecting. I peep into the bedroom and check the clock on the nightstand. I have about fifteen minutes, maybe seventeen minutes at best, to get in the car and make it to Julian's school bus stop on time. If we miss the bus, I will have to drive Julian all the way to school, which will make me late for my meeting. I can't let that happen.

I call out to the boys once more, telling Julian to step outside to check the weather. He needs to gauge whether he should wear his lighter jacket or his heavier coat. I race like a madwoman to make sure that both boys are on time. We all make it to the car with book bags, bananas, juice boxes, and Pop Tarts in hand. I have to neatly fold my suit jacket over in the front seat for fear that food will land on it in the back.

As soon as we turn the corner, I see the yellow school bus waiting, and I let out a huge sigh of relief to myself. I am grateful that we made it on time, even if by the skin of our teeth. I used to tug at Julian for a kiss before he got out of the car, but he thinks everyone on the bus is staring at him. I guess he doesn't want to be viewed as a momma's boy, so he has learned to move quickly when he's getting out of the car. There's no time to ask him for a kiss, but only enough time to say, "Love you and have a good day," before he moves away from earshot. Meanwhile, Jonathan is studying every move with that look on his face that says, "I want to ride the school bus with the big kids, too."

Jonathan's watching Julian causes a quick flashback about Josh. Josh has a knack for studying cars similar to how Jonathan examines Julian getting onto the school bus. Josh's eyes will constantly roam the streets for high-performance or luxury cars while he's riding in the car. Once he spots one, he goes wild with excitement. He always declares that a Porsche will be his first car.

As my flashback of Josh fades, I reach for the button to turn on the radio. Things aren't so intense now, so I can listen to a little music as I get Jonathan to school.

The traffic gods are on our side this particular morning and we make it to Jonathan's school quickly. Before I take him out of his car seat, I comb his hair and tidy up his face, as well. I take advantage of a nearby trash can, throwing out the empty juice boxes, wrappers, and banana peels from the backseat. I open the school door, and make eye contact with the teacher on duty. I kiss my baby good-bye, let go of his hand, and I tell him the same thing I told Julian, "Love you and have a good day."

I hop back into the car and begin my commute along the Kennedy Expressway. Unless there's a bad accident, I should make it to the office on time. Fortunately my commute is uneventful, so I make it to the office with just enough time to get a cup of coffee, make those last-minute edits to my presentation, and arrive promptly for my important meeting. This is a pretty good start for a Monday morning.

Today, my boss, Dave, and I are meeting with Mark Sutter, the head of the finance division. I stop by Dave's office so that we can walk into the meeting together. As we walk towards Mark's office, I can tell that Dave is somewhat nervous, too. Mark is a tall, thin man whose face seldom shows expressions. He's a nice man, but his demeanor can be intimidating at times. If he passes you in the hall he'll nod his head in acknowledgment of you, but don't expect to hear a sound from him. Mark keeps his work environment under tight control, and nothing is out of place in his office. His desk usually has an apple squarely placed on a small bar napkin in the top right-hand corner, and he always uses a yellow, legal-size pad with a mechanical pencil to record his meeting notes.

We get to Mark's office about three minutes early, giving me just enough time to power up my computer in case I need to access any additional files during the meeting. We start the meeting at 9:30 a.m. sharp, and I begin with the presentation. For the first thirty seconds or so, I'm a bit nervous, but I've given this presentation to several other division heads before, so my nervousness quickly subsides. Mark's assistant, Carolyn, steps in to give him his latest phone messages and lets him know that his 10 a.m. meeting has arrived.

Meanwhile, I begin to pack up and realize how anticlimactic this *big* meeting was and how I want my Saturday back again. If I had known that things were going to be this brief and straightforward, I would have relaxed more over the weekend. Unfortunately, I had this meeting playing in the background of my mind almost the entire time; thus, I never fully unwound.

It is another typically busy Monday, and I'm starving because I didn't eat breakfast. I almost miss lunch too, but I barely make it to the downstairs cafeteria before it closes. With a last request from Dave, I end up staying about an hour later, which I fear will put me in the thick of rush hour traffic headed back into the city.

I'm right. The travel gods may have been with me this morning, but they abandon me this evening and the traffic on the Kennedy is unbearable. Heavy traffic is exhausting, and when you get out of the car, the last thing you feel like doing is cooking dinner. I enjoy cooking when I am in the mood rather than having to cook on demand. I am usually inspired to cook on snowy or rainy days. During those times, I love finding a good recipe and taking my time to create a new concoction while I sip a little wine. On the other hand, there's nothing fun about driving in bumper-to-bumper traffic for more than an hour and then having to get creative about what to whip up for dinner.

I'm almost home. I have the option of taking a shortcut, but I decide not to. If I take the shortcut, I will drive directly in front of a McDonald's, and I am too weak to resist the drive-thru this evening. Just think, all of my dinner woes could be resolved as soon as I hear that lady say, "Hi, welcome to McDonald's. May I take your order?" On a night like tonight, her words would be music to my ears, but I know my weaknesses. I avoid the shortcut, and with the extra two minutes in the car, I ponder what I will cook tonight. Every meal option I consider would require that I'd taken something out of the freezer this morning, which I failed to do because I overslept.

As I put my key in the front door, I already hear the boys racing to the door to greet me. This is when I put on a bit of a performance as I hug them both and think to myself, "Round 2." Despite my exhaustion, I still have to put on a fresh face and ask specific questions about their days' stories. My heart is fully engaged, but my mind and body just aren't.

Before I change my clothes, I think about yelling downstairs to Webb, but I know he's on the phone. I decide to wait to greet him until he comes upstairs. We converted our smallest bedroom, which is downstairs, into an office for him, so he spends a lot of time down there. If we were in a place where I was feeling really connected to him, I would have gone downstairs and greeted him with a gentle kiss. No time for that now, because we're both in our own worlds these days. He is also in deal-making mode this week. Webb works in the world of private equity, and his team is pushing to close a deal by week's end. The last few days before closing are always intense, so it is best to relieve him of his kid duties and give him his space tonight.

I tell the boys that I'm going to change my clothes and I will hang out with them in the kitchen. They ignore that and talk to me through the bathroom door as I change clothes. I put on a comfortable T-shirt and a pair of leggings and head to the kitchen to prepare dinner. They've had only light snacks after school, so they have full appetites and are already questioning me about what we're having for dinner.

I decide that I will cook spaghetti and meatballs with corn and broccoli tonight. It's not exactly one of Webb's favorites, but the boys will love it. I begin to thaw the ground beef, which shouldn't take too long, and notice that I don't hear the boys. I peep in the den and see them both glued to the television, watching one of their favorite Nickelodeon shows. I think about interrupting Julian to make sure that his homework is complete, but I decide to let them watch TV for the next thirty minutes. This way I can work faster to get dinner on the table.

We're eating late again tonight as dinner hits the table shortly after 8:30 p.m. Webb joins us, and we have a nice family time together. Both boys come back for seconds, but now it's time to get them ready for bed. Julian can bathe himself with the exception of being reminded about the critical areas, but Jonathan cannot. I have to bathe him and get him ready for bed myself. Webb usually does this part, but tonight these things are all on me.

Once the boys are ready for bed, I'm back to the kitchen to clean. As I walk toward the kitchen, the phone rings; it's my mother. We haven't spoken in a few days, so a call that would normally take ten to fifteen minutes goes on for nearly forty-five. She recently got a job promotion that required her to move to Tennessee. Considering that she's no longer married and has no minor children, she jumped at the opportunity. Her phone calls are a priority, since we no longer live in the same city.

By the time I fall across the bed with the remote control in hand, it is well after 11 p.m. and my chance to decompress with a few laughs from a decent TV show is gone. Tomorrow, I will start all over again.

Even as I lie on the bed, there is a debate going on in my head. One voice says, "Get up and get ready for bed before you fall asleep in your clothes, Webb has to wake you up, and you have difficulty going back to sleep." The other one says, "Lie here for just a few more minutes; you won't oversleep tomorrow morning."

For the moment, the latter voice wins. I lie there thinking about how my life feels like a machine constantly operating for everyone else with little time leftover for me.

On the other hand, I have so much to be grateful for. I have what I always hoped for—a husband whom I love, great kids, and a decent, corporate job from which I can retire. I don't want to change what I already have. I just want to fill in the part about *me*. As a young girl, when I fantasized about the very life that I am living today, I thought this was the pinnacle. If I knew then what I feel now, I would have focused less on *looking* the part and more on *feeling* the part.

My deepest fear is that this is it—this is as good as it gets.

Coming Full Circle

Sometimes you can reach a crossroads where your life looks right to others but it doesn't feel right to you. This is a place where you likely have more questions than you have answers. The longer you go on like this, the longer you feel trapped between looking fulfilled and being fulfilled…between playing the part and actually feeling the part. You may even be very grateful for all that you have in your life, but you still sense that something is missing. Make no mistake, you have truly come to a fork in the road, and your question becomes: Will you move past the uncertainty in search of what's missing in your life, or will you continue to ignore that inner gnawing and pretend that you've already found it?

Have you neglected your innermost desires and are now sleepwalking through parts of your life?

"Come to me, all you who are weary and burdened, and I will give you rest."
(Matt. 11:28 NIV)

Chapter 2

Groundhog Sundays

IT HAS HAPPENED AGAIN. It will be another late morning thanks to my snooze button, another morning of hustle and bustle. The boys both turn over or groan when they hear my voice, but no one is moving to get out of bed.

"Both of you, put your feet on the floor. I need to see them now!"

Again, I have no idea what to wear and I need more time. I am visiting Mrs. Taplin, a mover and shaker in Chicago politics and its business community. She became my mentor when I started working in corporate nearly ten years ago. She's old enough to be my grandmother, and sometimes she acts like it. Trust me, she has no problem speaking her mind to me. She recently had surgery and I've been intending to visit her at home with flowers and her favorite dessert for the last several weeks. Each week I add it to my to-do list, and each week I end up putting if off until the next week. Now, she has recovered and is already back to work and I'm somewhat regretful that, yet again, I wasn't able to follow through on something that I said I would do.

Our paths recently crossed and she asked me if I would serve as a co-chair for her Annual Women's Day Luncheon this year. Needless to say, I was honored by her request. Our meeting today is for me to learn more about her expectations for the role.

Today, I can't decide between my light gray and charcoal gray suits. They're similar in color, but different in cut. I grab my pearls again and stick them in the zipper part of my purse.

"Wow!" I enter her office and I'm instantly stunned at how good she looks. I was positive the surgery would have taken a bigger toll on her than it seems.

"Suzette, get on in this office, girl. I had surgery—I'm not dead. And where have you been all this time?" She goes on, "Let me look at you. I can see that you've picked up a few pounds... but you look good. You're not having any more babies, are you?"

"No, I'm not! Do I look like I'm pregnant?"

With a half-sly smile on her face she says, "No, you look good."

About ten minutes into our conversation, I feel like we're really connecting. She asks about everything, from Webb and the boys to my job, and how life is treating me overall. I talk briefly about the boys and tell her that the job is going okay, but when I talk about my marriage, I do not sugarcoat things.

"What do you see as being the main issue in your marriage?"

It's funny how she cuts right to the chase with that question. Most people would have said something like, "If you don't mind me asking, what is the problem?" Not Mrs. Taplin. She goes right to the heart of the matter.

Initially, because our relationship has always been more of a professional one, I am hesitant to go into the details with her. However, I notice that her tone sounds more supportive, and this opens the door for me to candidly express my feelings to her.

"I believe that we both really love each other, but lately we haven't been on the same accord. He sees his way as better and I see mine as better. This leaves us in a perpetual state of striving to be right. Being right seems like it trumps everything else in our relationship. We have become masterful at making each other feel small when one of us is wrong.

"The strangest thing is that I really don't want to be with anyone else, and I believe Webb feels the same about me. We love each other, but we don't always act as if we're on the same team.

"So, sometimes the intimacy in our marriage is compromised. For example, when I'm in the mood to open up about my deepest desires, I will call a girlfriend and talk at length with her before I would tell him any of it. Unfortunately, I think he feels the same with me.

"Lately, things have been more transactional with us. We've become so overwhelmed with the actual tasks required to keep our family functioning that we spend less time connecting as a family."

I can tell by her eye contact that she's absorbing every word I'm saying, but it's hard to interpret her facial expressions. I'm not sure if she's thinking, "These are common marital issues, and as long as they love each other they'll be fine," "These folks have some real issues, and this marriage will never last," or "Suzette is not the strong young woman that I thought she was. She is not ready to serve as one of my co-chairs."

I continue to talk before she interrupts me. I think that she's about to weigh in with something real heavy, something that only a person who has been married for fifty-plus years could share. She cuts me off midstream.

"What's the name of your pastor again?"

I am tempted to tell a white lie, and give the pastor's name of the church that we used to attend when Jonathan was christened at six months, but I couldn't readily recall his name.

"I am not attending a church at this time."

Her mouth opens wide. A donut could have fit perfectly between her lips without touching either one of them. "Suzette, you're raising three young boys in these times, and you don't have a church home?"

I open my mouth to answer and she cuts me off again. "You and your husband are on separate pages, and you don't have a church home?"

I see that her line of questioning is rhetorical, thus I need to sit up and earnestly listen to what she is saying—or at least pretend that I'm earnestly listening. "You were raised in the church all of your life, and today you don't have a church home?"

She pauses longer.

"Yes, unfortunately, I do not currently have a church home."

"And, why is that?" Her eyes sort of bubble, which look a bit comical, but I dare not even crack a smile.

"I am not impressed with the teaching ability of many of the pastors today. I'm interested in more of a teaching pastor rather than a preaching one, and I haven't been able to find that type of church. I can tolerate preaching if it involves teaching, but generally speaking, that has not been my experience.

"I also feel that many churches today lack a vision. They meet on Sundays but seldom engage their congregation beyond Sundays. Weekly offerings are collected, but members rarely get to experience the fruits of those offerings."

"Why don't you visit my church? I consider our pastor to be a 'teaching pastor,' as you call it."

Feeling put on the spot, I could not decline her offer, so I halfheartedly smile and say, "Sure, Webb and I would love to visit your church."

"Good. I'll expect to see you and the family this Sunday."

Within seconds she reaches for the arm of her chair to brace herself as she stands to say good-bye. It's as if she is signaling that the purpose of our meeting has been fulfilled. I move around her desk to give her a big hug, and to thank her for her time.

"Are you able to serve as one my co-chairs for this year's luncheon?"

"Yes, I am honored to serve in any way that I can."

"Great, then are you available to meet with our planning committee here at my office this Saturday at 10 a.m.?"

"Absolutely, I'll be here!"

I accept her invitation realizing that as I commit myself, I am committing Webb too. I am trusting that he will be able to pick up my portion of the Saturday morning activities with the boys.

Just as I turn away from her, she pulls my hand and eyeballs me. "Suzette, I'd really like you to consider the value in belonging to a good church. It's the next step for your marriage and your family. You just need to find the right one."

I leave her office on a high. The time she spent with me this morning feels validating. We met for nearly an hour before she even mentioned her luncheon. Her next meeting might just be with the mayor of Chicago. Her plate is always full, yet she takes more time to discuss my needs rather than her own.

I drive to the office reflecting on her words. I was raised to go to church every Sunday, so how could I be raising children and not allow them the same advantage of having a church home? I also must admit that, for most of my adult life, I have only gone to church out of duty. Although, each time I go, it's with the expectation that this visit will be different than the last one. I go with the hope of learning something new, or at least being given a new perspective. Sadly, I have often thought the pastor's message seemed as if he prepared it on his drive to the church. He usually talks loudly but says nothing. I leave the church service feeling the same way I felt before, like I could have done a better job myself.

If I were teaching a congregation, I would keep the message enlightening and applicable to folks' everyday lives. My sermons would be rich in content. Each message would end with a good cliffhanger, inspiring members to come back next week.

As promised, that Sunday, I bring the entire family to Mrs. Taplin's church, and several Sundays later our family actually ends up joining her church. The congregation is warm and inviting and, most importantly, the pastor is a really good teacher.

Now, my Sundays have become just as regimented as my weekdays. We rarely miss going to church on Sundays. Over two years, we miss maybe three or four Sundays, even in Chicago's worst weather conditions. This is good for a family that used to only attend church for baptisms, Easter Sunday, and sometimes on Christmas Eve. From the outside, everything looks even more picture perfect.

Coming Full Circle

Your regimented weekdays have now extended into your Sundays. You look the part, and are going through all of the right motions while you continue to sense that something greater is missing. Are you going to your place of worship for the sake of appearances? Have you become more loyal to serving those appearances than you are to serving God? Hopefully, your exploration of these questions might lead you to finding your answers in the arms of God.

*Are you "sleepwalking" to your place of worship
and wishing there was more?*

*"…These people honor me with their lips, but their hearts
are far from me. They worship me in vain; their teachings are
merely human rules."
(Mark 7:6-7 NIV)*

Chapter 3

Sleepwalking with Credentials

It's 1:30 a.m. on a Tuesday morning and I'm just putting my key in the door. I'm trying to be super quiet, so I take my heels off at the front door. The last time I spoke to Webb I told him that I thought I would make it home before midnight, but he's already accustomed to tacking on another hour or two to whatever time I give him these days. Our team has intense homework assignments due at the end of the week, and I was at school fulfilling my portion of the assignments. To quench my enormous thirst for doing something new, and to quell those feelings of void, I decided to return to school to get my MBA.

When I applied to grad school, I thought this was a perfect way to learn more while enhancing my career options too. Webb agreed with this rationale and gave me his full support. Sometimes I have to really pitch Webb on what I believe is a good idea before he buys into it. Not this time. He immediately threw his support behind my pursuit of a higher education. Logistically, it works for our family because both boys are older and a little more self-sufficient.

Even with our hectic schedules we still manage to make it to church on Sundays. Rejoining church turned out to be a good move for our family. It is especially good for the boys because it teaches them the importance of service at a young age, and it helps them to develop new relationships on a different level. Furthermore, it is another wholesome community for them outside of school. It has also been good for our marriage; sometimes the pastor's message will nail an issue that Webb and I may be dealing with. We both appear to gain an enlightened perspective on the matter at hand. However, it has done little for me in terms of giving me comfort around my personal feelings of emptiness.

It's a bit hard to describe what I feel, or how these feelings even come about. I think it mostly occurs when I see someone else experiencing a sense of fulfillment. That person seems to fully grasp the meaning of their life and their purpose. I want exactly the same thing for my life. I want to understand my own life beyond the 365 days of each year filled with the same routine, sprinkled with a few holidays and special occasions here and there.

I've heard people ask, "What would you get up at 3 a.m. to do without pay and you'd still love doing?" In theory, if you can answer this question, you've found what you're passionate about, and possibly your life's calling. I struggle continuously with this. As many times as I've toiled over this question in my head, I remain clueless about my answer.

When I hit a brick wall, I live in my own silent sadness. In this place, my thoughts spiral downward even further:

Maybe a passionate, self-fulfilled life isn't in the cards for everyone. Maybe some people just have *it*, and others do not. Maybe I need to accept the reality that I may not have *it* and never will. I feel like I'm not special or that I was overlooked.

These thoughts and feelings only bring about a deeper sadness.

Lately, I especially feel that way. I am just wrapping up my final assignments and exams to finish the first year of a two-year program, and once again, I compare my life to others' lives. Specifically, I am comparing where I am in relation to some of my classmates.

I'm in the Executive MBA program at the Kellogg Graduate School of Business, where the average student's age is around thirty-seven or thirty-eight. Everyone has a full-time job (a requirement of the program) and most people are married with children. Given the rigor of this program and the work-life balance that is required, my class is a group of high-performing students. After only the first year, most students are being highly sought after. Some are being rewarded with a promotion within their own company, while others are being pursued by elite headhunters for higher-paying positions, with all the perks, at other companies.

Meanwhile, my once colorful career has turned into a joyless job. Several years ago, I resigned myself to being a lifetime corporate employee. I figured trying to climb one corporate ladder was just as good as the next, so I would stay with my current employer and further build my already established relationships until retirement. However, at the time, I didn't see myself as marketable enough to scale any corporate ladder with only a bachelor's degree. I knew someday I would have to pursue a graduate degree.

Given my feelings of emptiness and my desire to do something new, I figured now would be as good a time as any to begin my journey of scaling that corporate ladder. My hope is that with more education and hard work, I could transition from my current mid-level management position in Human Resources to one of the other business units. In the end, I could retire on a pretty decent salary.

Since the beginning of the second semester, I have been in hot pursuit of two new job leads at my company. I, too, feel that I am ready to advance. Unfortunately, my company recently filed for bankruptcy, so some departments are being disbanded while others are being revamped. According to Dave, the first position that I expressed interest in has not been funded yet, and the second position will actually fall under a new department, or may even be eliminated. After the first year of business school, still no career opportunities have opened up for me.

I'm actually glad those new positions have not opened. I walk around every day holding in two big secrets. The first is that after being in Bschool for just a year, I don't think I want to do the corporate thing anymore. This is a big secret because I believe that if Webb and my family found this out, they would flip out. I feel as though I've become exposed to too many other options. Maybe I've been bit by the entrepreneurial bug. Maybe I'm just completely burned out in my current job, and a new job would change my feelings? I actually go back and forth with this idea, but I don't think so. I think that I'm really done with the corporate experience, but I have no idea at this stage what else I want to do. It just becomes clearer by the day what I *don't* want to do anymore.

My second secret is that Bschool did not quite fill that void like I had hoped. In the beginning, everything was off to a very challenging start, and my plate was so filled that I had no time to experience any feelings of emptiness. As the year wore on, and the newness of Bschool wore off, the feeling that something was missing began to creep back in.

When these feelings hit, it always helps if I have some new plans to anticipate. We get two months off for the summer and I won't have any school material to read, but I have begun to read a couple of really good self-help books. Maybe I'm not asking the right questions and, after reading these books, I will be able to look at my life's purpose from a different perspective and answer that 3 a.m. question. For the moment, I am cautiously optimistic.

I am also looking forward to our class trip to Hong Kong and China. There's a general course that is geared toward doing business outside of the U.S. The classroom time and the time spent visiting various companies will take up most of the trip's agenda, but we will also have some downtime. One thing that we'll do is visit the Great Wall of China, where we will spend hours and, best of all, climb the Great Wall.

Karen, Hillary, and I are ecstatic about climbing the Great Wall. Karen and Hillary attend grad school with me, and have become my very close friends, almost sister-like, over the course of these two demanding years.

I never had any expectations about making new friends on this level after high school, but here they are, as I'm sure God put them both in my life at just the right time. Hillary is about six feet tall and has a laugh and a smile that light up a room. Her personality is infectious, and when she's on your team, things usually go well. Karen is strong, direct, and loyal, and you will never feel abandoned by her. Even though she may not always tell her girlfriends what they want to hear, we still seek out her advice. However, there is one thing that we all despise about Karen: it seems she can comfortably eat as many burgers and French fries as she wishes, and she never loses her toned figure.

Anyhow, we're all thrilled about our travels to Asia, and I am especially optimistic because I can't imagine traveling this great distance and not having some breakthrough in my dilemma. Maybe it's in God's plan for me that, through this last year of school coupled with the people that I will meet on my journey to China, I will have my "ah ha!" moment about my life's purpose. I also credit myself that I diligently use every angle I know to uncover my life's purpose, and God helps those who help themselves, right?

Coming Full Circle

Do you remember the song *"Lookin' for Love"* from *Urban Cowboy* that goes something like, "I was lookin' for love in all the wrong places...Lookin' for love in too many faces..."?

These lyrics remind me of how we can easily fall prey to searching for our value in all the wrong places. We look to external things, such as material possessions and credentials, to fill our hollow places within. When one possession or achievement doesn't do the trick, we quickly move on to the next. If we're not careful, we can end up on a perpetual path of chasing one pinnacle after the next while obtaining only a fraction of fulfillment at each juncture.

What badge of honor are you seeking
to validate your self-worth?

"For I know the plans I have for you," declares the Lord,
"plans to prosper you and not to harm you, plans to give you
hope and a future."
(Jer. 29:11 NIV)

Chapter 4

Dreaming from Prison

I AM MORE DISTRAUGHT THAN EVER. It is eight weeks after my graduation from Kellogg and I still have no answers on what direction my career is heading. My long-awaited trip to China has come and gone. Climbing the Great Wall of China was great, and I will surely live to tell my grandchildren all about it. Nevertheless, when it was over, it was over.

To top things off, I am still at the same stupid corporate job with no new leads and no new answers. I have just become tired. I am tired of trying to replace *seven of my bad habits with seven effective ones* while maintaining *four agreements* with myself and trying to pinpoint *who moved my cheese* and where they put it. Enough already with the self-help books! I am tired of trying, tired of asking, tired of searching, tired of putting a smile across my face every day when I don't feel like it. I am tired of feeling overlooked. I'm just plain *TIRED!*

I am also sick of Webb characterizing my situation as simple. This was our brief banter this morning while getting dressed for work:

"Why do you have that look on your face?"

"I don't feel like going in today."

"Why? What's up?"

"It's the same story warmed over. I am tired of feeling stuck. I am tired of trying to figure out what I am supposed to be doing next."

He responds sarcastically, "Your answer is not going to drop out of the sky. You never know which avenue God will work through, so you need to pursue several different options. I think your situation is pretty simple—start looking for jobs at other companies."

"Webb, are you really listening to me? I've been saying all of this time that I'm not even sure if another corporate job is what I really want, so why are you steering me to an area where I already think I am fed up?"

"Your real problem is that you're fed up with your current employer and your current job. You'll feel differently once you get a job at another company."

UGH! I'm so sick of that response. I want to scream! Instead, I withdraw by ending our banter.

As tired as I am of hearing Webb's response, I understand it. We moved into a new home about two months before I graduated. It is a beautiful gem nestled in one of Chicago's up-and-coming neighborhoods. For nearly a year we had been searching for a home that was affordable, a good fit for our family, located in a decent neighborhood, and would ideally appreciate in value. We worked with two different real estate agents, but at least one of those factors was always missing. Either we would find an affordable house that was not in a neighborhood where we wanted to raise the boys, or we found stunning homes in great neighborhoods that weren't affordable.

One Saturday morning, Webb left the house shortly after 6 a.m. as he had been doing for the past few weeks, inspired to search for our home on his own. He drove through certain neighborhoods street by street. About two hours into his hunt, he stumbled upon our home. He claims to this day that God woke him early that morning to lead him to the home that we live in today. That said, as much as I dread hearing his pitch to find another job, I understand it.

Later that morning, I run into my dear friend and colleague Andrea in the cafeteria at work. By the time our paths cross, I'm feeling really defeated. She waits until I get through the cashier line to ask how things are going. I confess that I am at a real low point. She knows about my current career dilemma.

"Have you ever done a dream board before?"

"No. I can't even say that I know what it is."

"It is a fun exercise that helps people gain more insight into where they currently are in life and where they'd like to go. Keep in mind that a lot of this is speculative, but the exercise may give you some clues."

"This sounds interesting. I'm in."

"Great. Can you start this weekend?"

"Sure."

"Gather several of your favorite magazines. Identify the images, and even the words that *speak* to you. Arrange your cut-outs on a poster board. Once you're done, we can steal a corner in the cafeteria or a conference room sometime Monday or Tuesday, to discuss your board."

"Sounds like a plan. See you Monday."

Seeing Andrea gives me a second wind. Before running into her, my Friday was off to a miserable start. After seeing her, I feel like I have something to look forward to. I am intrigued by this whole dream board idea.

To make sure that I do not rush putting my dream board together, I wait until Webb takes the boys to the sporting goods store. Jonathan needs new football cleats, and I'm sure Julian will find that he needs something new too. They will likely stop for lunch after their shopping, so I should have enough time to select those images that "speak" to me, as Andrea put it.

Unfortunately, I am not a big magazine subscriber. There are only two magazine subscriptions that come to our house: *O: The Oprah Magazine* and *Sports Illustrated*. I have a plethora of *O* magazines. I save these magazines because I always promise myself that I will read them when I treat myself to one of those *me* afternoons. Of course, this all remains a fantasy; hence the reason for so many magazines on hand.

A few hours and two glasses of wine later, I have finished my dream board assignment. I continue to study it over and over again. To someone else, I'm sure it looks like a collage of words and images neatly arranged on a red poster board. To me, there is much more meaning and symbolism on this board. For example, I have a passionate connection to animals, and I am especially drawn to horses. I found a picture of a beautiful white horse galloping in the darkness. It looks as if he has just broken free. This picture speaks to me. Given where I've been lately, I want to break free.

I review my board once more, and then hide it alongside the bottom rack in my closet. The only person I plan on sharing my board with is Andrea. I can't wait to see what comes of all of this. I am not sure how my love for horses, for example, will translate into an answer about my career, but I have an open mind.

Monday is finally here, and I can't wait to discuss this board with Andrea. I prefer to have a private space to discuss the board, so I reserve a conference room as soon as I get to the office. We take our lunch around 11:30 a.m. to ensure that we have enough time to eat and discuss the board. I have already accepted that I will end up working late tonight. At this point, I am only concerned with seeing what this whole exercise reveals.

We get into the conference room, I put my lunch off to the side, and I open the board. I want Andrea to begin deciphering the board right away. She studies it for a few minutes before inquiring about certain images. I notice that she is not only observing the words and images on my board, but she is also taking note of where I chose to arrange the images on the board.

I should have known this was going to be a deeper assignment with Andrea. I forgot to factor in that she holds a Ph.D. in psychology. Nothing is merely black and white to her. So, for example, she sees those images at the bottom of the board as what grounds and supports me. Whatever is at the top may indicate my future aspirations, and the words and images in the center might signal where I am currently, or even where I might be stuck.

Andrea enquires about the woman in the center of my board. This woman appears to be in prison, or some type of correctional facility. She is not behind bars, but she is wearing a dark green prison-like jumpsuit and a partial smile on her face. Just above the woman's picture, I have the words "BE EXCELLENT" in all capital letters, and to the left of her picture I have the number "10."

When Andrea asks me to explain why I chose the woman in the center of my board, my response is simple. I think the woman is in some type of prison or correctional facility, and I have a positive message for her. I believe that I can reach her. She asks me a few more questions, and then drops her bomb on me:

"The woman in the center of the board is you."

I should have seen this coming, but I didn't. I had no idea that how things were arranged on the board would matter. I just cut the pictures out, organized them on the board by size and shape, and pasted them to the damn board.

So while my facial expression says *WTF*, my immediate retort is:

"I am hurt, frustrated, and confused, but SCREW YOU, I am not in prison!"

Coming Full Circle

There are a myriad of ways to be imprisoned that can come in all shapes and sizes, so to speak. Sometimes we can be entrapped by an addiction, or a relationship, or by a certain economic or social status. In this instance, our greatest threat is fear. We fear digging deep. We fear opening up old wounds. We fear uncertainty, and losing a sense of control. First, we must realize that a situation of entrapment is not a situation of God. Second, as an adult you have choices, and if you would only seek Him, He will guide your path. If you find that you can only muster up a halfstep, go with it, and He will be there to guide you in taking the next. Your fears to change course may be overwhelming, but remind yourself that if your fear is great, the God you serve is greater.

What is imprisoning you, and where does it come from?

"So do not fear, for I am with you; do not be dismayed, for I am your God. I will strengthen you and help you; I will uphold you with my righteous right hand."
(Isa. 41:10 NIV)

Chapter 5

The Circumstantial Church

I CAN'T BELIEVE I JUST SAT for two hours of that! Today, of all days, I needed to hear a good message that I could latch onto before starting another laborious week. This is why I got up early and told Webb and the boys that they could sleep in this Sunday. I could only take care of myself this morning. I didn't want to risk getting to church late and end up being seated somewhere in the back where it's difficult to hear the message.

This morning I arrive at the church early to get a seat front and center. I even came with my pocket-size journal to take notes.

This all turned out to be for naught. Rev. Brown's sermon fell flat once again. I would've even appreciated a message that didn't teach me anything new, but reminded me of something important. But *noooo*, he used his sermon to strengthen his case for wanting to build a new church.

I am so sick of the bickering back and forth in this church. The pastor and his wife want to relocate the church to the suburbs to develop a mega-church. However, some key, longtime members (code for tithers) don't have the transportation means or the will to travel to the suburbs, so they are pushing back to the pastor and his wife.

For the last several Sundays, Rev. Brown has used the pulpit as his personal platform to build his case for a mega-church. He tailors his message to those who are completely unsupportive of his vision or to those who might be on the fence. He also targets those whom he believes spread rumors about his intentions. In the end, his sermon sounds like a frustrated sales pitch and rarely ties into the scripture that it was predicated upon.

Meanwhile, I'm sitting there thinking, "What about us members who don't have a dog in this fight? We don't care if you keep the church in the city or move it to the suburbs. We just want you to honor your role as pastor by leading the entire flock."

I recognize that it must be difficult to have a vision for an organization and have to wrestle with dissension from within. However, I see the church as a different type of organization. When a man of God steps into the pulpit, it is his responsibility to teach those who support his vision as well as those who oppose it. What a complete waste of his talent and my time. I think to myself, "Father, please send me to a teaching church."

I had a feeling that this Sunday would be no different than the last several Sundays, but I still held out hope. I was desperate to hear a good message this morning. I can't seem to get beyond the whole dream board exercise that I did with Andrea last week. I was hoping today's sermon might shed some light on my feelings, but it didn't.

After lashing out at Andrea for telling me that the imprisoned woman in the center of my dream board is really me, the tears trickle down my cheeks. I partially cover my face in shame. Andrea takes no offense to my remarks. She's well aware that my outburst is aimed at my circumstances and not her. She hands me a napkin to wipe my tears as I attempt to regain my composure, and to explain my feelings.

"I feel trapped in a job that I outgrew years ago. I've tried so hard to help myself by going back to school, and pursuing new job leads while continuing to deliver my best work in a job that I no longer find fulfilling. I've watched new opportunities come to those who were pursuing them and fall into the laps of others who weren't pursuing them. When I see all of this, I can't help but believe that even as hard as I try I must be doing something wrong. This all makes me feel hurt, frustrated, and disappointed, but not like I'm in prison."

"Suzette, it all depends on how you look at it. I've been your friend for a number of years. I watch you put this extraordinary pressure on yourself to fit in, achieve, and excel to be just what you placed on that board, a '10,' which could spell your own personal prison, or hell, or however you choose to define it."

I have regained my composure, and she has my full attention. She continues, "As humans we have a desire to control our situations. If we seek an opportunity, and the opportunity does not materialize, we assume that it didn't happen because there is something wrong with us. Another way to consider things is that Divine Order is at work.

"Suzette, I have watched you push, pull, and tug at every angle of your career trying to manipulate things to go your way. Maybe, the uplifting message that you have for the woman in the center of your board is really what you want to say to yourself. I know you're going to cringe when I distill this whole situation down to this singular point, but maybe it's time for you to let go and let God."

Andrea is correct. It feels like I've heard the words "Let go and let God" a thousand times before, so this is not what I was expecting to result from my dream board exercise. I was hoping for an answer to my career plight. This is not an answer.

More importantly, my dilemma produces another unexpected realization for me. After meeting with Andrea, I was in real pain. The crazy thing is that I've been waiting all week for Sunday to come around. This is the day of reckoning. This is the day when I physically get into my car and drive to an actual building to worship God. Somehow between hearing the pastor and being in the sanctuary, one or both of them will save me. It is here that I will be enlightened and set free from all of the negative messages that infiltrate my mind during the week.

Silly me. I've been using God as a supplement to going to church when it should be the other way. Going to church and hearing a good sermon is all a supplement to my relationship with God. I see this clearly now. The church can be circumstantial. The pastor may be going through his own issues, but God is there for me at every hour and with each page turn of my life. I can't depend solely on my spiritual feeding to come from a man, because he's human and we all fall short.

Coming Full Circle

Have you fallen into a spiritual trap of going through the motions and thinking they're sufficient? Do you allow your traditions to check your God box rather than actually experience God? Sometimes our traditions and the things we've been told about our religion prevent us from experiencing and discovering our faith for ourselves. When you seek something, you have to know that there is always something deeper to be sought.

Does your religion create
a barrier to your relationship with God?

"I have given them the glory you gave me, so they may be one as we are one. I am in them and you are in me. May they experience such perfect unity that the world will know that you sent me and that you love them as much as you love me."
(John 17:22-23 NLT)

Chapter 6

Those Two Voices

LATELY, I HAVE BEEN PREOCCUPIED with a pressing, time-sensitive decision that I need to make about my current job. I am really torn over what to do. One moment I feel decisive, and I know exactly what I want to do. The next moment I waffle and change course.

My company is going through a third round of layoffs due to its filing Chapter 11 last year. I am trying to decide whether I want to stay on with the company or take one of the severance packages. If I choose to leave the company, I would use the severance money to start my own business.

I am anxious about this decision, because this may be the last time the company will offer separation incentives like these. The severance packages are getting smaller with each subsequent round of layoffs. If my choice is to leave the company, I need to notify Dave by this Friday. Human Resources needs to know which jobs are being eliminated, who's getting severance packages, who are early retirees, and so on.

I'm also anxious about Dave's reaction if I choose to leave the company. I fear that he may pitch me hard on how this is such a critical time for the company and how he really needs me to stay for just a little longer. I guess I really fear my own inability to stand my ground with Dave if I decide to leave.

Adding to my stress is the fact that I have failed to tell Webb any of this. I think when he hears that I'm toying with the idea of leaving my current job to start a new venture, he may lose it. Webb has known for a long time how unhappy and unfulfilled I've been with my job. But leaving one job without a definite alternative is a much larger issue.

Webb's core skill is finance. Things need to add up for him. If they don't, you won't get to first base in a conversation with him. Thus, I need to have a solid plan when I go to him. I am nowhere near that point. However, this could all be a non-issue if I choose to stay with my company.

I continue to struggle with this decision because there are two conflicting voices constantly playing within me. The rational voice in my head says things such as, "Don't leave a job without having another job secured, especially in today's economy. You have a decent amount of seniority at this job. If you venture out on your own and this new venture doesn't work, then it could be difficult to find another job at the same salary level with similar benefits. Your current employer is a devil you know. A new devil, like a new employer or starting a new business in a tough economy, is just not worth all the risk."

The other voice that either belongs to my heart or my soul (I'm not sure which one) is telling me, "It's time for a change. Go for it."

I must admit that I spend far more time fantasizing about what things would be like being self-employed than I do about staying in my same job. Just when my fantasizing is getting good to me, my voice of reason abruptly interrupts. "The reality is that you are a parent with financial responsibilities. You must act on behalf of the greater good, and avoid taking selfish risks that could be bad for your family."

To quiet these voices, I invoke a common practice. I take out a pen and pad, draw a line down the middle of the page, and label the left column "pros" and the right column "cons." I stop the exercise when the cons far outweigh the pros.

My next move is to call one of my girlfriends (or others whom I respect) to solicit their thoughts. Of course, people avoid weighing in on such a personal decision. They listen, and politely offer their support for whatever my decision turns out to be.

The other part of my preoccupation involves determining how and when to have my conversations with both Webb and Dave. I think I must force myself off the fence. If I tell Webb that I want to sit down with him to discuss an important matter, this will force me to formulate a plan, at least a skeletal one. The same is true for Dave. If I call his assistant to get on his calendar for this Friday, I will be forced to make a decision by the time of our meeting.

While away on a short business trip, I decide to call both Dave and Webb. I am fortunate to get a spot on Dave's calendar for this Friday morning. I can use the time to inform him of my intentions to leave the company, or if I choose to stay, I can let him know I've made my decision. I have, at least, made a commitment to have a meeting this Friday.

I liken this to getting into a cool pool. There are two ways to get in. You can slowly wade your way in, or you can just jump in. I just dove head first into the deep end of a very cool pool.

I continue the same line of reasoning when I call Webb. I tell him that I'd like us to go to dinner in the neighborhood tonight because I'd like to discuss something important with him. Of course, he won't let me off the phone so quickly. He wants a heads-up on what's so important. To make the call short and sweet, I just tell him that I need his advice. I hang up, chastising myself for my lack of transparency: "You liar, you don't need his advice. You need his support if you decide to leave your company."

These two calls give me a temporary feeling of confidence. I feel productive in the moment, even if I've only kicked the can down the road, so to speak. I have done enough to compartmentalize my anxiety in the short term so that I can focus on my business affairs at hand.

On the day that I fly home from my business trip, Webb and I meet for dinner at the Italian bistro in our neighborhood that we often frequent. Webb really enjoys their food, and the dining area will accommodate our need to have a private conversation.

"So, what's up?"

These are Webb's first words to me as soon as we meet. I begin to talk about my trip, but he wants to know what's so important that we had to meet at a restaurant to talk instead of home. As much as I dislike being pressured to tell my secret, I also hate being kept in suspense, so I can relate to what he is feeling.

"You know that we're going through another round of layoffs at work."

"You're not losing your job, are you?"

"No."

I take note of his deep sigh of relief.

"The downsizing is what I want to talk with you about. I have a few things that I want to express to you, and I need you to hold your thoughts until the end. In fact, let's order now so we don't have any interruptions."

His eyebrows are raised. He senses something. This may not go well.

The waiter approaches. "Yes, I'll have the Rotina Santa Lucia."

He always defers to me to order first. This time he didn't. He's definitely distracted.

"And, what can I get for you this evening, ma'am?"

"I'll have the Farfalle Al Salmone."

I love the Rotina Santa Lucia dish, which is the corkscrew-like pasta with Italian sausage, peas, and mushrooms in a tomato cream-based sauce. Normally, I would order this. I am feeling different tonight so I went with the bowtie pasta with salmon in a vodka sauce.

"Okay, Suzette, so what's up?"

"The company is downsizing once more, and there's still no new job for me. I recently received a stellar performance review, so I had high hopes it would earn me a new position. It didn't. I'm fed up at this point. I feel like I'm becoming stagnant. I am no longer fulfilled by the work that I do each day. I'd like to be more purposeful, and what I'm doing now feels more like a job that anyone else could do. It isn't unique to me at all. I realize that when I went back to school, I went with the intention of staying put and retiring at this company.

"However, the truth is that I no longer want to retire at this company, or any other company for that matter. In fact, I've actually been thinking about venturing out on my own. I do recognize that we are a two-income family, so I won't abandon my role to honor our financial commitments. I just don't want to do *this* anymore.

"While I have a few ideas on what this new venture might look like, I don't have everything all figured out just yet. I thought that in the meantime, I could consult."

As I blurt out the heart of my issue, my neck feels warm and tingly. I feel the pressure rising within me. I also notice that he's honored my request to not interrupt me even though one of his brows remains higher than the other one. This brow will usually stay like that until he reaches a point of clarity. The fact that it's still up there tells me that he has a lot of questions.

"So, Webb, in no way am I trying to eliminate my financial contribution to the family. I just don't think I can continue to get up each day and stay sane when doing this work. I've outgrown my position and I want to explore new options. Because the company is doing another round of downsizing, I thought this would be the best time to think about something new. Therefore, I've planned to speak with Dave this Friday about being considered for voluntary separation."

"Are you finished?"

"Yes. For now, I'm finished."

Instinctively, I feel that by the end of our talk we will be on opposite sides of the table. I can tell by the tone that he used.

"Suzette, I can understand you feeling stagnant in a position that you've clearly outgrown. That's not uncommon. I can also understand your frustration, and probably even a little embarrassment that you experience when your classmates report their successes and you feel like you have none to report. I have feelings about this too, because when you're in a stagnant position your compensation remains the same. Let me remind you that going to graduate school was not only your decision. It was a family decision, because that was more than a $100K investment. So your advancement is the way that we realize a return on the family's investment. That said, I don't think your issue is your employer. Your issue is your actual job. So, I am all for you looking for another job. Hell, I'll even help you as much as I can with that. But, I think it's a mistake to leave your current job without another one in hand."

"Webb, did you not hear me? I am not feeling the corporate thing right now. One corporation is just like the other. I think I may be ready to do my own thing."

He responds coldly, "What is your own thing?"

"I don't have it all figured out, but I am thinking that I can consult while I create a plan."

He chuckles, and mumbles underneath his breath, "This is all emotional."

"What do you mean by that?"

His dismissive chuckle and characterization of my idea as being emotional ticks me off.

"Honey, you've busted your tail at your job the last couple of years to prove yourself, and the company has overlooked your efforts. So, you feel angry and hurt. These emotions are causing you to respond emotionally. You must be careful, though. You want to be smart about your actions. You can't take an action that hurts us financially, and sets you back professionally."

"Webb, I'm not sure if you really understand my intentions. I am not angry with anyone. I've actually had the urge to do my own thing after I completed my first year of grad school, but I suppressed those feelings.

"I think it's fair to say that Dave has made attempts to put me on the right trajectory, but for whatever reason, things just haven't worked out. You never know—things may not be falling into place because they're not *supposed* to fall into place."

Webb emphatically interjects, "If anything, this is a sign that you need to look for a new job outside your company, not to start a new venture. You don't have the liberty to walk away from a financially secure position after a $100K investment. Let's not forget that we have three boys still in elementary school, and three college funds to build, not to mention our mortgage and other living expenses. You asked me for my thoughts and I think your ideas are selfish and not well thought out. Leaving a decent job with benefits, because you are no longer 'fulfilled' to start an independent consulting firm while you figure matters out, just doesn't add up."

Momentarily entertaining my idea, he asks, "What is the core consulting service that you would offer?"

"Management consulting."

He gives that sly chuckle again, which hurts and frustrates me even more.

I quickly snap back, "Are you laughing at my ability to provide management consulting services?"

He tries to clean it up. "No, I think you could do well. If that's your interest, why not try for a job at McKinsey, one of the leading consulting firms in the country? In other words, if I'm a business why would I go to an independent consultant who is right out of Bschool with no proven track record versus going to one of the respected firms like McKinsey?"

"I would not target high-revenue firms. Specifically, I would target small businesses with annual revenues less than a million dollars that could not afford the McKinseys of the world."

I sharply conclude our discussion by saying, "There's no need to go on. You've made your position clear."

I shift the conversation to ask about his day. I am seething underneath when I ask this question. He knows it too. The rest of our conversation is reduced to one-word responses.

We leave the restaurant and walk home. As soon as he puts the key in the door, I hear the boys' voices. They stayed up to see us and tell us about their day. Their being awake tonight means I have to muster up the energy to have a good conversation with them before they go to bed, and honestly I am not in the mood. Tonight, I am hurting and confused. I don't have the level of energy to talk with anyone, not even my own kids. As awful as that might sound, it's true. I still manage to hold a brief, superficial conversation with them. Afterwards, my mother-in-law, Myrna, leaves. I set the burglar alarm and walk upstairs to bed.

I lie in bed with all sorts of thoughts roaming in my head. After a few moments of silence, I decide to make one final pitch to Webb.

"Haven't you ever made a decision based upon your feelings, or something just calling you in another direction?"

He responds with a sincere tone, "No, my feelings need to add up."

He tells me that he loves me, and he hopes that he has not hurt my feelings. He also pledges to call a few contacts to see if he can help me find new employment. I accept his response to avoid arguing.

Before I turn my nightstand light off, I reach for my cell phone to turn it off and realize that I have a text from Karen confirming breakfast tomorrow morning. Karen has been traveling and I haven't had the chance to really talk with her about my dilemma. She'll give me her honest thinking, and our breakfast could not come at a better time. She's a great listener and always has sound advice. Maybe she'll offer something that I have yet to consider. I take comfort in knowing that I may gain new insights from Karen.

Coming Full Circle

Fear prevents the ability to step into what lies ahead. Our fear paralyzes us. Ultimately, we stay where we are…unhappy with where we are, because we're too afraid to move forward despite our desire to do so. In order to conquer our fears and move forward, we must first be introspective enough to know what we truly fear.

What are you afraid of?

"Do not be anxious about anything, but in every situation, by prayer and petition, with thanksgiving, present your requests to God. And the peace of God, which transcends all understanding, will guard your hearts and your minds in Christ Jesus."
(Phil. 4:6-7 NIV)

Chapter 7

A Choir of Voices

I SLEEP WELL and need no alarm clock to awake me. I am eagerly looking forward to breakfast this morning with Karen. I want to hear her take on things. She may offer a new perspective that I have yet to consider.

However, one hour and ten minutes into our talk and she's distilled things down to whether I've prayed about the situation. How disappointing! I was hoping for some genuine counsel and I didn't receive it.

As soon as I get in the car, my cell phone is buzzing. It's my mother. I contemplate whether I want to take her call at the moment. Of course, I answer. The thought that this could be an emergency always creeps into my mind, and I'm never at peace until I return the call, anyway. We talk until I pull into my office parking lot.

As soon as I get to my desk, I see my voicemail light flashing. I check my messages and learn that Tanya, one of my friends in HR, has some news for me. After checking email, I pay Tanya a visit. We go into a nearby vacant conference room to talk privately. She tells me that my specific job is ineligible for voluntary separation.

I feel like my heart is dropping into my left shoe. Learning that I'm ineligible for voluntary separation makes me feel more trapped than ever.

On my way back to my desk, I notice that one of our company's tenured directors has kept her door open. Our eyes connect as I pass her office, so I spontaneously enter her office and make small talk about the reorganization. She begins to candidly open up about how much of a headache the actual process has become. Her availability to chat is inviting. I begin to confidentially share with her that I have been toying with the idea of whether I want to stay or request a voluntary separation package but that I recently learned that my position is exempt from these separation privileges.

I continue to share with her that I have outgrown my position, and how I am just no longer fulfilled by the work. At this point, she shares a phrase with me that I will never forget.

"Suzette, you should do what many of us have already done."

"What's that?"

She looks at me blankly and says, "When we became 'unfulfilled' as you say, and realized the system was not going to change, we changed our expectations of the system. We chose to quit and stay."

"Excuse me?"

"Yes, in terms of my heart and passion for the work, I quit years ago. But, I decided to stay at the company for other reasons, such as my retirement, pension, medical benefits, and other perks. In terms of my fulfillment, I get that outside of this place."

She smirks and finishes by saying, "All this place can do for me is to give me my paycheck every two weeks, and anything else is gravy."

Out of habit, I plaster on a smile and nod in agreement, but on the inside I am shocked. I leave shortly thereafter.

On my walk back to my desk, I think to myself, "How can a person show up to a place every day for decades of her life and not be engaged? How could someone not be fulfilled in what they are doing, and only come for a paycheck? What about all of the other things that they could be doing that they actually enjoyed, and making the same amount of money or maybe even more? The quality of life doesn't seem to be worth the pension, retirement, or other benefits. As the saying goes, different strokes for different folks—but I pray this is never me."

I am back at my desk, and the thoughts are swirling in my head. I'm still in deep thought about being ineligible for a voluntary separation package. Any hopes to leave this place now seem false.

I'm also still thinking about the whole "quit and stay" mentality. Sure, I've heard of people staying in bad relationships out of convenience or staying in a job because the pay and benefits are good. They may feel trapped by their circumstances. The "quit and stay" mindset feels more conscious, and more deliberate.

I get to the break room and notice that the coffeepots are empty; I need to brew more. While it brews, I stand there in a daze, recounting the various conversations that I've had with others throughout the day. I started this whole process with two voices playing in my head. However, after seeking advice from so many others, I now have a choir of voices singing in discord. I have solicited all of this feedback from a host of associates including Webb, Karen, my mother, and Doris' "quit and stay" mentality. This is just the tally for the last forty-eight hours. As I watch the coffee drip into the carafe, I ask myself, "Am I better off after seeking all of this outside advice?"

My grandfather, the late Bishop Howard Thomas Primm, would often say, "Buy corn from everyone, but grind it in your own mill." I did more than buy corn from others, though. I went to others seeking their answers to my issue.

Coming Full Circle

When things don't happen the way we want, believe, or expect them to, we turn to other people for guidance and validation. However, we forget that they often are just as lost as we are, and we ignore the guidance of God. In some instances, we pray for results but we don't ask questions. In other instances, we ask questions but fail to stop and listen for the answers. It seems futile to ask the creation about advice on how to handle the creation, and neglect to seek the wisdom of the Creator.

Who do you call on first, before you call on God?

"As for me, I look to the Lord for His help. I wait confidently for God to save me, and my God will certainly hear me."
(Mic. 7:7 NLT)

Chapter 8

Quit and Stay

IT'S NOT EVEN 5 A.M. and my eyes are open. My entire house is still asleep. If I stay in bed for five more minutes, those five minutes will easily turn into fifteen minutes, and so on. I can go back to sleep or I can take advantage of the total silence and stillness in my house to write in my journal. It's now or never. I decide to move.

I ease out of bed, slip my feet into my slippers, grab my robe, and head downstairs. As I make it to the last step, I realize that I just left my journal upstairs, but I decide to brew some coffee before I return upstairs to get it. I continue to move about quietly because I don't want to wake anyone.

After pouring what smells like a great cup of coffee, I grab my journal and get nestled into my writing spot. I begin to reflect on my job situation and the meeting that I have today with Dave.

Dear God,
I won't begin this journal entry trying to recap all that's been going on with me lately. That would be a waste of

53

time. You know exactly what's been going on with me. Instead, maybe in Your own way You could answer the following questions for me:

- Is there a way for me to earn my living by doing something that I enjoy and that maximizes my talents, but also helps others? If so, can You please lead me to it? I would be eternally grateful.
- If You would prefer me to continue at my job, then please remove the desire to leave it, and please fill me with the joy to stay.
- Is my purpose to serve the greater good?

I ask for answers to these questions in Your Name. Please give me a sign, so that I know it's You and not some figment of my imagination. Amen.

It's almost time to get the boys up, and I must stop writing. I squint to see the clock on the microwave. It looks like it's nearly 7 a.m., but it can't be. I squint more as I walk toward the microwave. "Shoot! It's nearly 7 a.m.!"

I leave my journal out on the table while I dash upstairs to wake up the boys. While I start to get myself ready, I remember that I left my journal open on the kitchen table. I immediately run back downstairs to grab my journal before someone spots it and feels tempted to read it.

Since today is Friday, it is a casual dress day at the office. I shower and get dressed in no time. I kiss Webb and tell the boys good-bye before I walk downstairs. Before I leave the house, I leave small juice boxes and Pop Tarts out on the kitchen table for Julian and Jonathan. Every time I'm in the grocery store I promise myself that I am done with this unhealthy eating, but it's mornings like these when I'm glad I have something quick to give the boys so they don't leave the house hungry.

I notice that I have a little more pep in my step this morning. Writing in my journal is therapeutic for me, so I feel lighter in general. I definitely must release my thoughts like this more often. I also like the idea of writing a letter to God. I've done this only a few times before, but I think it takes my journal writing to another level. I feel even better because I am not only releasing my issues, I am releasing them to God. I have to be careful, though, because sometimes my language can be so casual, and I don't want to come across as having little reverence for the Lord.

Anyhow, I'm feeling good this morning. This is great because I thought I would be feeling depressed since I am not leaving my job today. Maybe God is already answering my prayer by filling me with the joy to stay at the company. If He's answering my second question, then He is also answering my first question too. I avoid going down this path because I don't want to spoil my mood.

Traffic is lighter than normal this morning. I make it to the office in good time and I'm even able to secure a parking spot near the main entrance. This is rare. I stop in the cafeteria before going up to my floor and I run into Dave. He tells me that something has come up and he needs to reschedule our 10 a.m. meeting to 3 or 4 p.m. this afternoon.

The morning starts as an uneventful one, but things begin to take a turn closer to lunchtime. Several staff and management employees are beginning to learn their fate with the company. The energy is clearly shifting. I hear a few angry murmurs and muffled crying, which begin to trigger some emotions within me about my true desire to leave.

On my way to the cafeteria, I see a few of my colleagues whispering in a huddle. Of course, my inquisitive mind wants to know the latest news. I detour toward the huddle to find who's just been shot. Today, a large pool of employees will be notified as to whether they will retain their jobs or not. All this time I've been so focused on the voluntary separation packages that I'd nearly forgotten about those employees who were being forced into early retirement and others who were being fired.

Rita, one of the directors who has worked for the company for thirty-six years, has apparently just learned that she's being forced into early retirement. This news is shocking. She is a staple in the company. She is admired among leadership, rank, and file. The company already promised her a position in the reorganized company. They withdrew their offer and did not give her notice. One of my colleagues says that Rita is in her office falling apart from the news. Leadership reassured her repeatedly that she was "safe." She is also angry with herself for trusting leadership to the extent where she didn't see this coming.

After thirty-six years of hard work, dedication, and a slew of sacrifices, she is being kicked out just like the next guy. This is a revelation for me. I assume that eliminating her position is a business decision and not a personal one, but it is how she is being handled that makes me uncomfortable. If they treat Rita this way, I don't want to think about how I might be treated. After thirty-six long years of consistent job performance, a stellar reputation, and being an admirable team player, she is being terminated the same way as the person who joined the company six months ago and has mediocre job performance. In the final analysis, there was no difference at all. All of the sacrifices that resulted in multiple relocations to remote territories, and missed family time due to heavy travel, were all for naught.

I get back to my desk and recall what Doris said yesterday. I think more about what Rita must be going through in the confines of her office. I see both as amazing women whom I respect and admire, but I don't want to end up like either of them. The "quit and stay" mindset may work for many people, but it doesn't for me. Furthermore, I definitely would not want to give a company thirty-six years of my life only to be treated the way that Rita is being treated today.

I look up at the time, and it's nearly 3:30 p.m. There's been no word from Dave yet. I assume our meeting must be at 4 p.m. My agenda and key discussion points are all prepared, so I'm just waiting until two or three minutes before 4 p.m. to begin my walk over to his office.

I'm fine until about 3:50 p.m., then I become nervous. My heart beats a little faster. I feel that common tingling sensation in my arm. I cannot explain these feelings. I try to ignore them, but now it's time to walk over to Dave's office. The feeling persists. I stop in one of the coffee rooms and pick up a bottle of water. I still feel a bit nervous, so I whisper, "God, please guide me."

I get to his office. He is on the phone, but he still signals for me to come in. I sit down, and we engage in a little small talk first. Afterwards, I present him with a short list of my current projects. He looks up and says to me, "We'll get to that in a moment, Suzette. I'm actually glad that you put yourself on my calendar today, because I want to talk with you as well. Why don't you close my door."

"Okay."

I say this with a half smile as my nervous feelings return.

"Suzette, is everything okay with you?"

"Yes."

"And the family?"

"Yes, Dave, things are fine. Why do you ask?"

"Well, let me just get right to it. I didn't know if something was going on at home or something was wrong with one of the boys. I have noticed a drop-off in your performance lately. You know with this reorganization going on, everyone is being watched.

"Suzette, you're one of my star players, and I need you to set an example for the others."

To me, this is code for "Suck it up and perform for the greater good of the department."

Dave continues. "I know you earned the highest mark for your latest performance review, but if I had to rate your most recent performance today, it wouldn't even come close to your last rating."

Those last words make my blood boil. Even though I am wearing a turtleneck, I can feel my neck turning red. In a split second, I am furious, hurt, and confused, and I feel very misunderstood. I can't believe it. He is talking about my job performance, something that I take great pride in. When someone says my performance is bad, it feels like they're saying to me that I am bad.

My mind is racing, but I need to gather my thoughts and respond factually, not emotionally. Thank goodness I'm angry. If I wasn't, he would probably see me tear up and hear my voice crackle. Right now, I'm too offended and angry to tear up.

My first response is to politely disagree with his assessment. I rattle off my goals for the year and my view of how I am performing against those goals.

He starts to cut in, but I won't let him. I talk over him. "Dave, let me add one final point, and then I'll listen to you. I think it's important to factor in how much downsizing has occurred. The work has not decreased but the size of the staff has. This means whoever is left must take on this additional work."

He nods his head in agreement and says, "I can't argue with you there. But, it's something about your attitude that has changed, Suzette."

I respond bluntly, "Give me some examples."

He gives me a long, direct look, to signal that he does not appreciate my tone. "There have been several instances where I've really needed folks to volunteer for additional projects. I could always count on you for that. You have not volunteered for anything lately. It seems like you, Suzette, of all people, have taken on the attitude that if it's not in my job description, don't ask me to do it."

He pauses. "Suzette, I have never known that to be your attitude. Before, I would walk around your desk at 7 or 8 p.m. and you'd still be there, plugging away. That is not the case anymore. It seems that nowadays you're out of here right at 5 p.m. I know that you have the boys to deal with, but your attitude has definitely changed."

"So, Dave, this seems less about my performance, and more about my attitude."

"That might be a fair statement. Off the top of my head, I can't recall any missed deadlines or anything like that. I can, however, recall a few staff meetings where it seemed your mind was a million miles away."

"I do recall a few staff meetings where I was not totally present, so this is a fair assessment."

My heart is no longer pounding. I feel relieved, and less angry. This whole conversation is about my attitude. I put my heart into my work, and I haven't done that in a long time here. I better understand Dave's observation.

I respond, "Dave, you've said a lot, and I've had a chance to listen to you closely. Please allow me to respond."

He unfolds his arms and makes a gesture with his hands as if he's giving me the floor. "First, I am relieved to hear that your talk with me is not performancerelated. This is important to me, because as you know, I take my job performance very seriously. You referenced my last performance review, but the one thing that I've been for this company is consistent. I've always maintained solid performance reviews since joining the company.

"Now, on to my attitude. Since I announced to the company that I was going back to school for my MBA, I was promised to be put on a developmental career track that would enable me to learn multiple facets of the business. That promise was made over two years ago. To date, it has not been kept. I feel that I have so much to offer, but I am not being fully utilized. Every five to six months, a new opportunity is discussed, but discussions eventually fall flat due to budgetary constraints or more changes with the reorganization efforts. In the end, nothing changes. I am continually put on hold and told to remain patient. Given all of this, I have not been inspired to volunteer for more projects and take on more of the same.

"Dave, can you please take a moment to see things from my perspective?"

His response is short and simple. "Suzette, I don't know what else to say to you. I can't tell you when another job may become available. What I do know is that I need you to bring the *old Suzette* back. Since you're not volunteering for those special projects, I'll just have to put some of them on your plate."

My appeal to him is a complete waste of time. My blood pressure is beginning to tick upward again. Just as I am about to come back with a stronger response, this voice within me says, "It's time." That's it…nothing more. It rings crystal clear to me. I know beyond a doubt this is God directing me.

There is an uncomfortable pause on my part as I look down at my papers searching for the first words to say to Dave. "Dave, it has been a pleasure working with you, but I believe that it is time for me to move on."

He gives me a longer than normal stare. "Are you quitting, Suzette?"

"Yes."

"Suzette, I had no idea that my talk with you would lead to you quitting. The company is in such great transition. We really can't afford to lose you at this time. Wouldn't you like to take the weekend to think about this?"

"Dave, there would have been a time where all I needed to hear was that the company really needed me. This would have been enough for me to suppress my feelings, and to stay. For some reason, I can't do it anymore."

"Are you sure you don't want the weekend to think about this?"

Before I realize it, the word "No" just falls right out of my mouth. However, the thought of Webb enters my mind as I give him my response. I can't go there just yet. I need to maintain my game face as long as I'm in his office.

"Suzette, I can't help but feel like I've done something really wrong here. I never knew our conversation would lead to this. How do I explain that I let you get away from us?"

"Dave, in all fairness to you, I've been doing my own soul searching for some time, so don't feel like you forced me into this decision."

He stands, and walks around his desk to give me a very warm handshake/partial hug.

"I'm here if you need me for anything, so don't think twice about calling me, Suzette."

"Thanks, Dave, I will definitely do that. To make things official, two Fridays from today will be my last day, which I believe is the 28th. I will email you my resignation letter by this Monday."

I leave his office walking down the corridor to the elevator. I really want to skip. I feel major relief. A real weight has been lifted.

On the walk back to my desk the thought of "What have I just done?" begins to creep in. I quickly dismiss it. I waste no time in packing my things, and I head to the parking lot.

I get in the car and plug up my cell phone, deciding who to tell first. While I feel the first person should definitely be Webb, I consider calling Karen first. She could give me pointers on how to break the news to him. I dismiss that thought, too. There's only one way to talk to Webb—honestly and genuinely.

I look before I shift my car into gear and I say, "Thank You, God. Thank You. There will always be those who will doubt whether the voice I heard was really Yours, but I know for certain it was Yours. I guess that's all that matters. Now, I need Your help with Webb. Please give me the words to genuinely and honestly express to him what happened today, and please allow him to understand my actions."

I call Webb to tell him that I have some great news to share with him. We agree to meet at a little sports bar near his office. Fortunately, I am able to hang up the phone with him before he presses me for more details. My mother-in-law is at basketball practice with the boys. They will probably order a pizza when they return, so we don't need to rush home.

Friday evenings in Chicago usually mean heavy traffic. If the travel gods were with me this morning, they certainly are not during my evening commute.

I finally make it to the restaurant a little more than an hour later. I spot him seated at a table towards the rear of the restaurant.

Feeling quite nervous, I greet Webb with a kiss as soon as I see him, but I waste no time delivering the news. "Honey, something major happened today."

"What's up?"

"I quit today."

"What happened? Did they let you go, or did you really quit?"

My eyes are now filled with tears. One more blink and my welled-up tears will spill onto my cheeks. I use my quivering lips to say, "I quit on good terms. In fact, Dave hugged me before I left his office. Webb, I'm sorry. I didn't mean for things to happen the way they did. I had a meeting with Dave, and our conversation took a turn. He has noticed a change in my attitude, and he needs the 'old Suzette' to return. As simple as it may sound, I can't go backwards."

My tears finally tip over and begin their race down my cheeks. Webb reaches for my hand across the table. When I put my hand in his, he says to me in his baritone voice, "I understand why you did this more than you think I do. Don't worry, things will work out."

Now, I feel real relief. I get up to hug Webb's upper body while he's still seated at the table to thank him for his love and support.

The waiter observes that we're beginning to peruse the menus and stops by to take our drink orders. Normally I would order a martini, but today's events call for additional prayer time with God to genuinely thank Him. It doesn't feel right to have vodka in my system while I am communicating with God. I order only one glass of red wine.

By the time we get home, the boys are just finishing their pizza and several rounds of video games. Myrna is upstairs in the kitchen watching television. Webb reaches for his ski jacket and hat. This means he's going on the back deck to smoke a cigar.

Meanwhile, I go upstairs to steal a few moments in private thought with God, but my mind begins to wander. I am pondering what I will name my consulting practice if I really start one. I don't want to name it Webb Consulting. Maybe I need to come up with a catchy business phrase.

I snap back from my fantasizing to make God a priority. First, I need to thank Him properly for everything that He has done for me today. I walk from my closet into the bathroom. I give our tub a second look and decide that I will kneel in prayer at the tub. We have a Jacuzzi tub, so it is something about the height of the tub that allows me to drape my torso over it. It's not a church altar but it can serve my purpose tonight.

I kneel down at my tub and pray.

> Father, I just want to find a special way to thank You for what You did for me today. I talk to You more often now, and I certainly write to You more. Now, I want to find a special place in the house where I can pray to you. For now, let's pretend that this tub is my personal sanctuary.
>
> First, I want You to know once more that I heard You speak to me today during my meeting with Dave. I

will never doubt that. I knew it was You. I must admit that I am a little afraid, but after hearing You today, I will always trust that You will be there for me. In fact, as I lean my body over this tub, I imagine that I am placing my hand inside of Your palm. All I need to do is to hold onto You.

I have also been thinking that while I have a lot to learn, I also have a lot to contribute. I have been dancing to the beat of others for far too long. It is time for me to let my light shine.

As I say these words, the lyrics of the hymn "This Little Light of Mine" run through my mind: "This little light of mine, I'm gonna let it shine."

I will name my company Light of Mine Consulting. Well, I can't actually call it "Light of Mine," because people will think I'm crazy. I will call it LOM Consulting.

Father, You and I will both know the real meaning of L-O-M. I also see You as the chairman of my board. This will make it feel like I am really working for You.

Coming Full Circle

Sometimes we can take on a too-big-to-fail mentality when we put our faith in those things that appear impossible to perish, or in those relationships that we believed would never become disloyal. We place our bets on what we see and live for the here and now. We feel ultimate betrayal when things don't end up how we envisioned, or how they were promised to us. Putting your faith in man or man-made principles always has a risk of changing no matter how high the stakes are, because neither possesses the quality of everlastingness. The next time you feel betrayed by man because he didn't honor his word, there is still a Word that you can always look to stand on.

Have you ever invested your faith in the wrong thing only to find that it has let you down?

"Jesus looked at him and loved him. 'One thing you lack,' he said. 'Go, sell everything you have and give to the poor, and you will have treasure in heaven. Then come, follow me.' At this the man's face fell. He went away sad, because he had great wealth."
(Mark 10:21-22 NIV)

Chapter 9

A Sea of Darkness

SHOOT…who could that be ringing the doorbell? I'm not expecting anyone.

I think, for a second, that it could be someone selling something, or a child raising money for his school. The bell ringing turns to hard knocking on the door. I step down off the stepladder in my closet to make my way downstairs. I peep through the stained glass on the front door and see that it's Julian. Webb and the boys just left the house to run a few errands and to take Julian to a birthday party. They had to swing back to the house because Julian forgot the gift on the dining room table.

Today is a rarity in my house. I am home alone, which means that I have the entire house to myself…on a Saturday afternoon. This never happens. I think the reason for my getting an afternoon to myself is because it's been three months since I left my job, and nothing has opened up for me yet. As the days wear on, I am becoming increasingly stressed about the next chapter of my professional life. I fear what the future may hold for me. I think Webb felt my anxiety come to a peak yesterday. This is why he just took the boys out of the house today and is giving me my much-desired space.

Three months ago when I heard those words, "It's time," in that crystal clear voice when I was meeting with Dave, I knew those were from God. He was telling me that it was time to move on. I also swore to myself that I would never, ever doubt that those were God's instructions even if Webb or anybody else thought I was a bit looney for believing that. However, doubt has started to creep into my thinking. What I continue to ponder daily is that God wouldn't lead me *from* a place unless He had the *to* portion in place. Yet it is three months later and the *to* portion is not evident. This leads to my greatest fear, which is that those words "it's time" were my own words and not God's.

I feel like I'm living each week in limbo. I am powerless over what's going to happen next. Unproductive weeks turn into unproductive months. When I look up, I have nothing to show for this particular period in my life. The job application process is similar to my life's experiences. I do my part, but I have to wait for someone else's response. This causes me anxiety because I have no control in the situation. I reach for something that I control to feel that my life is not just sitting idle, and that I am a productive being.

This was my mindset last month when I decided to sign up for the Chicago Marathon with Karen and Hillary. The marathon was not my idea. In fact, the thought of running a marathon never crossed my mind before, but it was something that came along just at the right time to make me feel like I was reaching for a goal, even if it wasn't necessarily the wisest use of my time. I did not have a deep-rooted desire to run a marathon. I just figured if all else failed on the professional end this year, at least I will be able to say I accomplished something that most others have not accomplished.

When I am not taking on such Herculean tasks as training for a marathon, I do other things. This can involve single-handedly cleaning the garage by myself from top to bottom. Doing things like this does two things for me: it distracts me from the very thing that I am stressing over, and it makes me feel empowered. At least I am accomplishing something, even if it's on a smaller scale. It is what I call mindless yet productive activity.

The lucky pick today is my closet. Several weeks ago, I was watching one of those home makeover channels and they talked about how efficient it is to color coordinate your closet. Apparently, reorganizing my closet will shave time off of getting dressed, and I will be able to create more wardrobe combinations. I think since I'm going to be doing more interviewing or meeting with potential consultant clients (you just never know), it would be beneficial for me to organize my entire closet, especially my business attire.

When Julian was knocking at the front door, I was moving the last few items from the top shelf in my closet out into my bedroom, so that I could begin my reorganizing efforts. Coordinating by color is a completely new exercise for me. I have always just organized my clothes as "winter" and "summer" clothes. Since it is spring, I can also make this a spring cleaning effort by choosing those items that I wish to donate, creating a more purposeful distraction for myself.

As I begin to organize things on my bed and the chaise lounge chair that sits catty-corner to my bed, I separate the donation items from the clothes that I plan to keep. I also separate the casual clothes from the work clothes. As I toss a suit to my right, my eyes catch a glimpse of the mound of all dark-colored suits, dresses, and skirts in the "work clothes" pile on the bed. At first I ignore it, but as my mind begins to envision my closet organized by color, I am quickly realizing that there isn't a whole lot of color here. I dismiss this and keep pulling out the donation items. It will all come together once I begin to put things back into the closet. I remind myself that I have a few colored silk blouses that are probably on the bottom of the pile, so "just wait" is what I tell myself.

Two hours and two very full bags of donation items later, everything is back in the closet, arranged by color. It did not come together. I am standing in a sea of navy and charcoal gray suits. I am surrounded by dark, lifeless suits. There are all dark-colored suits, dresses, and skirts on one side of the closet, and there are beige-, cream-, or oatmeal-colored blouses on the next rack over. I realize that I have just spent hours reorganizing a collection of uniforms, not a wardrobe of savvy business attire. I choose to donate two of the bright-colored blouses. I never wear these blouses but, after seeing all of the listlessness in my closet, I am tempted to pull them from the donation bag.

Perhaps, I associate color with more of an unprofessional look. No, that doesn't make any sense, because a person can have color in their business wardrobe and still look professional as long as the color isn't neon.

I'm dumbfounded by the appearance of my closet. I walk out into the bedroom and push the casual pile of clothes over to make room for myself on the bed. I quickly see that the "casual clothes" pile doesn't lack color. I guess with these colorful pieces mixed in, I didn't see that the majority of my work clothes were all dark-colored. I'm sure that someone off the street could have walked in here and seen that immediately. The people whom I work with must have witnessed this about me daily, but never said a word.

As I recline on the bed, I do recall Karen and Hillary inquiring about the way that I dress. They never asked me about the color of my suits, but they did ask me why I dressed so businesslike for class and why I always had a conservative, buttoned-up look about myself. Karen suggested that I try more open-necked, free-flowing blouses.

My initial reaction was a bit defensive. I felt like I was just dressing professionally. I was in one of the most elite, executive business school programs in the country. I took everything about that program seriously. I would never show up in a T-shirt and jeans to class, even when class was in session on Saturday. However, after reflecting on their question a bit more, I had to admit that I was completely oblivious to being buttoned up until they brought it to my attention. When I gave it a second thought, I realized that I do wear a lot of men-tailored button-down shirts with my suits. During my trip to China, I was even able to get some high-quality shirts with the French cuffs and my initials monogrammed on them at really cheap prices.

I get up from the bed with an I'm-not-going-to-take-this-sitting-down attitude and march barefoot back into the closet. I think to myself that when I walk out my door every morning, I have one objective in mind, and this is to look like a well-groomed, business professional. I am not focused on the color. I am not focused on how buttoned up something is or isn't. I just want the entire outfit to look appropriate.

But the toughness in me wears off quickly, and I begin to nervously curl and uncurl my toes on my right foot backwards and forwards in a rocking-like motion. I begin to take on a defeated posture. I've mastered looking professional, but I give into the truth, which is that each day I go out of this house and I look like the same, well-manicured Plain Jane.

I wonder if Webb notices this. If he does, what does he think? Maybe he finds these clothes completely unattractive but has never expressed his true feelings to me.

I encourage myself by pointing out how the cut and style of most of the suits and blazers vary. There's top stitching on some and unique cuts and designs on others. In other words, these are quality suits, and not your average boring attire.

My self-rationalization isn't working. My brain experiences a rush of fragmented thoughts and questions. I take advantage of the fact that I'm home alone and begin to talk out loud to myself.

This talking aloud to myself starts out in a very rational, controlled tone. It's as if I'm talking to a six-year-old little girl. I'm trying to find out what's hurting her. "Okay, navy and gray are not your favorite colors, so why did you purchase so many navy and gray suits?"

I can noticeably feel my temples pulsating. I feel that same tingly feeling that I felt on my walk to Dave's office on the day I quit.

Because I am distracted by what I am feeling physically, there is a long silence before I begin to answer myself. My mind wanders back to when I was preparing for my first interview right out of college. Someone said to me that I would need a good navy or gray suit to interview in. From that moment on, I must have thought those were the colors of the corporate workplace. If I wanted to conform, or to show that I was one of them, I needed to conform on every level. So, it appears that I religiously acquired these same suits over the years just as a parochial school student would purchase the school uniform for her school years.

After recalling this, I begin to utter, "To fit in, I purchased both navy and gray suits. To be acceptable. To conform by looking the part. To become one of them. To play it safe. To remain predictable. To appear non-threatening...all in a concerted effort to receive their stamp of *FRICKIN' APPROVAL!*"

My tears are back. I swallow, and I feel the pain in my throat. I resist the opportunity to cry out loud. I weep to myself as if someone is in the next room.

I look around in the closet, I walk back to the bedroom, then back again to the closet, and I continue, "You made a royal mistake, girl! You equated looking *appropriate* with *acceptance*! You're fluttering around here in all of these dreary-ass-looking suits saying *accept me...please accept me...*and where did it get *YOU*? Where did it get *YOU, SUZETTE*?

"Nowhere! It got you flat-out nowhere! You've been in the same damn job after going to one of the elite grad schools. You were wearing this same old crap everyday when you started school and even when you finished, and it has all led to *NOTHING...* absolutely *NOTHING!*

"Where's your payoff? Didn't they teach you that in business school about getting a *RETURN* on your investment? Well, it seems like you've invested a whole lot of time and effort in exchange for *NO FRICKIN' RETURN* for *YOURSELF!*

"They didn't appreciate you then, and surely don't appreciate you *now!* This is why no one is calling you back!"

My dismay about my clothes has turned to pure, unadulterated anger at myself.

I roughly brush my tears away. I revert back to my monotone voice, and I say to myself out loud, "The real question is not why you bought so many of the same colored suits. The real question is what do you really like?

"Suzette, are you ready to get real in here? The question of the FRICKIN' DAY *is* what do *you* really like?"

The river of tears is right there to just flow out of me, accompanied by a hurtful moan like a wounded animal. They are caught in my chest just waiting on the next breath to unleash them. I can do this, because no one is at home. But, I fear that if I let go and go to *this* place, that I may not be able to put myself back together by the time Webb and the boys return home.

Instead, I just run down the stairs barefooted and head to the kitchen. I whip off the ponytail holder that is holding my hair together while en route. As soon as my feet feel the cold of the kitchen hardwood floors, I reach for the largest wine goblet I can find to pour myself a very large glass of wine. I would prefer vodka, but we don't keep hard liquor in the house.

I take two huge gulps of wine, almost drinking nearly half the goblet in the first swallow. I quickly remove the stopper in the bottle and nearly fill the glass again. Then, I move over to the pantry as I'm looking for something salty to bite. Chips never last in this house with the boys, but I do find a bag of pretzels. I grab the pretzels and head back upstairs to lick my wounds.

I enter my bedroom and walk by my closet without looking inside. I sit on the bed in the same spot that I cleared away earlier, and I lay my head on one of the pillows. I reflect on things, and begin to sob into my pillow. For the next thirty minutes or so it's just sobbing, sipping, and eating an entire bag of pretzels. Eventually, I peek over at the clock and realize that Webb and the boys could be coming home soon. I need to hang the remainder of casual clothes back in the closet and put my bedroom back together before Webb and the boys return.

As I'm putting everything back, I see some red cardboard sticking out from the bottom rack. For curiosity's sake, I push back the clothes on the bottom rack and notice that it's the dream board that I created with Andrea last year. I reach for it, open it up, and see the lady in the center of my board who is in prison. I immediately recall that Andrea's take on my dream board was that the imprisoned woman in the center of my board was actually me. I also recall getting offended and dismissing her comments as absurd.

I can hear her now. "The positive and uplifting words you think you have for this woman are the words that you should tell yourself."

I pick up the board and hold it at my side while I look up at all of the order that I created in my closet: the dark-colored suits on one side, the beige- and cream-colored blouses on the rack below, and the casual clothes on the opposite side. My closet tells a nauseating story. I could never look at these suits and blouses again without seeing them as uniforms.

My four-cornered closet feels like a four-cornered prison cell. I see now what Andrea saw a long time ago, and what Karen and Hillary sensed. I specifically recall Karen suggesting that I try "free-flowing" blouses, but there was nothing free about the way I was living.

I lift the board from my side, open it once more, and look into the eyes of this woman on my board. "The words that I thought I had for you, I don't anymore. I don't have words for you, because I don't even know what to tell myself. I thought I had encouragement for you because I saw myself in a better place than you. I wanted to say something inspiring and uplifting that you could cling to when you got out of prison. I now see that I am in a prison myself, a self-inflicted solitary confinement. This closet or jail cell is a reflection of how I've been living my life. I have to figure out how to get out of this thing myself before I'm in a position to advise you."

As I experience this moment of truth, on the inside I feel like what I've just professed to do sounds monumental. I have decades of experience being a peoplepleaser and valuing other folks' way over my own. I have to lead with my own way, and I don't know what's real anymore. I feel lost and don't even know where to begin.

For the last few years, I have been searching for my life's purpose. I see now why God has not revealed it to me. I think He's saying that somewhere along the way, I lost me. In order to find my purpose, I need to first find myself.

I sink down in the center of my sea of darkness.

Coming Full Circle

The behaviors at our core are the toughest to face, and ultimately the toughest to change. They help to define ourselves for better or for worse. These behaviors are to us what software is to a computer. They are the reason that we are wired a certain way. Sometimes this behavior is the only one we've ever been exposed to or practiced. Going in to rewrite parts of your software can feel scary, overwhelming, and even invalidating. The good news is that sometimes God will go to great lengths to point out a new way forward. He can shine His light on something as insignificant as a wardrobe to reveal an inauthentic thread that is running throughout one's life. No need to run scared. The fact that He shined His light on this opportunity to change means that He will also supply you with what you need to pull it off.

What problems in your life do you ignore,
because they are too overwhelming to confront?

"I can do all things through him who strengthens me."
(Phil. 4:13 NIV)

Chapter 10

The Revolution

I REACH FOR MY CELL PHONE to call Webb and the boys. They should have been home at least an hour ago. As I reach for my phone, a reminder on my calendar pops up. I see that I am scheduled to meet Karen, Hillary, and a few other girls for drinks within the hour. I completely forgot about this. One of Hillary's friends is moving to town and we are all welcoming her to Chicago. There's a part of me that could definitely go for a night out with the girls to have a few laughs; the other part of me feels like I'm in no mood to laugh, or to be funny.

I arrive at the restaurant in an-all tan outfit, little makeup, and my hair brushed back into a bun. I had little energy to indulge a curling iron prior to dinner. Karen, Hillary, and her friend Alicia, who is moving to Chicago, are already seated at a table. The hostess directs me to the table. I can see from the hostess stand what each woman is wearing. As soon as I see them, I feel that I'm too conservatively dressed. Everyone is dressed casually, yet hip, and there is zero hipness to my look. Instantly, I feel inferior. This takes me right back to my closet experience.

To ensure that I drown out that thought, I speed up my pace to the table. I want to catch the server before he leaves so I can place my drink order now. I order a large margarita with a shot of Cuervo Gold tequila.

I put my purse down and greet everyone individually before taking my seat at the table. Just as Alicia starts to tell everyone about her new job, the other two ladies arrive. We share another round of drinks, but I soon realize that I am still reeling from my closet experience. I signal to Alicia across the table, and tap my watch simultaneously to tell her that I have to leave. Of course, I put it all on the fact that Webb has had the boys all day. I give my farewell and make sure that Alicia has my contact information. I can't get out of that restaurant fast enough.

When I return home, Webb is on the back deck smoking a cigar and talking on the phone. The boys are downstairs watching television. I walk up to Webb and softly kiss his forehead to thank him again for giving me a free afternoon. He puts his friend on hold and says, "It looks like you hit your closet pretty hard."

"Yes, it was a lot of work, but it needed to be done."

"I'll be in shortly."

"No rush. I'm pretty tired, so I'm heading to bed."

Before getting into bed, I remove my cell phone from my purse. I see that I missed a call from Hillary. I call her back and embarrassingly disclose my closet meltdown to her. I confess that I feel like such a fool for not knowing that I was so buttoned up, and in some ways locked up in these corporate-like uniforms weekly. Second, I also admit that I have been holding myself to some corporate standard of dress for so long that I really haven't developed a style of my own.

Just as I'm pouring it all out, Hillary quickly cuts in and says, "Girl, you're being way too hard on yourself. I completely disagree with you that you don't have your own style. Now, I will say that

Karen and I thought you were aware that you dressed that way, which is why we questioned you about it."

"Yes, and if you recall, I always responded defensively at the time, so I guess I didn't hear or appreciate what you were both trying to communicate to me."

"We all live and we learn. You know you don't need to ask me twice to go shopping with you if you want to add more color to your closet. I am glad to help you with that."

I thank her, and we talk only for a few more minutes. I'm glad that I called her back when I did. Her words were comforting and nonjudgmental. I feel like I just hung up the phone with a true friend.

My body's alarm clock goes off even when my physical alarm clock doesn't. It's nearly 6 a.m., and the tape recorder in my head is pressed to "play." The scene from my closet is already playing. I also realize that I did not even say my prayers last night before going to bed.

I am really in the mood for hearing a good sermon today. I know it will be a waste of time to go to my church, so I'm wondering if I should try to go Rev. Joseph's church on the South Side. He will often have a good message, although his church is pretty far away, so I don't visit more often. I am so hungry for a good message that I think I am willing to make the drive this morning.

If I'm going, I need to get a move on, because the early service starts within the hour. I'll let Webb and the boys sleep in. They can meet me somewhere for breakfast after church. The boys will love the idea of sleeping in and going to breakfast later. I nudge Webb and share my plan. He's fine with it as he appreciates the chance to sleep in, too.

Getting dressed for church is pretty hassle-free. I decide to wear a black dress that is simple and easy to wear. I don't need to bother Webb with zipping or buttoning me up. I get in my car and realize that service has already started. I am guilty of only going for the sermon portion, so there's still time to stop and get Starbucks on the way.

There's no traffic this early, but parking is somewhat of a challenge since I'm arriving late. I get a parking spot two blocks away. This church is large, and each service is usually filled to capacity. I can't just walk in and seat myself, especially after the service has already started, so I have to wait until an usher seats me.

The usher sees my gesture and sticks up one finger to ask if I am a party of one. I give an affirmative nod and get a pretty decent seat. Now, I just need to hear a great sermon so that I can stop obsessing about yesterday.

I get situated and look around to see if there's anyone I know, but there isn't. While flipping through the church bulletin to pass time until the pastor comes on, I hear his voice on the P.A. system. He is traveling today and is not here to deliver the message. But, we're in good hands, because Pastor Sean McMillan will be the one delivering today's sermon.

Before I can catch myself, somehow the words "I can't win for frickin' losing" tumble right out of my mouth. I quickly chastise myself. "Oh my goodness, Father, please forgive me. Please, Father, forgive me. I just swore in the church!" I sit and silently say, "Father, you know that I have never, ever done anything like this before. I am just trying to understand my life more. I came to church early this morning to hear a good sermon. Yet on the very day that I come all the way out here, so hungry for a message that I leave Webb and the kids at home, the pastor that I came to hear is traveling.'" I am gravely disappointed because visiting pastors rarely deliver good messages.

I am looking for a path to make a quick exit. I am nearly in the center of my pew. I study whether it would be less disruptive to exit on the left versus the right.

As I'm thinking about my next move, I hear a voice say, "Jesus emerges after forty days of suffering in the desert with clarity of purpose.... Please turn to Luke, the 4th chapter, verses 16-21."

I think, "Wait, did he just say the word 'purpose'? Well, I can't leave during the reading of the scripture, and I think he just said the word 'purpose.' I'll hang out a bit to see where he's going with this."

I didn't bring a Bible, so I move over to my neighbor on my left. I read Luke 4:16-21 along with her.

Pastor McMillan repeats, "Jesus emerges after forty days of suffering in the desert with clarity of purpose. He's had to deal with Himself in the darkness.... He's been torn, tested, and tried. He's had to encounter demonic engagement, and now He's ready to assume the mantel of His ministry. So after Jesus' forty days in the desert, He went to the synagogue, took the scriptures, and opened the book. He read, 'The Spirit of the Lord is upon me.'

"God will work with us in similar ways, and sometimes the time that we spend in the darkness will press out of our mouths a clarity that we wouldn't have unless we had experienced the darkness."

I need to be taking notes, but I quickly remind myself that I can buy the tape at the end of service. I am enthralled by everything that Pastor McMillan is saying. Every word is critical to my soul. Just as he opens his mouth again, a baby starts to cry. My eyes automatically begin to roam for the mother of this baby to make eye contact (friendly, of course). I want my eyes to communicate to quiet her child down, or to temporarily step outside until her child quiets down.

He continues, "This is important to understand, beloved, because God will continually test us behind closed doors. He does not want us to come out in public until we have dealt with some things in private."

My closet experience was my private battle. My search for my purpose is my private battle. "Wait, maybe God is saying to me..."

I can't analyze what God is saying yet, because I'll miss where Pastor McMillan is going next.

He asks the congregation, "Can I preach it like I want to?"

The church roars back a resounding "Yes!"

I also say "yes," and I rise to my feet at the same time.

He says, "You don't want your gifts to take you places where your character cannot keep you."

I respond, "Bada bing, bada boom!"

My neighbor who appears friendly and just as engaged as I am says to me, "This young man is really preaching." I squeeze her hand back, and nod my head affirmatively again.

To bring silence back over the church again, he brings his commander-like tone back and goes on to say, "We live from one day to the next…we pay bills…we raise children…we go to work from one day to the next, but nothing has claimed us and nothing has called us…and nothing has raised us and nothing has engaged us. We live from one day to the next of eating, drinking, and sleeping, but nothing has called us in the midnight hour."

I rise to my feet. The tears are streaming so fast down my cheeks that they have rolled under my chin to my neck. The handful of tissues I was holding now looks like two small cotton balls. I am standing and crying profusely, two things that I have never done during any sermon. I try to sit down a couple of times, but I keep popping back up. Each time I am concerned about blocking the view of the person sitting directly behind me. I turn and apologize for standing so much. I receive the most comforting assurance that I'm just fine. My tears pour out even more.

He goes on. "We all want to know what we should be doing with our life. I have this job…. I have these kids…. I have this degree…. I have this marriage, but what should I be doing?"

I respond, "Yes! Yes!"

He is preaching directly to everything that I have been going through since before I went back to grad school. Finally, I get

82

to hear a message that teaches directly to my story. My tears are everywhere, but my soul is being cleansed. I will forever treasure God for ordering my steps to this church this morning.

Pastor McMillan goes on to say, "We try to find ourselves in the acquisition of things and titles. I am my car. I am my title. I am my degree."

Yep, that would be me too. I treat my value and self-worth as if they were a composite score of my job title, my credentials, the places I've traveled, the neighborhood that I live in—you name it. If just one of these things goes away, I see myself as less. In other words, I increase and decrease in value as the things in my life that I deem valuable increase and decrease.

This is happening to me right now. I am unemployed; hence, I see myself as less, so I sign up to run a marathon race. This is something I never had even the slightest desire to do. I sign up mostly to keep the scale of my achievements somewhat balanced. One way to view things is that being unemployed and running a marathon race are like comparing apples to oranges. Another viewpoint is that I would be replacing one missed goal (rising to the executive ranks in my company) to achieving another goal (running and finishing a marathon race, a goal that less than 1% of the human population achieves). Again, these are apples and oranges, but it is achievement that I can take on, and control for now.

He animatedly lifts the Bible and says, "Every page of this book is about *you*! I know you thought the Bible was about Abraham and Sarah, but I came to tell you this morning that this great book is about you!"

"You are not a mistake. You are not illegitimate."

Whew, I needed to be reminded of that, because my parents were never married.

He brings it full circle. "You are not a mess. You are a child of the living God."

He is teaching us that when we look at the text Luke 4:16-21, we are supposed to see ourselves. Too often we think the Bible is about all of the great people who came before us, and not us. He shows us how Jesus knew this text was about Him.

This is *it*. I have been valuing what others say and elevating *their* way over my own way as if it were the Gospel. Luke 4:16-21 is the only Gospel.

He wraps up by asking the congregation if we want a revolution or just another change in our lives. I think to myself, "I want a revolution, Father. I am standing with you and trusting you until things are further revealed to me about my life's course. I will work hard each day. Just guide me, Father."

As the pianist begins to play, which is a real sign that the sermon is over, I come full circle with my final "ah ha!" moment of the hour. I have been trying to succeed in my life only by trying to change those things outside me. I've been unconscious to the fact that a shift needs to take place within me. I think that as much as I seek God about my purpose, He's trying to teach me that if I focus on finding and uncovering the real Suzette, I will see my purpose as clearly as I see the light of day.

There's a long line waiting to greet the pastor after church. I know that I told Webb and the boys that we could go to breakfast immediately following the service, but there's no way that I can leave this church without greeting the pastor. While I'm waiting in the line to meet Pastor McMillan, I recall my request to God about sending me to a "teaching" pastor. He surely answered my prayer this morning.

While walking back to the car, I call Webb to tell him that I just met the most amazing pastor who just preached a sermon like I never heard before. He has a small church here in Chicago, and I'd like us to visit his church next Sunday.

After breakfast and a stop at the grocery store, we finally make it home. As I'm changing out of my dress, it dawns on me that this is the same dress that I wore to my graduation last year. I smile to

84

myself and think that I may have walked across a stage to graduate in this dress last year, but I sat in a pew today, and graduated all over again.

Coming Full Circle

Past disappointments and hurts leave us not only afraid of the future, but afraid of the deepest parts of ourselves. We fear that our true selves won't be accepted. We fear that our true selves can't be loved. We fear that our true selves are not good enough. Even more so, we fear that if we leave behind the only façade that we've ever known, we're unaware of how life will accept our true selves. It's one thing to have your façade rejected. It's another thing to experience the rejection of your true self. Your question of the hour is: "Do you have the courage to allow the person that you truly are to step forward, and present what only you can offer to the world?"

Do you have the courage to fight for your deepest self?

"And we know that in all things God works for the good of those who love Him, who have been called according to His purpose."
(Romans 8:28 NIV)

Part Two

Preparation

Overview

THE SECOND PHASE of the butterfly's life is a tremendous stage of growth. After the butterfly egg hatches, a tiny caterpillar emerges and its sole purpose at this stage is to eat and to grow. The caterpillar's exoskeleton or skin does not expand to accommodate the caterpillar's growth, so he is forced to shed his skin. This shedding process is called molting, and is pretty hassle-free for the caterpillar to endure. In particular, monarch butterflies shed their skin five times.

Each layer of skin is larger than the next so as soon as he sheds one layer, the new skin is right underneath the one he just shed. The caterpillar has such a hearty appetite during this time that he even eats the skin that he sheds. But, as God would have it, there's a purpose for that too. His skin turns out to be good for him because it is filled with nutrients, which further facilitate his growth. When the caterpillar is fully grown, he will eventually leave the plant that he has been feeding on to enter his next stage of development.

Similar to the caterpillar outgrowing his own skin, we too can feel like we've outgrown our current place in life and will ask for more. You know this period. It feels like your efforts don't equal your results. It's like you're running in place—moving, but not progressing. This leads to you having more questions than answers, and you wonder if *your time* will ever come. You petition God over and over again but you get no response. You may even begin to compare yourself to others as you observe opportunities opening up for them but not for you. This drought-like period can cause you to doubt yourself and question whether you did, or didn't, do something to deserve all of this.

The caterpillar will live and feed off of the *same* plant during this stage, and will only advance to his next phase of development when it is time for him to do so. Unbeknownst to him, this phase was in place to prepare him for the great work he has ahead. It is possible that the same holds true for you.

Chapter 11

Out of Step

FOR THE LAST TWO MORNINGS, the only thing I've looked forward to with Webb is seeing his back as he leaves for the office. Lately, we've been at odds about my approach to finding employment. Our approaches are such polar opposites that his might as well be from Mars and mine from Venus.

Two weeks ago, I tried to switch things up. I spontaneously suggested that we walk to a fun spot in our neighborhood for lunch. I thought we could use that time to have a more intimate discussion about what we really want out of life, what we fear most, and what's holding us back from achieving our life goals. This idea backfires. Webb feels like a discussion about our deepest fears and life goals is separate from the present reality of me getting a job. In fact, I think he wants the reverse. If I get a job, we can talk all day about goals, but monetize that MBA today. Of course, he never says that to me, but I believe that's what he's really thinking. I have come to avoid these types of conversations, too.

This morning, however, feels pleasantly different. A few months ago, our dear friend Louis invited us to this year's Essence

Music Festival in New Orleans. This morning is the eve of our trip. We both appear ready to bury the hatchet so that we can focus on our weekend escapade to the "*Big Easy.*"

Coming Full Circle

There are times when you will reach that proverbial fork in life's road, and you will only get a feeling about which direction you should or shouldn't go. You won't have any explanations to offer, just a feeling. In addition to being challenged by life itself, you are also challenged by those around you. They have expectations of you, and they expect you to justify your position about taking one course over the other beyond your feelings. At this point, you almost wish you could take those feelings rested on your heart and belly and share them, so they could experience themselves why you hold your position. Of course, you cannot do that because God only gave you those feelings. The conflict ensues as they continue to solicit you to change course, and you continue to solicit their trust and support.

Asking someone to fly blind with you, especially when you don't possess a clear understanding of matters yourself, can be a tough ask. During this phase of your life, you will be tasked with the great balancing act of continuing to respond to them with love and respect (even if it's a distant love) while remaining true to your vision. One navigation tip: Continue to seek direction from the One who gave you the feelings in the first place.

Today, I am taking action to protect my hopes.

"Stand firm, and you will win life."
(Luke 21:19 NIV)

Chapter 12

In Step

I WONDER IF IT'S JUST ME, but I have observed that certain cities have their own smell to them. New Orleans is definitely one of those cities. My senses are triggered as soon as the wheels of the plane touch the tarmac. It's like seeing a pickle—your taste buds are instantly stimulated before you actually put the pickle into your mouth. In a similar way, I automatically recall the unique aroma that is New Orleans.

While I can effortlessly recall the city's scent, I struggle to describe it. There is no single description for it. I wish I could use a pretty metaphor and say it smells like half-finished roux and fresh magnolias. It does not. Instead, the smell that is reminiscent to me reeks of stale doughnuts doused in a whiskey sour with fresh drizzles of rain in the air. New Orleans is not really a place you can experience vicariously through another. This is one of those places on the planet that requires you to experience it firsthand.

As I eagerly walk onto the jet bridge to confirm the city's scent, the heat index is confirmed for me, too. I forgot how hot this city can get before noon. As much as I miss the summer temperatures, my hair does not miss the humidity. I can already feel my curls loosening. Nevertheless, I will not let a bad hair day alter my mood. If necessary, I will pull my hair back into a ponytail, and keep moving.

Webb and I are famished. We briskly walk down the concourse, through the baggage claim area, and toward the rental car counters to pick up our car. We intentionally did not eat this morning to save ourselves for our first New Orleans meal of the weekend. I think Webb wants to go to Acme Oyster House in the French Quarter. Acme is one of my favorite spots. My grandmother Millie and I would go to Acme and sometimes eat three to four dozen oysters in one sitting. Unfortunately, we'll have to squeeze Acme's into our schedule at another time, because it isn't open yet. I'll take Webb to Le Richelieu. It's another spot in the Quarter that I don't think I've taken him to before. The restaurant's indoor patio overlooks a picturesque pool, and we can get a decent breakfast. (Mostly I can nurture my craving for a Tequila Sunrise.) When I get to New Orleans, I crave both the food and the liquor.

En route to the restaurant, Webb tries to recall our last visit to New Orleans. I count backwards and calculate five years. I can't believe it. Five years doesn't seem correct, so I use my fingers to count again. I conclude that it truly has been five years since I've been home. When I moved away, I never thought I could survive being away from home for one year, much less five. This only escalates my desires to reconnect with everyone. Even though I no longer have family here, my close friends and their families are like my own family, so it all feels the same.

While it has been five years since we've seen each other, it has not been five years since we've communicated. We always reconnect on special occasions like our birthdays, Christmas, and especially at Thanksgiving. Michelle is such a good cook, always daring to try new recipes and to spruce up old ones. Typically, I will call her when I'm in the mood to concoct something new to add to our traditional holiday staples.

Thank goodness Louis and Hillary have taken the lead to get everyone together for this year's Essence Festival. Initially, we couldn't afford this trip, because I am not working. However, when Dr. Louis Barrington does something, he does it right. He not only invites us to spend the weekend with him at his home, which we've dubbed *Chez Louis*, but he has provided us with premium tickets for the entire weekend. Hillary's attendance to this weekend festival puts the icing on the cake. Hillary invited Karen and her husband, so I couldn't pass up the opportunity to connect my girlfriends from grad school with my girlfriends from high school.

We're already seated at the restaurant, and I'm just about to order my second Tequila Sunrise, but I feel as though I need to give my waiter better instructions.

I say to him, "This time, please have your guy make it good."

Webb adds, "What she really means is stronger…. She wants you to ask your bartender to make her drink stronger."

I defer to Webb with sort of a sheepish grin.

We continue our small talk about the latest, greatest updates in everyone's lives until we're interrupted by the ringing of Webb's cell phone. I often refer to it as that little animal. It never seems to stop, but I understand this is a call that he needs to take. The break in our conversation frees my mouth to savor this second cocktail and allows my mind to drift to what I will wear tonight.

I honestly think I overpacked because I brought at least two different wardrobe options for each night. My look is important for several reasons. First, I want to show myself that I am completely over my closet meltdown. Secondly, I sort of want to show my girlfriends whom I haven't seen in five years that I still *have it*. Furthermore, Karen and Hillary still accuse me of dressing too corporate-like. That comment actually gets underneath my skin, so I definitely don't want to hear that this weekend. Finally, I don't want it to appear as if I'm trying too hard. In other words, I don't want to get my look too perfect, because then it will be obvious that I've been wrestling with the idea for too long. Instead, I want a well-coordinated look that falls naturally on my frame and appears effortless.

In the same way, I want my behavior around my two different sets of girlfriends to also be effortless. Even though I am always Suzette, I can sometimes behave differently around different sets of friends. If I am around girlfriends who like to have a few good martinis and let their hair down a bit, I can enjoy that and fit right in with no problem. If I'm around girlfriends who are a bit more reserved and will call it quits after having one glass of wine, I can fit right in there, too.

This is a little more than just going with the flow. I really do act differently. I call this my water syndrome. Just as water takes on the shape of its vessel, I can take on the shape of any social setting that I'm in. I have become a master at this, and I can't really say where I learned how to behave like this. I can dial it up or dial it down in an instant. It becomes like second nature to me. Most often, I appreciate my social-butterfly nature. The delicate dance comes when I have to manage *which* Suzette will be more pronounced when I am trying to appeal to different groups in one setting.

I return from my daydreaming and notice that Webb is still on the phone. I decide that I will drive us to Louis' house. I dread riding with Webb while he is talking on the phone because he is too preoccupied. I want to get from Point A to Point B in the most expeditious way. Webb will be on the phone more focused on making a point rather than making the light that's ahead. To avoid all of this, I choose to drive.

I put the key in the ignition, glad that I did not order a third Tequila Sunrise. I hardly feel anything after drinking two, but three likely would have given me a buzz.

96

Just as we are exiting The Quarter, Webb points back and mouths to me that he wants to stop at the cigar shop that he often frequents when he is here. It's not a place that I readily recall so I get somewhat lost, but eventually I stumble upon it.

While I'm waiting in the car for Webb, I make a quick call to Louis to let him know that we're on the way. I end our call so quickly that I forget to ask him about the details for tonight. Will we go directly to the concert, or will we go to dinner first?

Knowing Louis, he made dinner reservations last week at a swank New Orleans restaurant at which we will dine before to-night's concert. If that's the case, then my outfit is decided. I will wear my white pantsuit with the hot pink halter top. This will give me a great dual look for both dinner and the festival. I can sport the suit at dinner, and the halter top at the festival. The halter top will showcase my softly defined biceps, which will definitely show that I still have *it*. Webb loves me in this suit, too.

I am so relieved that I do not have the pressure of having to plan Webb's outfit too. I have a couple of girlfriends who dress their guys for special events. They coordinate everything from the suit and tie right on down to the shoes. Webb is not that kind of guy. He had an excellent teacher early in life: his mother, Myrna. He is such a smart dresser that, sometimes, I feel pressed to stay on my toes so that he doesn't out-dress me. Whenever I become antsy about my outfit after seeing his, he fondly tells me, "Baby girl, no man could ever out-dress you."

As this last thought crosses my mind, I look up and see Webb. He's sauntering out of the cigar shop like a kid coming out of a candy store. Of course, he's on the phone yet again. From what I can see, he has at least eight to ten cigars in a clear Ziploc-like bag. When he gets in the car, he covers the mouthpiece and whispers that we should make one final stop at the grocery store to avoid going to Louis' empty-handed. I rule that out. I am eager to get to Louis', so we drive directly there.

Louis walks out to greet us as soon as we pull into the driveway. He times our arrival perfectly after buzzing us into his gated community. I greet him warmly, but I am looking for his wife, Lisa. I am eager to meet her. Actually, I am only eager to see her... to see how she compares to Liz, who is one tough act to follow. I know already. This is terribly shallow of me. Shallow, but true.

We enter to the sounds of Pat Metheny softly piped throughout the house. Once inside and situated in the guest room, I still see no sign of Lisa. I inquire as to her whereabouts with Louis, and learn that she's still working. In fact, because she has a full workday there won't be time to go to a fancy dinner before the first concert starts. Lisa has cooked dinner in advance for everyone.

Even though I have yet to meet her in person, she is introducing herself to me as I walk through her home. Entering a woman's home can tell you a lot about her. Lisa's home is spotless, and the extra detail given to the guest bedroom and bathroom to welcome Webb and me is duly noted. Even though she doesn't have to work, she chooses to do so anyway. And, instead of conveniently ordering out for food, she chose to cook in advance.

The afternoon goes pretty quickly. Initially, I sit out at the pool with Webb and Louis while Louis drinks a glass of champagne and Webb smokes his cigar. However, I realize that Louis and Webb would prefer to catch up on their own. This is fine with me, because I could use a nap.

Before lying down to take a nap, I check in with Michelle to find out her plans for the weekend. Unfortunately, I learn that she won't be able to make it to town. Michelle works in media and lives in Shreveport, LA, which is about a four- to five-hour drive away. Because she has to work today, she wouldn't arrive until midday Saturday only to have to drive back midday Sunday to be refreshed for Monday. Therefore, a long drive over a short weekend doesn't make sense for her. She'll have to catch us the next time.

I absolutely hate to hear this. Michelle and I have been friends since freshman year of high school, and she is also Julian's godmother. She is the one girlfriend who knows just about everything about me. She is the girlfriend who I've likely cried the most with, and also laughed the hardest with. Among all of my high school girlfriends that I wanted to introduce to Karen and Hillary, Michelle is the most important.

Webb gently rubs my shoulder to wake me up and let me know that it's time to start getting ready. I get up and begin to lay my clothes out on the unslept side of the bed. I will stick with my white pantsuit/halter top ensemble even though we're not going to a fancy restaurant for dinner. The feelings that I have about putting this outfit together is reminiscent of when Webb and I were dating. We're in such a good place that it feels like he's courting me, like I am experiencing the newness of our relationship. I feel as though I am getting dressed for a date with him as his girlfriend, and not his wife. This feeling is really refreshing, given where we've been the last several weeks.

We get to the Essence Festival just moments before the first concert kicks off the weekend. Only seconds after entering the main stage seating area, the Superdome lights flash on and off. That's a sure sign that we're moments away from showtime. Our plan was to arrive early to avoid being rushed, but parking turned out to be worse than traffic. The lights flicker on and off once more. The crowd roars in anticipation, and I begin to watch the Bic lighters go up in the air.

Everyone is fixated on the stage, and out comes the one and only Alicia Keys. Webb and I have an affinity for great talent, and she exceeds every aspect of our expectations. She performs tunes that I know well, and some new ones that I don't know as well, but appreciate nonetheless. I sing along to the tunes with which I am familiar, and I just sort of groove in place to the ones with which I am not familiar. All in all, her performance is magnificent, and my only complaint is that it wasn't longer.

As Alicia wraps up her last tune and starts to bid her farewell to New Orleans, Webb and I excuse ourselves and start to make our way to the superlounges. We want to catch The Roots, a neo-soul group that is one of our favorites.

On the way to the superlounges, we run into Karen and Rick. They, too, are exploring things before the next main stage act comes on. We greet each other with warm embraces, but I can see a hint of a question mark on Karen's face as her eyes shift from Webb to me, as if to say, "Sue, what in the world are you doing at the Essence Fest with a suit on?" I, of course, pretend that I don't notice it, and I immediately switch to Louis' and Lisa's barbecue tomorrow. They told us earlier that they were going to give a barbecue/pool party tomorrow during the day, and that I should invite my Chicago friends. Karen says that she's not sure what Rick has planned, but she and Hillary will definitely be there.

We finally find the superlounge where The Roots are performing, and the show is already underway. As soon as we walk into the lounge, their sound becomes instantly mesmerizing. I need this. I need the distraction from how much my feet are aching me at this very moment. Webb is mesmerized too, because he catches me off guard and takes my hand, and leads me into a romantic two-step dance with him.

His love for me is evident in the way he grips my hand. This latest move reaffirms that we are finally *in step* with each other. Not too distant are those times when we were out of step.

I surrender first to his embrace, and second to the idea that my understanding of real love is evolving. Most of my life, I have pined for the romantic, problem-free version of love while discounting the value of tough love. Tough love is necessary to endure the tough times. I'm sure each of us wanted to throw in the towel at one point or another, but we didn't. I take humble pride in us being able to press ourselves to this point, not giving up when we were out of step, but we hung in there with each other until we came around to being in step once again. Getting to the other side feels rewarding. It makes all of the disagreements, and those Men-are-from-Mars, Women-are-from-Venus idiosyncrasies, worth it.

I think that's how Louis must feel, too. There have been many more years of his life when he wasn't able to put on a party like the one he is planning for tomorrow due to medical school, his residency, the many holidays that he actually worked or was "on call," which is the same thing. I am sure there have been many times on his journey when he, too, wanted to throw in the towel, but he didn't. I think the next time I am striving toward something that is really worth it, and the difficult times have me hostage, I will remind myself that today's **Blues** pale in comparison to tomorrow's **Blessings**.

Coming Full Circle

If we had a choice between experiencing the blues or the blessings of life, most likely we would always choose the blessings. However, we cannot overlook all that is happening behind the scenes when the blues take center stage. The blues come to teach, strengthen, enable us to make different choices, push us to endure, etc. However, when we become too immersed in our blues, we can miss all of the great work that, in turn, is helping to set the stage for our blessings.

Imagine that you're in a movie theater, and you're in the center seat of Row 1. You're nearly enveloped by the movie screen. Now, if you move back several rows to be seated more towards the center of the theater, you see there is more to appreciate. Up front, it may have been difficult to follow the story line, to appreciate the film's cinematography, special effects, etc., but you can appreciate more when you bring more into view. Don't let your blues cloud or confuse you. Trust that God has not abandoned you during this time, and that there is truly more at work if you just step back and enjoy The View.

Today, I am taking action to press forward out of the darkness until I see some light.

"So take a new grip with your tired hands and strengthen your weak knees. Mark out a straight path for your feet so that those who are weak and lame will not fall but become strong."
Heb. 12:12-13 (NLT)

Chapter 13

Out of the Blue

BEING INTIMATELY IN STEP WITH WEBB motivates me to share more of my unknowns with him. As long as we've been together, it's hard to imagine that there are any remaining unknowns about myself, but there are. When I take him back home to New Orleans with me, we always end up going to hot spots both old and new, but I never take him to those childhood spots that give color to my life's story. This last visit was the perfect opportunity to do this, and I blew it. I guess I avoid these spots, because some aren't too colorful. In fact, some are pretty dark. That's why it feels easier to really open up about them when we're in sync with each other than when we're not.

One case in point is that I grew up living between two houses most of my childhood. I always lived between my mother's house and my mother's childhood house. Each time I return home to New Orleans with Webb, I always drive by my mother's childhood house where I did spend a lot of my early years, but I never take him to any of the other houses that I grew up in with my mother. This time I was ready to revisit some of those places, but failed to do it.

For example, I have a long scar on my left calf that required me to get seventeen stitches when I was about seven years old. Webb knows about the scar, but he doesn't know how or where I got it. This scar comes from a biking accident that happened when I was seven years old outside of the apartment that I lived in with my mother, my younger brother Sam, and his father Samuel. We lived at this apartment for only a short time; Samuel turned out to be an alcoholic. Once he progressed from a functional alcoholic to a dysfunctional, raging one, my mother left him and never looked back.

Even though I ended up in the emergency room that day, I still have some fond memories of the incident. After the kickstand on the bike goes through my leg, I burst into the front door. My mother and Samuel were sitting in the front room watching television. My mother was eight months pregnant at the time with my brother Sam. When she saw the shock on my little face, and blood everywhere with the "white part" hanging out, she sprung up from the sofa as if she were younger than I was. She grabbed two dish towels hanging on the oven door, her purse, and keys from the kitchen counter and flew out of the back door to the car. Samuel picked me up and carried me in his arms, gently lying me down on the backseat while instructing me to keep my leg elevated across my mother's lap. We were riding in my mother's prized possession—her Volkswagen Bug. She absolutely loved this car, except when she was pregnant, because her belly felt every street bump and pothole the car rolled over. As Samuel raced me to the emergency room, I recall him apologizing to my mother for hitting so many potholes. As she was cupping the bottom of her belly with her right arm, and helping to elevate my leg with her left arm, she said, "You hit as many bumps as you need to. Just get her there!"

This is so like my mother. She will sacrifice all of herself for me. If I am hurting, she is hurting. If I am in need, she makes it her mission to help me whether that's by her own means or if she has to become resourceful in some way. Even today as an adult, when she may not always agree with my approach to something, I can always expect to have her unconditional love, no matter what.

For that short car ride to the hospital, I was the focus, and not Sam's drinking. For that short car ride, it felt like we were a genuine family.

Recalling this bike accident and living in this apartment reminds me of something else I could have shared with Webb. I was an only child up until the age of seven before Sam was born. I spent a lot of time looking for other children my age to play with. When I didn't have playmates, I spent a lot of time riding my bike. My mother only allowed me to ride within the apartment complex, but sometimes when I was in a more adventurous and mischievous mood, I would ride outside of the complex up to Gentilly Boulevard. I was always fascinated by a large white house with black iron bars that is situated on the corner. Compared to our small apartment, this house resembled a little castle to me. The rear entrance is on one street, and the front entrance is on another. When I rode by this house, I would stop my bike hoping to see signs of kids my age coming out of the house. Each time, I would only see an older couple entering or leaving the house. Little did I know that several years later, I would end up spending many days and nights in that house. My dearest friend Michelle, and her older sister Joakima, whom we fondly call "Jo," would eventually move to this house to live with that older couple, their aunt, and uncle, after losing both of their parents. Jo is also like my older sister.

Just as I have taken Webb to only one house, I also have only taken him to one school—my high school, Ursuline Academy. This time, I wanted to take him to my middle school, St. Matthias. It was at St. Matthias where I was nicknamed *Cinderella*. I dreaded being called this.

One evening there was an event at the school where we were allowed to wear our regular clothes. This was a big thing for us, because we wore our school uniform year round. I was in the sixth grade at the time. I came to the event sporting a nice "little girl" dress with flat, black patent leather shoes. My family was old school. To them, flat patent leather shoes were age appropriate shoes for an eleven-year-old girl. Wearing heels of any height at this age was off limits in my house. To the contrary, most of the other sixth grade girls wore low to medium heels, and a couple even wore high heels. I was the only one wearing flat shoes; hence, the nickname "Cinderella" was born. For the next two years, I would be called Cinderella day in and day out. Ironically, by this time, I was living in one of those houses where I have never taken Webb, and being Cinderella was the least of my problems.

This last trip, I felt more inclined than ever before to open up, and to take Webb down a few of my own memory lanes. But, I blew it.... I didn't act on my intentions. I told myself that I would take him next time. Given the way things look in New Orleans today, I feel as though there won't be a next time. Things have changed and seem as if they will never be the same.

My precious city, where I am always proud to come home, has been struck by Hurricane Katrina, and is currently enduring the devastating aftermath with the breach of the levees. People are found dead in their homes and on the streets. Others are on their rooftops with rescue signs trying to escape death. Some are heat-stricken and famished in front of the convention center while others are held up in the Superdome. To escape these horrific conditions, many are being forced to leave the city with or without their loved ones.

It's hard to imagine that just a few short weeks ago we were in the Superdome grooving to the sweet sounds of some of music's greats. Now with the looting on the streets, and some of the lurid acts being reported out of the Superdome, not only have those sweet sounds faded, but the pride and sweetness of our spirit–that spirit that makes New Orleans *New Orleans*–seems to be fading too.

In this moment I am grateful for two things. First, I am grateful that my friends and their families are all safe. A lot of property has been lost and the rebuilding efforts will be long, but they are all alive and well. I could not be more grateful for that. I am also grateful for God's impeccable timing. I haven't been home in five years, and out of the blue, when I am unemployed, God makes a way for me to see my great city once more before this vicious storm hits. My memory lanes may be flooded, and others may be completely washed away, but my memories are sealed tight.

Coming Full Circle

Some things in our past may seem trivial. Some things in our past may seem shameful, but it is important to remember that everything in our past has shaped us into who we are. It's easy to show gratitude for blessings, but it's important to also show gratitude for the situations that have helped carve your identity, perspective, and fortitude.

Today, I am taking action to remember and appreciate where God has brought me.

"And all the trees will know that it is I, the Lord, who cuts the tall tree down and makes the short tree to grow tall. It is I who makes the green tree wither and gives the dead tree new life. I, the Lord, have spoken, and I will do what I said!"
(Ezek. 17:24 NLT)

Chapter 14

Uprooted

"Sue, it's Michelle."

"Girl, I am so glad to hear from you! I've been trying to get an update on what's going on down there for days."

"Yes, I know, but I still didn't call to talk. I'm just leaving the station and heading home, because I've got seventeen folks coming to my house from New Orleans and I'm trying to get things ready for them as best I can."

"Wow! Seventeen people?"

"Yes, girl, count them—seventeen! Things feel so surreal, Sue. I feel like I'm living in a twilight zone."

"I know you guys have a pretty spacious home down there, but you will definitely have your hands full with trying to accommodate seventeen people under one roof. What can I do from here?"

"I've got men, women, and children staying with me for the next few days until they can figure out next steps. The goal is to keep everyone fed and in clean clothes. Jot these sizes down, which may not be exact, but will be a good place to start. Any financial gifts or clothing donations will be a big help."

"Webb and I will do what we can."

"I know, girl. I know."

"Okay, I've got a pen and pad, so shoot."

"Girl sizes: 6x, 8, and 14. Boy sizes: 12, 14, and 18-20. Women: a few 10s but mostly 12s, 14s, and maybe a 16. Men: shirt sizes would be L, XL, and maybe one or two XXL. I'm not sure of their pant sizes."

"Okay, got it. Have you heard from Sandy?"

"I have not spoken with her directly, but I heard that she and her entire family are safe."

"The Labats?"

"They're also good, and Liz is on her way from D.C. to be with them."

"Good."

"How about Cheri? I've been calling her for the last few days, but haven't been able to get through."

"Well, you know she and Verge are in Baton Rouge, so everyone is headed to their house, too."

"Good! Please give her my love when you talk to her."

"Okay, girl. Like I said, I didn't call to talk, but just remember to keep everyone in your prayers."

"Okay, we will and we love you so much!"

"Love you too."

I hang up with Michelle and run upstairs to give Webb the status on everyone. I tell him about her seventeen houseguests, and his reaction is similar to mine. I also express to him again how it's so difficult to believe that we were just there last month when things seemed in such perfect order, and here we are today when things could not be more out of order. I start to summarize what I've been hearing officials on the news predict about the city's recovery process. I can sense Webb withdrawing, because he knows this could likely turn into another two-hour-long conversation.

I take his lead to end my talk, because I have no time for it, either. I need to call Angelique to give her the update from Michelle. Angelique is another dear sister-like girlfriend who lives in

New York. I call Angelique only to learn that she's already on top of things. She and her kids have been walking the neighborhood to collect financial gifts and donations to put with her and James' gift. All she needs is an address for where to send everything. With great pride, I call Michelle back to alert her that a package from New York is on the way that is filled with a few checks, gift cards, and clothing donations.

My joy about being able to help make a tiny difference is short-lived. For one, I want to do so much more, but it feels like my hands are tied. I am also revisiting all of my friends' homes and some of their parents' homes that have been totally destroyed. In fact, I have a running mental list of them. The Blancs' (Joakima's family) home is gone. The Labats' (Liz's family) home and all of their children's homes are gone. The Labats' home, in particular, is a real heartbreaker for me, because I have so many memories from that house with Liz and her parents, Peggy and Eliot Labat. The Hagans' (Dru's parents) home is gone too. Fortunately, Bondy's home is not gone, but it has sustained its share of damages. I'm sure many more will dawn on me.

With the round-the-clock coverage that I've been watching all week, my mind is beginning to make analogies of some of the images it is seeing over and over again. For instance, when I see how so many beautiful trees have been uprooted, I can't help but compare how Katrina survivors have been uprooted in similar ways. A tree's roots are broad and deep, so when it is uprooted its entire root system is impacted. In the same way, homes, families, businesses, and lifestyles have all been toppled.

To rebuild from such shock and brokenness will require exponentially more. Rebuilding property is only a part of the equation. Lives and families are being restructured. This is the place where many relationships will be tested. Some will temporarily relocate, and will eventually return to rebuild better than before, but they won't have the same network in place to share their rebound with.

Many will rebuild, but not to the same standard. Others have fled the city with good intentions to return, but will never become residents of New Orleans again. All of this represents loss—the death of one's vision of how the future was supposed to be.

Uncovering loss of this enormity will be a slow process for many. While property loss is obvious, some is intangible and is not so obvious until you have to experience being without it. For example, Louis did not lose his home; he is fortunate to only have some roof damage. However, the spontaneity to fill that home with all the love and good times we had just last month looks like it will be gone for some time. It's hard to fill your home with that kind of love and joy when your family and friends are scattered about and consumed by the daily toll of rebuilding their lives. Their journey has just begun.

Coming Full Circle

We set ourselves up when we set our foundations on man-made ideas, and those things that will fall apart. Sometimes building our foundation on something tangible will cause us to feel intangible loss, should it fall apart. Instead, we can embrace the opportunity to build our foundation on God-made principles that will never fall apart. Loss does not equal being forsaken. Remember, excessive attachment to anything is what opens up the space for it to become a part of your foundation.

Today, I am taking action to embrace loss and change as an opportunity for growth.

"For the Son of Man came to seek and save those who are lost."
(Luke 19:10 NLT)

Chapter 15

One Step Forward, Two Steps Back

FINALLY, I think the answer to the question that has dogged me for years, the one that I dread being put on the spot to answer, the same one that I ultimately became a master at dancing around, is being revealed to me. Now, I can look someone squarely in the eye without blinking and tell them what I would be willing to get out of bed at 3 a.m. to do without pay and still be fulfilled. Supposedly, if I can answer this question, I have just discovered my life's purpose or calling.

My life's calling is to inspire people to look up, and not down, about whatever negative life occurrence they may be dealing with at the time. The glass is always half full to me. When I get into the mode of trying to inspire someone, I can feel those goose bumps come alive on my arms as the words of inspiration just roll off my tongue. I guess that I've always known that lifting the spirit of others is a passion of mine, but I've never seen it as work that I could commit my life to. I see that very differently since Hurricane Katrina.

Several years ago, I self-published a little affirmations book titled *Moments of Truth: A Spiritual Journey & Journal for Everyday Life Encounters*. The second affirmation in the book is entitled "*Blues to Blessings,*"and the quote I wrote for this affirmation goes like this: "*Misfortunes today are often unforeseen blessings for tomorrow.*" Of all the affirmations, "*Blues to Blessings*" resonated the most for my readers.

I had been feeling that my hands are so tied as it relates to Hurricane Katrina, but not anymore.

The "*Blues to Blessings*" concept could be a great vehicle to uplift and inspire Katrina survivors as they work toward rebuilding their lives. The fact that I am a native New Orleanian makes this fit all the better. Maybe I could start the *Blues to Blessings* website, which could serve as an inspirational hub for Katrina survivors in particular, filled with the most powerfully uplifting stories and messages of the day. Maybe it could also serve the purpose of reconnecting loved ones who've been separated since the storm.

I don't know what the possibilities are at this stage, but my head is much more into pondering these possibilities than it is into writing a cover letter for a job that I have no desire to do.

I am sitting at my computer and I am struggling to write a cover letter for a software sales job in the restaurant industry that I really don't want. On the one hand, I am grateful for the opportunity. I have been out of work for nearly a year, and I can't continue to rest our family's entire financial burden on Webb's shoulders along with my student loan debt. On the other hand, taking this job feels like I am taking a step backward professionally. I already had a sales job in the restaurant industry more than a decade ago.

I seem to always come back to the same conclusion: the corporate world has never been the most attractive to me, which is why I always fantasize about the entrepreneurial side. The *Blues to Blessings* website could be a win-win idea. It would be a positive and useful tool for users of the site (not limited to Katrina survivors).

It would definitely allow me to work in my life's purpose, and I would even venture to say that this would be pleasing to God.

As my mind is more preoccupied with planning the *Blues to Blessings* website and less into writing a meaningless cover letter, I begin to write out key action steps for the website in the margin of my writing pad. When I finally finish the letter, I can't help but release my frustrated feelings through journaling. What starts as a journal entry ends up being a letter to God. Here's an excerpt of my letter to Him:

> Father, I have such a desire and capacity to offer so much more. You know my heart. Even though I am just beginning to understand my life's purpose, You have known my purpose all along. You gave it to me. So, why aren't You making things happen for me? Why haven't the right doors opened for me yet? The last thing I want to do is to sign up for a job that I really do not want, and lose another chunk of my life stuck in a position that has absolutely nothing to do with why I was put here. Why would you allow this to happen, Father?

Coming Full Circle

Each year, Jesus would attend the Passover Festival in Jerusalem with his parents. This particular year, Jesus was around the age of twelve when he separated from his parents. They got all the way home and realized he was not with them, nor was he traveling close behind them. Mary and Joseph had to return to Jerusalem at once in search of Jesus.

"Three days later they finally discovered him. He was in the Temple, sitting among the religious teachers, discussing deep questions with them." (Luke 2:46 NLT)

It seems, at the tender age of twelve, Jesus' passion was already coming into light. It is easy to infer that Jesus would have preferred to stay engaged in his passion rather than to return home with his parents. However, returning home with Mary and Joseph was what he had to do. Even though he was passionate and he knew clearly what his life's calling was, he still had a course to follow.

There is a difference in being passionate, and being prepared. Being passionate is good, but now you must become prepared to fulfill that passion. God's idea of preparation and our human understanding of preparation are quite different. One key difference is that God knows each day of your life, so He can perfectly prepare you for all that lies ahead. You don't know what each day of your life holds. Even though you don't have that inside information, you have something better—an inside track. Let Him be your Compass for understanding and direction.

Today, I am taking action to seek understanding from God.

"Trust in the Lord with all thine heart; and lean not unto thine own understanding. In all thy ways acknowledge Him and He shall direct thy paths."
(Prov. 3:5-6 KJV)

Chapter 16

Bypass One, But Land in Another

FOR AS LONG AS I CAN REMEMBER, I have lived by the words "You can do anything you put your mind to." Those words have always inspired and motivated me to believe that I could achieve whichever Herculean goal I set, such as running a marathon despite the fact that I am not a runner. These nine little words have always helped me keep my eye on the prize. Blocking out all else and continually envisioning the end goal, like crossing that marathon finish line, is what keeps me fueled up. I have never seen a flaw in this thinking until now.

As I lie in bed with my leg iced and propped up, I am reflecting on the events that led to my current state.

Flashback to earlier this day

Karen and I were doing our normal run along Lake Shore Drive this morning, as we're both still training for Chicago's upcoming marathon, when I injured my knee. When the first sharp shooting pain struck, I tried to run through it but to no avail. Once I stopped running, I was never able to regain even a trotting pace. I was forced to stop training, and call Webb to pick me up.

Fortunately, I was able to secure an afternoon appointment with the boys' orthopaedist. When I hobbled into the doctor's office, his hunch was that I injured my iliotibial (IT) band. This is the band of muscle that runs from the hip down the outside of the leg, and it can cause excruciating pain when you injure it. My x-rays would confirm his prognosis. He gave me a cortisone shot and prescribed therapy three times per week for the next two to three weeks. Of course, my primary concern is whether my knee will be healed in time to run in the marathon next month. His initial thoughts were that I would still be able to run provided that I followed his prescribed plan. Any deviation from this plan could prevent me from either finishing the race or from being able to participate in it at all.

Before leaving Dr. Garelick's office, I asked him what could have caused the injury. Of course, I was hoping to hear a response that would leave me faultless. No luck. His explanation nearly mirrored Karen's assessment of things. Apparently, IT band injuries are common for runners, and can typically occur when the runner does too much at one time. My mind immediately drifts back to my earlier exchange with Karen while we were waiting for Webb to pick me up.

"Karen, I just talked to Webb and he will be here shortly, so I'll be fine. You should go on, so that you don't lose your momentum. It doesn't make sense for both of us to miss out on training today."

"Speaking of training, Suzette, how many miles did you run the last time?"

"I think like eight or nine."

"And you were trying to run thirteen miles today?"

"Yes."

"That's your problem, Suzette! You have not run twelve miles, or even ten for that matter, but you expect to skip over that portion of the training, and show up this morning and successfully run thirteen miles nonstop."

"Yes, that's how I see it. I had a good night's rest, a good breakfast, and I am well hydrated. I've also been training for months; therefore, if I ran eight or nine miles the last time, what's another four or five miles if I really put my mind to it?"

"You are not following the training guidelines, but you expect to reach your goal without any injuries just because 'you put your mind to it'? The fact that you're well rested and had a good breakfast this morning has nothing to do with your knees having not been prepared to run thirteen miles today. Let's remember that running a marathon requires both mental and physical preparation; both are necessary to succeed."

Glancing down at my knee, I respond, "I see your point. Okay, I think I see Webb turning in over there."

"I know that's your way of saying, 'Enough Karen…you can shut up now.'"

"That might be partially true."

"You're not upset with me, are you?"

"No. I guess I'm somewhat upset with myself. My mind is always wired to focus on the end goal, and less on the details of a process."

"Well, Sue, there may be some processes in life that can be short-circuited, but training for a marathon ain't one of them.

So, why do I resist the process? Because it usually takes too long, and sometimes I don't feel like doing every step that is required. In my mind, following each step is usually not really what's required to achieve the end goal. If I am to be totally honest, I guess I have treated a process with some degree of arrogance—as if following "all" steps applies to those who are more risk-averse or who may not be as driven as I am, or may not be as smart as I am; hence, my arrogant path of reasoning begins. Therefore, I will cherry-pick those steps that I feel apply to me, and will toss the rest.

Running in the Chicago Marathon was the one major accomplishment that I was counting on this year. Given that things have not advanced for me professionally, I needed at least one major accomplishment. Now, if this race doesn't happen for me, I will really feel unaccomplished. I think my ultimate point of frustration is that I brought this all on myself.

I also feel like I'm somehow moving backwards. Instead of training, I'm stuck here in bed with my leg propped up, trying to heal it. Instead of my career advancing, it appears that on Monday I will be taking a job that's similar to what I did more than twelve years ago. I cannot begin to express the overall aggravation that I feel.

I realize that I cannot stay in a place of complete frustration. I must think about what lessons I've learned. I think the first lesson is a newfound respect for the "process." Following each step of a process requires discipline, and seeing the journey through to the end requires a commitment. I can see now that I lacked both in training for this race. I shouldn't just choose certain steps, do them only when I feel like doing them, and ignore everything else. I have to discipline myself to do them even when I don't feel like it.

Finally, Karen was correct to point out that something as mundane as a process can also serve a purpose. The obvious purpose for the marathon training process is to prevent injury. I didn't respect that process, and here I lie, paying the price. I will apply this same line of reasoning to the new job that I will start this Monday. Even though I cannot see it now, the new job will likely serve a purpose, too. I will trust that it will. So, rather than dismiss it, I will embrace it even if I have to do so one hour at a time.

Coming Full Circle

I once heard a sermon about King David. As a shepherd boy, he was tasked with working the fields daily. In comparison to his brothers, it seemed as though David's job held little meaning. David likely had his own growing pains in that shepherd's field. His day probably consisted of going up and down that field, back and forth, time and again. The pastor's point was that what may appear as simply "going back and forth" to the human eye looks another way to God.

When you feel as though you're going backwards, or you're running in place and not advancing, try to remember there are always two depths of understanding. There is your human understanding, and then there is God's. Based on your human understanding, David's field work may appear purposeless and mundane, but to God it was a way for Him to teach David discipline. It was one of the many ways God was preparing David to be used in His service. You can't reach this depth of understanding using your human eye. When you can take on a situation that you feel you've outgrown or have little desire for, but can still choose to give your best (no shortcuts), and trust that God is doing a greater work within you, you are not only on your way to realizing God's blessings, you are learning how to hold on to them once you receive them.

Today, I am taking time to value and respect my life's process.

"Wait patiently for the Lord. Be brave and courageous. Yes, wait patiently for the Lord."
(Ps. 27:14 NLT)

Chapter 17

52,400 Necessary Steps

D-DAY IS FINALLY HERE, and I could not be more nervous. The stakes feel so high. I have been waiting all year with great anticipation for this day to come, and now that it is here I wish I could push it back another two weeks.

Webb is driving me towards Columbus Drive, which is the starting place for the Chicago Marathon. I don't mind if he takes the long way, because I am petrified to get out of this car! The next time I get back in this car, I will either be a woman who finished her race or one who gave it a valiant effort but didn't finish. I also feel that once I get out of the car, I won't be alone, given the tens of thousands of other runners, but I will be all on my own.

Webb pulls up to a side street that runs perpendicular to Chicago's famous State Street. I tell him that I'll just walk from this point. He unfastens his seatbelt, and reaches over to give me a hug. I reciprocate by holding on to him tightly for a few seconds. I can feel a few tears coming, but I suck it up. I know that I cannot let my heart and mind become somber for one second. Before I exit the car, he reminds me that he and the boys will be standing near his office building. Myrna is coming over this morning to help the boys make signs to wave at me as I run past them. She is always on top of creating those memorable moments for our family. Webb says a few words of encouragement and running tips before he goes deeper into his distinct baritone voice to warn me not to push myself too hard. I leave him with a dry peck on the lips, and I promise him that I won't, even as I know that I will. I will push myself to the limits and beyond (if there is such a place) to finish this race.

I get out of the car, and walk into a sea of smiles and poster boards. I want to smile, but my facial muscles feel too tense to even hold a smile. Strangers are high-fiving each other everywhere. One stranger just attempted to high-five me, and my whole hand missed his.

I am still too shaky. I think that I am really nervous about my knee holding up. I became *scared straight* after my knee injury last month, so I followed the doctor's orders step by step, and I received my final cortisone shot two days ago. Dr. Garelick believes that I am fit to run this race, so I'll just keep replaying his words in my head to help calm my nerves.

I walk briskly through the crowd to the designated spot where I am supposed to meet the other ladies in our running group. Karen is supposed to lead the group in prayer before the race, and I need this prayer to help relieve my jitters.

Our group began with twenty-nine ladies who committed in late January to run in the Chicago Marathon this October. There are five of us here this morning ready to run our race. Karen, Hillary, and I live in the city, so we trained together, while Terry, Wanda, and Deborah trained together in the suburbs where they live and work. However, Hillary got a great job promotion that required her to relocate in late summer, so she is not running today.

Mostly everyone else ended up with injuries or other conflicts that would not allow them to honor their initial commitment.

While we're all running the same race, I've noticed that we have different goals beyond finishing the race injury-free. For example, Terry, Wanda, and Karen all run a faster mile than I do, so they are more focused on finishing their run within a certain timeframe. My goal is far less ambitious. I want to be able to run the entire 26.2 miles, or to honor all 52,400 steps of my race, while the officials are still recording the runners' finishing times and before the street cleaners take over the streets.

I spot Terry as soon as I walk around a set of barricades. Unlike me, Terry doesn't appear nervous at all. I walk up to her, and she greets me with a high-five. I make sure not to miss her hand. Terry points me to where the others are gathered and she lets me know that Karen is about to lead a quick prayer in a few moments.

Karen begins her prayer, and starts by thanking God first for today's beautiful weather. Although the temperature feels a little chilly now, this is a good temperature for running, and it will only warm up throughout the day. She continues to thank Him for our good health to run this race, and for all of those on the sidelines cheering us on. Following this, she begins to ask for His blessings over us, and closes by calling each of our names individually to finish the race safely.

We finish our prayer, and give each other more well wishes and high-fives as we prepare to walk towards the starting line. Before our group disbands, Karen reminds everyone that we will run directly in front of Curt and Sharon's home on Jackson Boulevard, which should be between Miles 14 and 15. These are longtime friends of Karen and Terry, and they always have water and marathon goodies displayed on a table in front of their house for runners. Curt and Sharon are also hosting a party for us, so we are to meet at their house after the race.

As we give our final waves good-bye, my earlier feelings about being on my own come back. My jitters also return. Because we all run different miles per minute, we are in different starting groups. I think Wanda is in the fastest group, so she will be starting towards the front of the pack of runners. Terry and Karen are likely in the next group. All I can hope for at this point is to find another person who is nice and has the jitters like me. Maybe we can help to calm each other down.

My mind also wanders to the next familiar face that I will see. My teammate from business school, Rob, is expected to meet up with me on Broadway Street around Mile 7 or 8. He has successfully run several marathons, and has promised to run a few miles alongside me. I think what worries me is mostly the timing of everything. If someone who is supposed to meet me on the route looks away for one second, we could miss each other.

The gun is fired, and we're all off. I start my run, and there's a lot of self-talk going on in my head. Sometimes when Webb and I workout together, and he's pushing me to do more, he will say something to the effect of, "Come on, baby girl, give me five more.... Keep your form.... Finish strong." All of these little sayings are running through my mind. I even refer to myself as "baby girl" aloud a few times, but I refrain from doing this much because I don't want to use my breath unnecessarily.

The first five miles feel great. I hit Mile 7, and I become slightly distracted as I am already searching for Rob. I run several more blocks, and I hear my name called. I know this must be Rob. His girlfriend, Laura, has even created a nice sign to wave at me. I am pleasantly surprised that she would take the time to prepare a sign for me, because we've only met once before. Because I cannot afford to lose any momentum, there is no time to stop at all. I can only lift both my arms above my head to give her a whopping "thank you" as I run right past her. Meanwhile, Rob has already started to run next to me.

I really want to talk to Rob more, but I know that I cannot risk becoming out of breath. Since our communication is limited, I am selective about what I ask him. Rob has run a few marathons before, so I am curious to know how fast he runs.

"Hey, Rob, what mile per minute do you run?"

"I usually run somewhere between a four- or five-minute mile."

Whew! I knew he ran fast, but not that fast.

If Rob were a Robin, I would be seriously comparing myself to her right now. However, since he's a guy, I don't feel the urge to compare myself as much.

"So, Suzette, where will you meet up with Webb and the boys?"

"They will be waiting for me, with signs, downtown near Webb's office at Franklin and Adams Streets."

"Okay, I think I should be able to run with you pretty close to Webb's office."

I give him a firm thumbs-up. This is another pleasant surprise that I am truly grateful for, because this is at least five miles away.

"Will anyone else meet up with you after you pass Webb and the boys?"

"This lady named Meg may meet me at the halfway mark."

Meg is the mother of one of Julian's classmates. As my luck would have it, I learn that Meg is not only a runner but also a certified masseuse who works with a lot of runners. She inquired about the exercises that I was doing outside of my physical therapy treatments. When I told her, she quickly reached inside her purse for something to jot down a few more exercises for me. She also included her home and cell phone numbers.

When I called to check in with her after my final doctor's visit this week, and also because I began to feel my nerves building, she told me that she would meet me at the marathon's halfway mark.

"Hey, Suzette, I think we're about a half mile from Webb's office. I need to turn off here to get back to Laura, because we're going out this afternoon. Will you be okay?"

"Sure, Rob, I'll be just fine. Thanks so much for everything, and please give Laura my best."

"Take care, and let me know how you do."

I smile and give him another thumbs-up. I am feeling a little shaky again. My knee is beginning to ache slightly, but I feel I can't stop. If I stop, I may not be able to resume my run, so I can't risk it. I attempt to ease the pain by slowing my pace to a little more than a trot. I figure if I slow it down but keep moving I can likely run through the pain.

The truth is that I am beginning to feel the pressure beyond my knee. I feel like I need to get outside of my head, because the "what ifs" are beginning to dominate my thoughts. What if Meg doesn't show? What if my knee gives out on me? What if this causes me to not finish the race? What if I'm the only one who shows up at the celebration later with nothing to celebrate?

Rob's presence distracted me from these thoughts. Now that I am running alone, I feel inundated by them. I don't think I felt as much pain in my knee as I do now. Immediately, I shift to gratitude. This is a tactic that I have learned to use to pull myself out of a rut. There is a slight breeze blowing. I give thanks for this. Maybe this is why Karen started by giving thanks first? Anyhow, I need something to work. In a few more blocks I will be running by Webb and the boys, and I will need to have my game face on.

I approach the bend at Franklin and Adams Streets and I hear, "You look good, baby girl!" As soon as I hear Webb's voice, I quickly straighten up my form like I do when we work out together. I am in more pain now, but I am a master at plastering a smile on my face in spite of it.

I follow Webb's voice and see the boys are going crazy with their neon poster boards. I wish that I could stop and embrace all of them and tell them how much I appreciate them being here for me today. I also want to compliment the boys on their signs, but I must move on. All I can do is give another wide thank you with my arms. Before I get out of Webb's earshot, he tells me that he and the boys will see me at the finish line. His last words are confirmation to me. I will finish this race. Not finishing is no longer an option.

While I am grateful to see Webb and the boys, I am pleasantly surprised once again. Standing next to the boys are Meg and her son. I am grateful to see my family, but I am ecstatic to see Meg!

I keep running past everyone, but I am also looking back. I can see that Meg and Webb appear to be working out some logistics. When Meg runs up to me, I learn that she and Webb were exchanging cell phone numbers so that he could track us.

As soon as we move away from Webb and the boys, I confess to Meg that my knee is really bothering me. I tell her that I am not sure how much further I can run on it the way that it is. She tells me to stop so she can massage my muscles. Initially, I am afraid to stop, because I recall what happened the morning I was training with Karen. Once I stopped, that was it. She assures me that her massaging my muscles will only help. I heed her advice and stop running.

It feels like things are finally falling into place, and I can't ask for more at this point. First, Meg honors her word and comes prepared to help me in any way that she can to finish my race. Secondly, with hardly any direction from me, she zeroes in on my pain points, which have been screaming for relief. Next, she is wearing a fanny pack on her waistline from which she pulls two Ibuprofen tablets for me. I run a few more paces and there's a water table. I simply cannot ask for more than this. I've been worrying about the timing of things, yet everything has been falling into place, one after the other.

Even though there is not a lot of talking going on between Meg and me, she is doing an excellent job of boosting my confidence and distracting my thoughts. She knows one's mental condition is equally important to one's physical condition when it comes to running a marathon. In fact, she is doing such a great job that I just ran by a mile marker and I see the number 18. I immediately ask Meg if I read that sign correctly. With a gleeful look on her face, she tells me that I am not seeing things, and yes, we just ran past Mile Marker 18. She met me at Mile 13. I can't believe that I have run the last six miles problem-free. Jokingly, I ask her if she's sure she only gave me Ibuprofen. She smiles back at me, but doesn't even dignify my question with a response.

Running past Mile Marker 18 is when that "knowing" feeling clicks on the inside of me. Up until this point, I have been very hopeful and prayerful that I would finish. I feel certain at this point that I will finish this race. I contrast these feelings against all the times when I did not know. For example, when I got out of the car this morning, I felt overwhelmed by the unknown. I could only hope that I would connect with Karen and the other ladies. I could only hope that Rob and Meg would show up today. I could only hope that my knee would hold up. In fact, today is turning out to be far better than I could have ever anticipated or asked for. I have been pleasantly surprised in several instances.

It's funny how the predictability of our circumstances gives us comfort, and the unpredictability of things does just the opposite. I run alongside Meg and realize that while some things in life can be predicted, there are so many others that can't. I would have never guessed in a million years that when I started this journey some ten months ago that the person seeing me through to the finish line would not be my spouse or a best friend, but would be the parent of my son's friend.

Running this marathon has gone from a figment of my imagination ten months ago, to running past Mile Marker 18 and seeing light at the end of the tunnel, to running into that glorious light as I cross the finish line at 5:59:39! My time is officially recorded, my photo is taken, and the street cleaners are nowhere in sight. For this, I am humbled, grateful, and in the mood for a great celebration.

Coming Full Circle

Most of us are familiar with the idiom "Seeing is believing." What happens when we can't see? Unfortunately, many noble life endeavors are postponed or never embarked upon because we can't see in advance how things will play out. We spend more energy fantasizing or talking to others about our dreams than we do in taking the necessary steps to actualize them. The irony is that we prefer to have our *whats*, *whens*, and *hows* answered before we take our leap of faith. Year in and year out, we apply this same logic and move farther and farther away from realizing what's in our heart.

Knowing the details becomes a contingency to acting. We feel empowered and in control when we know, and at a loss and disadvantage when we don't. The truth is that we will never know all of the answers upfront, and the ones we know, or think we know, are subject to change. We are not in control despite how much we believe that we are. As much as we fear the unknown and not being in control, we ultimately become trapped by the known. Our quest for knowing inevitably leads to complacency. The next time you feel that God has put something on your heart to do, but you need to see that all of your bases are covered before you can act, reverse your thinking. Know that *you* are covered more than your bases ever will be.

Today, I let go of my desire to see and I cling to God.

"Then Jesus asked them, "When I sent you out to preach the Good News and you did not have money, a traveler's bag, or extra clothing, did you lack anything? No, they replied."
(Luke 22:35 NLT)

Chapter 18

Blue Diamond

It is nearly six months after Hurricane Katrina, and I have traveled home to New Orleans for a weekend to see friends, and to conduct one-on-one interviews with some Katrina survivors for the **Blues to Blessings** website. So far, I hear very gripping stories. One thing each story has in common is the invisible hand of God in each situation. These are the stories that I want to make known to the world. My vision for the website is to reconnect Katrina survivors who still may be scattered across multiple states and to use these powerful stories to inspire not only other Katrina survivors but even those who may be dealing with other life storms.

I have just conducted my last interview for the day, and I'm on my way back to Jo's (Joakima's) and Ben's place, because I am spending the weekend with them. Jo and Ben lost their home in Katrina, and are now renting an apartment on the Westbank while their home is being rebuilt. They were residents of New Orleans East, an area of town that was severely impacted by Katrina and the levee breakage. Jo and Ben have been married for nearly twenty years, and while I always assumed they had a good marriage,

I have witnessed the strength of their togetherness up close this weekend.

Driving back to their apartment will require that I drive through some of the hardest hit areas. There is a part of me that wants to see the devastation up close, and a part of me that doesn't. A similar feeling came over me when I went to see how severely Katrina and the levee aftermath impacted my childhood home.

When I was in Chicago watching the nonstop coverage on television, I was certain that as soon as it was feasible I wanted to travel to New Orleans, especially to those places most familiar to me to see the destruction firsthand. I would envision flying to the city, renting a car, and making my old neighborhood my first stop. However, once in New Orleans and sitting in my rental car only a block away from my old house, I was no longer so certain. I feared turning the corner to see everything for fear of *seeing everything*.

Eventually I would find the courage to drive down my block and even introduce myself to the new homeowner, but it was not without trepidation. In other words, from afar things looked straightforward, but the closer my moment of truth came, my emotions would come into greater play than I anticipated.

Some of these same feelings are coming up for me again, as I drive through the more bleak areas. I even notice that I am driving in silence. This is odd for me, because I always fill the car with music as soon as I turn the engine on. I feel different this evening. I feel a need to process what I've seen and heard this weekend.

My first observation is that there is a difference between devastation and defeat. While I know most have been devastated by Katrina, I have yet to meet one person this weekend who appears defeated by it. Despite the obstacles and inconveniences, most are still rising to the occasion to do what is necessary for their families.

Ben has exemplified this point for me as their home is a complete tear-down and rebuilding effort, a profile that fits many residents. For many, their rebuilding efforts are like another full-time job that is tacked onto the end of their regular workday, including weekends. Even though I claim to have come here to listen and to show my support, my deepest desire was to uplift people's spirits with my words. Instead, their actions are speaking volumes to me.

The work ethic that I've witnessed this weekend is shedding a bright light on my own work ethic recently. I took the software sales consulting job about six months ago, and the contract was abruptly terminated earlier this month. I have never been fired from a job before. Up until this point, I have not even wanted to acknowledge that I was fired. Initially, I took solace in that most members of the sales team were let go, too, or funneled to other areas in the company. But, the truth is that my contract was not renewed because I didn't offer my best work. It's as simple as that. I didn't do my part, because my heart wasn't in it. I'm sure there are many days when these folks' hearts aren't in it either, but you would never know it.

This reminds me of my last interview of the day.

Story from a Katrina survivor

One particular Sunday my wife and I went to church, and afterwards we visited a nearby Walmart to pick up a few things for the kids. This day was not one of my better days. I had a lot on my mind, I was physically tired and somewhat emotionally drained. To add to these feelings we were shopping for things that we already had, but needed to repurchase because they were lost in Katrina. This can be a depressing experience in and of itself.

As my wife and I were leaving the store, we were approached by a man who was also a Katrina evacuee. He and his family were staying at the motel just next door to the Walmart, but were being evicted. They needed money to stay for Sunday and Monday nights, but the man's funds would not arrive until Tuesday. He asked us if we could help him in any way.

I walked back to the motel with the man, confirmed his story, and told him that I would pay for his two nights. However, I told him that I needed to return to my apartment to get my credit card, so I would see him in about 15 minutes or so.

Well, on the way back to the motel, I got lost. I did not get back to the motel until nearly an hour later. To me, I was only 40 or 45 minutes late, but to the man waiting it must have felt like forever.

As I approached the motel, I could see him pacing back and forth. He told me that he was preparing for the worst because he didn't think I was going to come back. When the man's eyes caught a glimpse of me, it seemed that they were not big enough to see me. He genuinely expressed his thanks for keeping my word to him, and his family.

What he didn't realize is that he meant just as much to me that day as I probably meant to him. Sometimes when we think of the concept of blessings we think of being blessed rather than being a blessing. That day, being a blessing to someone else was the farthest thing from my mind. He taught me that even when I am feeling powerless, I am still powerful!

I conclude after this weekend that I traveled home to be a blessing to the blue, and the blue ended up blessing me.

Coming Full Circle

Being a blessing to another person is likely the last thing on your mind when you are feeling defeated and powerless over your current circumstances. You reason that under normal conditions you could likely be a blessing to many, but in your current crisis you are just not equipped. It is at this time when you are moving about with no real plans for the moment that you can wander into another's life and be a memorable blessing to them. Whether you are troubled or not, if God chooses, He can always use you in His purpose. Never underestimate your inner power even when it feels like it is being backed up by a generator.

Today, I will take time to remember
the power of my light within.

"Now all glory to God, who is able, through His
mighty power at work within us, to accomplish
infinitely more than we might ask or think."
(Eph. 3:20 NLT)

Chapter 19

Light of Mine

LIFE IS GOOD! After visiting New Orleans, I returned to Chicago with a newfound perspective, and it is paying off. Approximately one month after my visit, I secured another six-month management consulting opportunity. It was small, but within four months I am led to another consulting arrangement that has a one-year term. Because I'm officially consulting now, I've decided to use the name LOM (Light of Mine) Consulting that was born at my tub nearly two years ago. It feels so good to see my monthly earnings statement with the name of LOM Consulting printed on them. In addition to my consulting efforts, the beta version of the Blues to Blessings website has just launched.

I have landed in New York City to meet with Hillary, who is now a marketing executive at a multinational company in the media industry, and Joyce, who has a great deal of experience with today's online properties, to discuss the website.

I see the Blues to Blessings website as one that is more for women, so it is positioned as a woman's online escape for inspiration. It is where the *blue* and the *blessed* connect. Users will seek beyond "what is" (often *their blues)* and will begin to embrace "what is possible"—*their unforeseen blessings.* The site will be continually refreshed as users share and exchange testimonials of how their *blues turned to blessings*—eventually, connecting those users who are currently experiencing the blues in a given situation with another user who has come *full circle*, having experienced both the blues and a blessing in a similar situation.

Some are giving the site high marks, while others are confused by what action to take once they reach the site's home page. One person in particular even said the site looks like a "busy magazine cover." Today's meeting with heavyweights Hillary and Joyce is an opportunity to get their professional opinions.

Hillary is an ideal counterpart for these discussions as I will often refer to her as "wicked smart." She can come into most situations and add value. She can also be tough, but sensitive at the same time. I see her as a risk taker with style, which is why you know when something has been touched by her. I know for sure that she sincerely wants my efforts to succeed, so she will give me no less than her honest opinion.

Joyce is a media titan recognized for heading up an industry-leading online property, and developing marketing strategies at some of the world's foremost corporations. She, too, will offer her honest insights, and will not waste time doing so.

When I get to Joyce's home, she is already perusing the Blues to Blessings website on her laptop. Hillary's flight from Atlanta was slightly delayed, so she arrives about thirty minutes later. Joyce points out why some of the larger sites have failed, and why others succeeded. When I think the time is right, I ask for her specific feedback about the Blues to Blessings website. I listen intently to Joyce while observing the affirmative head nods from Hillary, and she gives me a response that I did not see coming. "The tone of this site is obviously spiritual in nature, so, Suzette, why don't you just be who you are?"

Coming Full Circle

Sometimes you may get caught up in the rigmarole of doing, and we forget why we're doing it and who we're doing it for. You're less effective when you mimic what's around you rather than offering something original. Sometimes, mimicking feels safer than trusting your own gut. Always remember that your talents and originality are gifts that come from God. He would not have bestowed them upon you if He did not intend for you to use them.

*Today, I will work for the One
who has given me the talent to do so.*

*"But my life is worth nothing unless I use it for doing the work
assigned me by the Lord Jesus—the work of telling others the
Good News about God's wonderful kindness and love."
(Acts 20:24 NLT)*

Chapter 20

All Hell Breaks Loose

OVER THE LAST TWO YEARS, LOM has become a viable entity; I have a lofty contract in one hand, and a lawsuit in the other.

After securing my fourth management consultant contract, I approached a few other consultants to see how they sustained their businesses during an economic downturn. One consultant in particular mentioned that she consults for the federal government, where there is always a plethora of opportunities, especially for small businesses. Shortly thereafter, I went through the process to become a federal contractor.

LOM recently won a contract to supply high-performance lighting systems to the Department of Defense. This is the contract that I have in one hand. The lawsuit that I have in the other hand is from a competitor who is suing LOM for inappropriately obtaining their pricing to underbid their company on this contract. They are both correct and incorrect. We did not obtain their pricing inappropriately. However, we do have it. We simply viewed their company website where it was posted, which they later removed. In preparing to submit LOM's proposal response and conducting our own due diligence, Mike, our chief operating officer, located their pricing. As soon as he found this information, he emailed the team. That was proof that information was not obtained inappropriately, but I guess that will all be explained in court.

I have never been sued before in my life. I am quickly learning that if you allow it, this process can rob your peace of mind entirely. You can easily become sucked into this entire process, where you are incapable of being productive anywhere else because you are completely consumed by the lawsuit.

Our competitor has been around a little longer than we have, so if they can take us out with one lawsuit, their money was well spent. We've obviously had to hire attorneys, but I see their objective might be to distract and to dismantle LOM. I refuse to let that happen. Webb refuses to allow it to happen, too, but we have very different approaches to the same problem.

All that said, the business side of things has definitely spilled over into our marriage and things have not been good for us lately. In fact, if there was ever a time when we hit rock bottom, this is it.

There is also another set of legal papers that are sitting on the kitchen counter that neither one of us has addressed yet.

I have a list of issues with Webb that are as long as my arm, and I'm sure he will confess the same for me. He has reached out to his confidants, and I have reached out to mine. Earlier this morning I spoke to Steven, who knows us both, and he ended up giving me advice that I am still processing.

He said the following to me. "Suzette, I've been listening to you talk for the last thirty minutes about Webb. You know that I care about you both, but I think the time has come for you, Suzette, to do your own work."

"Steven, Webb is so wrong about so much, so how can you say that to me?"

"Suzette, Webb has his own work to do, too, but it is time for you to begin yours."

Coming Full Circle

When you find yourself under attack from multiple directions and in a chaotic situation, allowing fear to manifest within you in the form of self-doubt, then victimhood, confusion, rage, and anxiety will only add to the chaos. You must first work toward where you can be centered if only for a few moments at a time, so that you can hear what your Father has next for you. Take real solace in knowing that no man can dismantle what God intends for you, despite how the odds may look in the moment. All God's seasons serve a purpose, so He will not allow something to happen to you without it serving a greater purpose for your life. Your role is to get to a place where you can hear His Truth and feel His Love.

Today, I will stand strong in my faith in God,
especially when I feel under attack.

"What, then, shall we say in response to these things?
If God is for us, who can be against us?"
(Rom. 8:31 NIV)

Part Three

Transformation

Overview

SOMETIMES YOU PRAY TO GOD to change your circumstances; however, He is more interested in changing you. That nightmare situation you wish would go away could be the very one that He is using to humble you and position you for the great work He has planned for your life. It is difficult to grow and to benefit from your experiences if your mind is closed to viewing matters through a different lens. In other words, your mind is open to the situation and other people changing, but it is not quite open to changing yourself. When the amazing conversion from caterpillar to butterfly takes place, it all happens inside the pupa, not outside.

Instinctively, the caterpillar knows that in order to achieve real transformation he must commit to real change. Real change can only be achieved by making different choices. The first important choice the caterpillar makes is to change his environment. Once he becomes full grown, he will leave behind the comforts of his habitat, sometimes venturing thirty feet away into unknown territory, to find a safe place to transform. Secondly, the caterpillar chooses to protect himself. After settling into his new territory, the caterpillar will form a camouflaged pupa (or chrysalis), which is the hard, protective casing it encloses itself in during its conversion. Third, the caterpillar chooses to stay the course during the difficult times. Undergoing a series of significant changes to transform his entire look and shape can sometimes bring about discomfort, such as the cramping of his wings inside his tight casing. Nevertheless, this soon-to-be-butterfly presses through the discomfort and the ugliness of his own process. There is no reverting back to the familiar stages of his life, such as life as an egg or a caterpillar. His next destination is butterfly, and *only* butterfly.

The same holds true for you. A few small changes here and there won't be sufficient to reach the life that is destined for you. A commitment to real change may be the next step for you. Similar to the caterpillar, you may have to choose to journey away from what is known and comfortable for transformation to take place in your life. Then, it will be important for you to protect your mind and spirit along the way. "Don't copy the behavior and customs of this world, but let God transform you into a new person by changing the way you think. Then you will learn to know God's will for you, which is good and pleasing and perfect." (Rom. 12:2 NLT)

Finally, you will have to continually choose to stay the course on your journey even when your terrain is patchy and unknown. Just as the caterpillar's commitment to transformation yields an entirely new look and shape, so will your overall presence and posture shift when you choose to be who you are and permit your light to shine. As the Apostle Paul teaches, "Let us not become weary in doing good, for the proper time we will reap a harvest if we do not give up." (Gal. 6:9 NIV)

Chapters 21-23 are actual journals that I kept private for years. These were my true feelings at the time that I never expressed aloud.

Chapter 21

Wounded

Old Wounds

I awake from my sleep
To find my old wounds
Are not buried deep
They are near
Fear
Unsealed
Unhealed
How to heal?
Where to start?
The band-aid of time did its part
The sting is gone
But the job remains undone
Healing and forgiveness
Are intertwined
Like ivy on a vine

Time did its part
Will I choose to do mine?

8/8/04

Dear Journal,

Webb and the boys are in D.C., so this morning I finally got a chance to take some much needed time for me. I got up around 7:30 a.m. and began my normal activities, but then decided to take my nature walk as Andrea had suggested.

I decided to walk the neighborhood, initially not knowing which specific direction I would take, ultimately deciding it would be nice to have breakfast at Toast near Val's house. I began the walk and recalled Andrea's comments about being aware of my surroundings, so I decided to pay closer attention to the passersby and to nature, in general. On my way to Toast, I noticed the farmer's market in the park. I promised myself that I would take time to stop at the market on my way back home. I had to *promise* myself just in case I changed my mind after eating. I shouldn't have to promise myself that I will come back to do something as simple as walk through the farmer's market, but unfortunately I do.

Toast wasn't crowded, so I was able to get seated pretty quickly. I was seated in a small booth for two which gave me just enough room to eat and spread out with the newspaper. My server also kept the coffee coming, which I always love.

After breakfast, I stopped at the market and became instantly attracted to a bunch of flowers. It was as if they called out to me. I decided to purchase them and to be on my way. I sniffed these flowers so much on my walk home it was as if I was trying to store their fragrance in my memory. As I reflected on the beauty and fragrance of these flowers, the scripture that goes something like, "If God took care of the lilies of the field, then you can only imagine how much he will take care of you," came to mind.

Then, I had an "ah-ha" moment! I thought about how my mind for more than 20 years has performed in a vertical manner. It's functioned this way for good reason, because it protected me during my trials and tribulations. I would often feel ashamed of this linear thinking, but now I am beginning to feel a strong appreciation and kinship to it. I recognize my mind as a "beautiful mind" that would protect me in such a way. I also realized that as everything in life has a season, the season for my linear way of thinking has expired, and now it is time for me to give way to a new approach.

5/17/06

Dear Father,

As a result of what happened today at my client's office, I believe that I can no longer work with this man. He is already behaving as if he owns me, and I am only consulting for him. I can only imagine how he would behave if I worked for him long term. I will not renew my contract with him. I cannot stand this man. He reminds me of Tim—always wanting to have someone under his thumb, as he had my mother and me for years. Watching Katie and Tony jump around him brings back feelings of how we jumped around Tim whenever he came home. Once I got out of that environment, I assured myself that as an adult I would never be in that position again. I think it is important to be true to myself.

Another thing that I claim, Father, is that whatever You have for me is for me, and no man can interfere with that. In other words, You can replace the income loss from this contract through another source if I choose to let this contract go for good reason.

Coming Full Circle

Imagine you are wearing one of your favorite sweaters and you're just about to leave the house when you notice a pinhole near the armpit of your sweater. You don't tend to it in the moment because it's so tiny, and no one knows it's there but you. You reach for this same sweater to wear again weeks later, only this time the hole has grown, because you never mended it.

As peculiar as it sounds, emotional wounds can start like a hole in a sweater. At first, it can start out the size of a pinhole, and likely no one else knows it's there but you. It is a small hole that is pierced on the inside of you by someone else's words and/or actions, or your interpretation thereof. Your wounds only deepen over time, and the short-term fixes you use to anesthetize your pain—overworking, excessive spending, overeating, your insatiable need for approval, and the list goes on—will never lead to true healing. Will you continue to walk around with your hole hoping that no one notices it as it grows bigger, or will you go after your hole today from the inside out?

I choose to stop ignoring my wounds,
and start my healing process.

"The Lord is my light and my salvation; whom shall I fear?
The Lord is the strength of my life; of whom shall I be afraid?"
(Ps. 27:1 KJV)

Chapter 22

Self-Worth

I Come from Scratch

I grew up in the Big Easy
Where folks say "work with what'cha got"
Where we take it easy and make it all look easy
It is not
The good stuff
The Big stuff
Takes time
We cook from scratch
Mixin' a lil' bit of this with a lil' bit of that
Nursing that pot 'til it's just right
Our music is homegrown
Good jam sessions aren't born
'Til sometime around 4 in the morn
But I come from scratch

No fancy, three-syllable Creole last name that rhymes with
    Gautier
No two-car garage
No mom on the PTA
Just a loving uncle
Who cooks for me
And sings to me
And gets to me by canoe
I come from scratch
Where the good stuff, the Big stuff takes time
but is worth every second of the wait

8/15/04 (Trip to Greensboro, NC)

This is a trip that I definitely did not want to take. Josh didn't
want to take this trip either, because he was invited to a sleepover
in Rochester. Early Thursday morning, I resigned myself to taking this journey and soon changed my attitude. To my surprise,
I had a wonderful time. The highlight of my trip was observing
the Dancer. Her courage to get up and dance in front of everyone
spoke to my soul. It also reminded me about my desire to please
and to be accepted. Pleasing and acceptance seem to be the least of
this carefree woman's desires. What it appeared that she *did* desire
was to have a great time, and to do some good dancing. So, while
everyone was seated and listening to the band, she politely began
dancing directly in front of the crowd.

Initially, I said to myself, "Who is this girl? Isn't she concerned
about what others will think?" Yet, before I knew it, the "others"
had joined her in the dance. The Dancer did what most people
wanted to do. The only difference is that she had the courage, and
the rest of us didn't.

Coming Full Circle

For some of us it is difficult to acknowledge the good in ourselves, especially knowing that the good within us is God Himself. It requires a renewing of the mind to acknowledge that you carry the light of the Living God. Once you know this, however, to carry this and do nothing with it is literally to take God's name in vain. It is useless and pointless to have access to an all-loving, all-knowing, all-powerful God, and not share the beauty of all that comes with this relationship to help improve and heal others' lives.

I choose to accept the fact that I have a light,
and assume my responsibility to let it shine.

"You are the light of the world—like a city on a hilltop that
cannot be hidden. No one lights a lamp and then puts it under
a basket. Instead, a lamp is placed on a stand, where it gives
light to everyone in the house. In the same way, let your good
deeds shine out for all to see, so that everyone will praise your
heavenly Father."
(Matt. 5:14-16 NLT)

Chapter 23

Codependence

Reaching Outside

Feeling hollowness inside
Fearing little worth is here
I reach outside
Stretching the tentacles of my being
Far and wide

Seeking those things
Especially, to
define me
elevate me
make me
give meaning to me

When my efforts
bear no fruit

and I am left holding
nothing that is true

I reach for you
Especially, to
fill me
complete me
give meaning to me

But when you don't
Because you can't
I reach outside once more
Seeking those things
Especially, to
soothe me
comfort me
numb me

Yet to no avail
the hole I set out to mend
is deeper and wider
and hurts more
than before

I see now
Just as making a house a home
Can't be outsourced
Going from hollowness to Wholeness
Is an inside job
And *only* an inside job

8/17/04

Dear Journal,

Today, I did not feel the best at work. I felt that I invited Leroy into a meeting with me where he shined and I didn't. Lynn used a word that Leroy knew and I didn't. Although it was a "psych" term, I still felt I should have known its meaning. By the end of the day, I was really down and frustrated about just everything in general. On the drive to the city, I really began to doubt myself. I had an appointment with Tanith, and afterwards I decided to wash my painful feelings away with a little wine.

10/4/04

Dear God,

God, it has been on my mind to write to You since last night. Here I am starting another week frustrated and confused. I am becoming more convinced that I must search for my true purpose in life. I am just having a very difficult time defining what that is. It's becoming clearer what I don't want, but I am still unclear as to what I do want.

I continue to have to remind myself that the answer lies within me. Yet, when I'm meeting with others, I'm constantly expecting an answer from them. I'm satisfied even if it's just a clue. Nonetheless, I should be firm that the answer really lies within me. I often feel frustrated, thinking that I'm inadequate in so many instances. I constantly postpone things that I should handle immediately. I set goals for myself, and I often fall off track. My eating is again out of control. I'm just lacking the overall discipline to get necessary things done. At times, I feel unworthy to ask for Your direction again, but I know that's the enemy working against me. I ask, Father, that You show me the Way. What is your divine plan for me?

What is it that I shall do next with my life and career? I ask that my next career move use my core strengths, coupled with my skills, to serve in the purpose that You, Father, have designed for me. I am ready to relinquish this need for perfection, but I need Your help.

Lovingly,

Your daughter Suzette

Coming Full Circle

Many of us are familiar with the old adage "Tell me who your friends are, and I will tell you who you are." A person can also tell you a lot about who they are by what they choose to reach for outside of themselves to bolster their name, and to ease their pain. It's important to avoid the judgment trap here. While there are many illicit ways to purport one's status and to self-medicate pain, there are many behaviors that appear normal, but done excessively and for the wrong reasons end up being unhealthy, too. What and who do you reach for outside of yourself to give you status and to ease your pain?

I choose to search within for my truth.

"Therefore everyone who hears these words of mine and puts them into practice is like a wise man who built his house on the rock. The rain came down, the streams rose, and the winds blew and beat against that house; yet it did not fall, because it had its foundation on the rock. But everyone who hears these words of mine and does not put them into practice is like a foolish man who built his house on sand. The rain came down, the streams rose, and the winds blew and beat against that house, and it fell with a great crash."
(Matt. 7:24-27 NIV)

Chapter 24

Jumping into the Deep End

It's 2 A.M., and I'm staring at the half sleeping pill on the nightstand. If I take it this late my morning will be terrible, but if I don't take it I won't have a morning. It's one of those "damned if you do, damned if you don't" scenarios.

I can't sleep because I am stressing about my first appointment to see a therapist. After Steven told me, "Suzette, you need to do your own work," he referred me to Ann, a therapist. Ann, in turn, refers me to one of her workshops. Tomorrow morning is the first day of this workshop. Seeing an actual therapist or attending a therapeutic workshop is all the same to me. I am still in disbelief that someone has actually referred me to a therapist. This is something that I feel I cannot explain to anyone, not even to my closest girlfriends. I wish he would have referred us to a marriage counselor. Marriage counseling says *we* have issues; seeing a therapist alone says that *I* have issues.

What is it that Steven sees in me that I can't see in myself? This is the question that I continue to ask myself. I'm sure I have my idiosyncrasies just like the next person, but things have not gone to the point where good, old-fashioned prayer couldn't fix them.

If I have my work to do, Webb surely has his work to do, too. This "Suzette, you need to do your own work" makes me feel singled out. Though in all fairness, Steven has likely prescribed some course of action for Webb, too, and if we were on speaking terms, I would know more specifics.

Thoughts of Webb begin to creep in. I sort of miss him. "No, you don't!" the intrusive voice in my heads snaps. I need to feel anger. It gives me the strength to do the tough stuff. I need to stand my ground with Webb, and the way to fuel that is to continually remind myself of our last argument. When I am fueled, I can keep my distance from him much longer.

What if things between Webb and me can't be mended and things escalate toward divorce? How will it be raising two boys on my own? How will we all be impacted financially and emotionally? Will the boys be able to adjust to living between two households? What if Webb remarries? What if the boys end up calling someone else "Mom," too? I can't sleep because of all these depressing questions flooding my brain.

The brochure doesn't help much:

> "Recovering Misplaced Miracles (RMM) is an intensive workshop that uses experiential group techniques. Participants will explore family-of-origin issues to break free of traumatic wounds, behaviors, and beliefs that have been holding them back. The hope is that participants will recover *miracles and treasures* that may have been lost."

I still can't picture this. I understand the therapist model: I talk, and the therapist weighs in. I don't understand the group model. I don't see how a group of perfect strangers who are not trained professionals in the field, and who do not know my story, can assist me with my issues.

Thoughts of backing out enter my mind. Unfortunately, this is not a serious option for me, because I've already given my word. I have taken the last space in this workshop. Ann is expecting me, and Steven went the extra mile to set things up for me. I must go, even though I am dreading it every step of the way.

RMM starts in less than five minutes, and I am scrambling to get to Ann's office building on time. This is absolutely insane. There is no other word for this but *insane*. I arrived downtown nearly forty-five minutes ago, but to avoid having to shoot the breeze with perfect strangers (this is out of character for me), I decided to kill time in the Starbucks around the corner. I chose to get coffee, check email, and peruse the *New York Times*.

I walk into Ann's office at 8:58 a.m., just two minutes before the session begins, and it's a non-event. Most people are still making their last-minute phone calls and dashes to the bathroom before RMM begins. Everyone appears so involved in their own affairs that I don't think anyone has even noticed that I arrived with only two minutes to spare. It is not the picture that I had envisioned of everyone sitting in their places being outwardly patient but inwardly irritated at the latecomer.

To the contrary, I am greeted with warm smiles and handshakes upon entering the room. Most participants have made their way back to the room in their sock feet and are seated in a circle on plush, large-enough-to-swallow-you-sized pillows. There appears to be a total of seven participants—three guys and four ladies, including myself.

Just as I am removing my shoes, this tall, slender lady walks into the room and sits down Indian style at the top of the circle.

She introduces herself as Cathi, and announces that she will be working with us over the next few days. Instantly, her words sound like gibberish to me. I think loudly to myself, "WHAT! Where is Ann?" Cathi tells us about herself, but I can't make it through her introduction without knowing where Ann is. I hate to be rude, but I must. While Cathi's still talking, I lean over to the guy sitting to my left (I have forgotten his name already) to inquire about Ann. He responds, "This is my first RMM, but I don't think Ann participates in these workshops."

I want out! Ann knows me, Cathi doesn't. My story is so long and convoluted it would take me the entire workshop just to bring her up to speed, and I'm not the only participant. Well, Ann doesn't really know me. I've never laid eyes on her, but I had a connection with her over the phone. I felt it. There is no connection with Cathi. If I'm going to do this work, and pay this amount of money, I need Ann to facilitate, and that's that! I want O-U-T of RMM! I will leave during the first break.

The room has turned silent, and I am clueless to what's going on. I have been in my head this entire time, so I have no idea what Cathi has said. She reaches for the remote control to what appears to be a large boom box. She presses a button, filling the room with music that sounds like music I would hear in a spa. She asks us to close our eyes and to take a few deep breaths in preparation for a short meditation. I am definitely not in the mood for this. The only thing that I want to meditate on is formulating my excuse to leave during the break.

The meditation exercise is less than five minutes, which is good. That's about all I could take at this point. I must say that I am disappointed.

I assume that since Cathi has introduced herself, she will invite everyone else to briefly introduce themselves. She takes a different route. Tucked away behind this small sofa in the room are white poster boards. She gets up to distribute one to each of us, and she puts a few small wicker baskets filled with Crayola markers in the center of the floor. She asks us to think back to our childhood and draw a picture of ourselves at one of our favorite spots. Before I realize it, she has again reached for the remote control to the boom box to turn on what sounds to me like very melodramatic music. The playing of this music only makes this situation all the more unbearable. It is so obvious that she is using the music to evoke our emotions. Case in point: one lady is already beginning to weep. I'm sure Cathi will take complete credit for this.

As I acquiesce to the moment and reach for one marker (unlike the others who are using a rainbow of markers) to draw this silly picture, I am pleasantly surprised. One of the female participants (I can't recall her name, either) asks Cathi directly to turn the music off. Cathi is obviously taken aback, and appears to be somewhat put off her own rhythm. She quips, "Sure, I can turn it off if the group is okay with it." I take full advantage of the moment. "Absolutely, there is no need for this music. I see it as a distraction, too." Even though I use a matter-of-fact tone with Cathi, I use my eyes to show deference to the lady across the room, who apparently was equally frustrated by the music and had the courage to speak up as I sat silent.

Cathi takes a hopscotch path over to the boom box, because everyone's posters and markers are all spread out on the floor, to turn the player off. A few others nod their heads in agreement, and two more say it really doesn't matter to them one way or the other. She simultaneously hits the off button on the player as she engages the group with a bright smile and says, "If this group wants no music, there will be no music." My final assessment is that she handled things as best she could in the moment.

To avoid being completely obstinate, I scribbled an image onto the poster board using one brown marker. I'm not sure this will qualify as an actual drawing, but it's my response to a very bizarre request. My picture shows me as a little girl floating in a small boat in the bayou at New Orleans' City Park. It is a place that has always pulled me into it. The park is overflowing with these beautiful oak trees, and their presence is so grand, it's impossible to walk by one of them and not feel its energy. Some oaks are draped in moss that hangs beautifully and freely from them. Others have these wide, low-hanging branches that reach out into the bayou. It's like the branch is reaching out to you, specifically. That's where I am in the image that I have drawn. I am floating on a little boat, and this God-like arm of a tree branch is inviting me to come over.

Because I have put very little effort into this kindergarten exercise, I have had more time to observe others' drawings. There's a mixture of concepts here. Some drawings are elaborate and more destination-focused, while others appear more people-centric.

The chatter among participants has started. Cathi brings the exercise to a close and restores order to what feels like a romper room. She points to the masking tape in one of the baskets, and instructs everyone to tape their posters to the wall. Once the boards are all taped, she invites the first guinea pig to discuss his or her picture. The lady who made the remark about the music volunteers to go first.

I think I better understand Cathi's approach now. Rather than have everyone do a verbal introduction that most would likely forget, the person has a visual to support their introduction.

The next three and a half hours are spent discussing these drawings. Each participant is invited to discuss their image and to share what they hope to get from the RMM workshop. I am a little surprised by how much individual time is being given to each participant. This better explains the reason for a small group.

Because I have yet to discuss my poster board, I have had more time to listen to the others describe their drawings. I also notice that my mind is not wandering this morning. I am grateful for this because when you see a person demonstrate the courage to be vulnerable, all you want to do is to support them in that moment.

You can't be available to them at that level if your mind is preoccupied.

Another observation is that the pain we share is more similar than I imagined. My initial concern was that if I was asked to work with someone whose background differed greatly from mine, there was little chance that we could connect and, ultimately, help each other.

My opinion about that is changing. I am in the room with one person who has an eating disorder. Another is recovering from a prescription pill addiction. Another is a child of a physically abusive father. I knew that I could have compassion for a person who appeared to be my polar opposite, but I didn't realize that I would be able to bond with them as much. However, when the white lady sitting across from me who was raised agnostic, in a rural town with both of her parents, and who struggled with an eating disorder began to discuss her picture, I hung onto and related to her every word. While our life experiences are very different, our pain is the same. The diversity in the room turns out to be a bonus, because it only adds a sense of richness and authenticity to the group experience. I am also witnessing empathy transcend race, religion, socio-economic status, and sexual orientation, those barriers that usually thwart it and keep us disconnected.

Cathi has just announced that she will break for lunch for one hour. She will discuss the balance of the pictures when she returns. I notice her quickly glance my way as she makes her last statement. Somewhere between the last two drawings being discussed, I decided to stay.

I reversed course for a few reasons. First, I am fortunate to be in the company of some very courageous people. No one here appears to be talking around their issues. Instead they are addressing them head on, with a willingness to heal and eventually live healthier lives. I could learn something here, because I often find it very difficult to address my issues head on. I also recall that when Steven called Ann, there was only one open spot left for the workshop. Maybe that was God keeping that spot open for me. If I walk out now, I might be turning down an opportunity that He created for me. Finally, I have already begun to connect with a few people here. I am eager to see what unfolds for them, too.

The group disbands for lunch, and I approach Cathi. I tell her that I will volunteer to go once we return from lunch. She gives me a bright smile and a thumbs-up.

The group reconvenes promptly at 1 p.m. per Cathi's request. She resumes the session with a two- to three-minute meditation. For some reason, I am not a fan of the meditation. I know that I should be, but I am not there yet. Too many thoughts roam through my mind during the meditation piece.

As the music is silenced and the light is restored in the room, Cathi looks out into the group and says, "Suzette will discuss her drawing next."

She then turns to me and says, "Suzette, you can begin whenever you are ready."

I glance at the clock to do a time check. She suspects that I might be concerned about how long it might take to explain my upbringing, so to put me at ease she says, "Don't worry. You can take as much time as you need to."

Nervously, I look up at the group, and I envision myself jumping into the deep end of a pool when I blurt out, "Okay, my childhood is not your traditional childhood. I was raised in two different households. And, Chicago is not my home. I was raised in New Orleans."

At this point, my thoughts and words are not flowing (even though I rehearsed some of these points during lunch). I also am not looking down at my drawing. Unlike the other drawings, I am the only one in my picture.

"Well, first let me go back to my mother's childhood. I don't have a relationship with my father, because my parents were never married.

"My mother, Arnette, was born to Sue and Thaddeus (Buddy) Willis in New Orleans. She had one older brother, Eddie, who was twenty-one years her senior and lived in New York."

I pause for a moment as I recall my mother always referring to herself as an "accident," because Sue had her so late in life.

"Sue and Buddy were in a tragic car accident when my mother was nine years old. It was a head-on collision. There were six passengers between both cars, and the only survivor was Sue. Buddy, Sue's mother, her sister, and nephew were all killed in the crash. Sue sustained critical injuries, and was placed in a body cast for a year."

Cathi interjects, "Wow, Suzette. That's a pretty significant tragedy for a nine-year-old girl to endure."

"Yes, I would agree, but she rarely talks about it. My mother was supposed to be in the car on the night of the crash, but at the last minute she decided not to go."

I was told that Sue was a heavy drinker in her younger years. I assume things were too unbearable after the loss of her husband, mother, and sister so, eventually, she returned to drinking. After the accident, she was never able to care for my mother again. She died just before my mother's high school graduation.

"So, at age nine in one horrific night, my mother lost both of her parents. The blessing is that the Nash family would take her in."

The Nashes were Sue and Buddy's neighbors and good friends. My mother spent a lot of her childhood years with the Nashes. In fact, she was staying with them on the night of the accident.

"There were five members of the Nash household. There was Wiss Nash, Sr., fondly known as Papa. His wife, Annie Nash, whom my mother called 'Muddy' when she was too young to pronounce 'Mother.' And, their three college-aged children: Harold, George, and Mildred."

I pause briefly, and one of the group members asks, "So, is it fair to say that your mom, Arnette, was a part of the Nash family since she was a baby?"

"Yes, she really had been part of that family since birth. After the car crash, she began to live with them permanently. In fact, she lived with them until she became pregnant with me."

To avoid disgracing herself, my mother chose to move to New York to live with Eddie and his wife, Nita, and to give birth to me. Unfortunately, Eddie was an alcoholic, so she only stayed with him until I was born. After that, she moved into a small apartment of her own. That, too, was short-lived. It was too expensive for my mother to work and to pay childcare, so when I was around six months old, she brought me back to New Orleans to live with the Nashes while she returned to her job in New York.

"By the time I was born, Muddy and Papa had died. In fact, Papa died just two months before I was born. However, Harold, George, and Mildred still lived in the house, and they were the ones who took care of me.

"Mildred (Millie) is my grandmother, and she is still living. I refer to Harold (Hawee) and George (Georgie) as my two uncles who helped to raise me. Today, my uncles are both deceased."

My tears start.

Cathi asks, "Suzette, what's coming up for you?"

"My uncles, Hawee and Georgie. Those men were a Godsend to me. I've always felt that God filled the absence of one man with two. He took my grandmother Sue, but He gave me Millie who is everything and more that a girl could wish for in a grandmother. The Nash family was God-given to both me and my mother. I often wonder what our lives would be like if God's Hand had not been on us."

I pause to wipe my tears, and I spend a few seconds reflecting on my relationship with Leslie. I know this is why I have always seen her as my daughter. Even though she did not come through my womb, she came to me in the same divine way that my mother and I came to the Nash family. For this reason alone, I will always honor her and the lovely young woman she has become.

Cathi gently interrupts my few seconds of silence to ask if I would like to take a break, but I decline. I do another time check, and I take a few sips of the bottle of water that I've been nervously gripping before I resume my story. I look to Cathi and ask, "In the interest of time, maybe it would be best to give you a chronological snapshot of my childhood?"

"That's fine, Suzette, whatever you prefer."

In this moment, I am really feeling like I am being heard by this small group of strangers. My eyes have caught glimpses of their faces, and they seem to be holding on to my every word, too.

"Preschool years—my mother returns to New Orleans to live when I am a year old. She works full-time during the day, and goes to school at night. I live with the Nashes during the week, and go to my mother's apartment on the weekend.

"First grade: my mother marries Samuel Jones, Jr.

"Second grade: my brother Samuel Jones III (Sam) is born. Unfortunately, my mother married an alcoholic, so the marriage is short-lived.

"I recall the night the marriage blew up. Samuel came home drunk in the middle of the night after wrecking my mother's Volkswagen Bug, her pride and joy. Their fighting and arguing woke me up. When I first heard their voices, I remained silent and motionless trying to decipher their argument. That lasted only a few moments. I leapt out of my bed and burst into their room when I heard my mother crashing into the venetian blinds. I remember clinging onto his shirttail with my little fingers screaming and crying to leave my mother alone. Sam was also awakened and started to cry from his crib. As soon as my mother realized that I was in the room, and Sam was crying, she surrendered her battle for the keys. Before leaving the room, he hurled the keys at my mother and went downstairs to sleep on the couch. That night, Sam and I slept with my mother. The next morning, she put Samuel out. I didn't see him again until years later.

"Fourth grade: Millie marries and moves to Denver, Colorado. She marries Bishop Howard Thomas Primm of the African Methodist Episcopal (A.M.E.) Church. After Millie moves away, my uncles Hawee and Georgie are the only ones left in the Nash household.

"Fifth grade: my mother starts living with a police officer named Tim.

"There was a period in my mother's life when she constantly fantasized about owning her own home one day. After divorcing Samuel, she was never in a financial position to realize this dream solely on her income. Enter Tim. I can't recall how my mother and Tim met, but they started dating exclusively pretty soon after they met. Tim moved in with us within the first year of their relationship. He seemed like he wanted nothing more than to help my mother realize her dream to become a homeowner. My mother had both full-time and part-time jobs, and Tim worked as much overtime and as many police details that he could secure until they had enough money for the down payment. Marriage was talked about early on in their relationship, but the longer they lived together the less marriage was discussed, at least in my presence.

"About two years later, my mother and Tim purchased a home together. Even though they purchased the home together, it always felt like we were living in Tim's home. He was the classic control freak. When he was in the mood, he would blast his blues and Richard Pryor albums any time of the day or night. He played Richard Pryor so often that by my early teens, I knew every Richard Pryor album by heart. Tim rarely allowed us to have our friends visit. He was of the mindset that a visitor today, even if she was a classmate or a neighbor, could be a set-up for the house being burglarized in the future. All of it was very weird. It was obvious to me that he got his jollies from always maintaining a certain level of dominion over us. He succeeded, because I often felt like a prisoner in that house.

"Eighth grade: the saddest, most horrific tragedy of my life happens.

"This particular Sunday started out like most Sundays. A typical Sunday for us would include going to church and going to breakfast afterwards. While we were getting ready for church, Sam began to sing his favorite hymn, 'We're Going to See the King.'

"After going to church and breakfast, I asked for permission to go to the roller skating rink. My mother drove me to the nearby rink, and when she returned home, she put on her gown and got into bed to relax and to read the Sunday paper. Shortly after, Sam asked if he could go to the park across the street from our house to play with his new Star Wars case that he recently got for Christmas. He was fascinated by the whole Star Wars phenomenon. As she began to put on her jogging suit to walk him across the street, Tim told her that he was old enough to cross the street on his own. Apparently, he was playing with one of the characters as he was crossing the street, and was struck by a car. The impact of the car on his little body killed him instantly."

The group gives off a regretful sigh, almost in unison.

"Two neighbors rushed to get my mother and Tim, telling them, 'We think your little boy has been hit by a car!'

"My mother flies to the end of the corner at the speed of light and is unaware that my brother has already passed when she is kneeling at his side, begging him to tell her where it hurts. Even after the paramedics cover his body with a white sheet, it has not hit her that he is gone. As a police officer, Tim knew he was gone before the paramedics even arrived on the scene. As Sam's body was being loaded into the ambulance, Tim had to nearly carry my mother back to the house.

"Another neighbor rushed to pick me up from the skating rink. When I got home, I saw Tim and my mother. I have never seen a grown man cry the way that I saw Tim cry that day. Sam always begged me to tag along to the roller skating rink with me, but I would always tell him 'next time.' To this day, I think that I still live with some level of guilt. If I would have invited him skating with me this Sunday, he would still be among us.

"On Sunday, February 3, 1980, my brother Sam is struck by a car and killed. He was only six years old at the time. I've always felt like a part of my mother left with Sam that day. It is a day that I will never forget."

The group gives off another unison sigh.

Adam, a group member asks, "Suzette, how old did you say you were when your brother was killed?"

"I was thirteen. I was also between the ages of ten and sixteen when Tim molested me. I never told a soul during this time."

I hear one or two more sighs in the room but I am looking down, so I can't see who made them.

"So, most of my childhood was spent between these two houses. In my uncles' house, I wore the persona Suzette, the *little girl*, and in my mother's and Tim's house I was Suzette, the *little woman*."

I think Cathi senses that this is the last piece of information that I want to share. She begins to conclude my session with a few questions of her own. "Suzette, I know that you have not done this type of work before, so let me acknowledge your courage to tell your story before a group of strangers."

"Thanks, Cathi."

"Now, what would you like to get out of RMM?"

"As tragic and as ugly as my past may sound, I think that I have been able to put that all behind me."

"You do, Suzette?"

"Yes, I have already put those things behind me.

"My issue today is with my marriage. My husband and I love each other deeply. I know that for sure. But, I feel as though we are both headed in opposite directions. He wants one thing, and I want something different. I feel as though I cannot live another day on this divided path. One possible outcome is divorce. This would be a major decision for me, because I have my children to consider. This is when I feel trapped. I can either take care of myself or take care of the greater good."

I look up to the group to state my hopes and desires from the RMM workshop. "By the end of RMM, I want to know definitively what I will do about my marriage. I also want to be able to make decisions that are in my best interests, and to not feel torn about those decisions."

Jennifer lifts her head to say something to me that played in the back of my mind for the remainder of the workshop:

"It's almost like you're torn between those two houses. In one house you were the *little girl*, and in the other house, you were the *little woman*. It sounds like these two personas are at odds."

Coming Full Circle

What's familiar is usually what feels comfortable, but seldom does it satisfy; otherwise you would stop seeking new opportunities and experiences. In other words, you desire something more but you settle for what you know. There's a disconnect when you can acknowledge that growth is necessary and you know that it will not occur in your current place, yet you remain unwilling to move. Stepping outside of what feels comfortable requires that you trust that God will direct your path and your next steps. What's miraculous is not only where you're going, but that you're building a relationship with God as you go.

I choose to step outside of my comfort zone into my miracle.

"Therefore, my dear friends, as you have always obeyed—not only in my presence, but now much more in my absence—continue to work out your salvation with fear and trembling, for it is God who works in you to will and to act in order to fulfill His good purpose."
(Phil. 2:12-13 NIV)

Chapter 25

The Greater Good

I'M HERE. Well, I'm actually on the elevator riding up to her office. The time shows 10:56 a.m. on my cell phone. My appointment is for 11 a.m. so I'm a few minutes early, which is rare, because I usually run late by a few minutes. As I sit down in her lobby area, I feel that tingly feeling near my heart, which means I'm nervous. RMM ended just a few days ago and today is my first therapist visit with Ann.

I am seated for only a few moments when she calls me back to her private office. She greets me with a warm handshake and offers me a bottle of spring water, which I accept. She is younger and more energetic than I envisioned.

Her office is not dark, cold, and sterile as I anticipated. On the contrary, her space is quite cozy. She has a few pictures of the beach and the sunset on her wall, nice floating bookshelves, and a very plush sofa that resembles a loveseat; there's no long, dark leather couch waiting to swallow me.

As an icebreaker, she starts to talk about her practice. Her calm tone invites my heart to stop racing, and to return to its normal state. The first part of what she says to me is all a blur, because I am thinking more about what I will say to her. However, she does catch my attention toward the end of her introduction when she says, "…no matter a person's struggles, healing and freedom are always possible." The word "freedom" feels new and refreshing.

Then, she gently turns the spotlight to me. "So, Suzette, tell me what brings you here today."

My first session with a therapist begins (April 2009)

I glance at the clock to do a time check. In an assuring tone, she says, "Don't worry, I won't let you run out of time."

It's now my turn to talk, and when I open my mouth, I feel an overwhelming sensation to burst into tears. This is a cry that has been building for the last several days. I resist the urge.

"I am here because I want to leave my husband. It's all his fault."

"Yes, Steven mentioned that. Let me suggest that before you get into what's going on between you and your husband—you call him 'Webb,' right?"

"Yes."

"Let's focus on Suzette first. For starters, Cathi has brought me up to speed on your RMM experience. She did share some significant childhood experiences that surfaced during RMM."

"I'm sure she mentioned the part about the molestation."

"Yes, she did."

"Yes, it is true. Tim molested me from the ages ten to sixteen. During this time, I never told a soul. However, in terms of…"

"Wait a minute, Suzette. Please back up for a moment. You just shared a traumatic life experience with me, but it felt like you were talking about someone else. You showed no emotion at all."

"Ann, that's because this happened a very long time ago. I have moved on, and I have forgiven Tim many moons ago. I am more interested in dealing with the here and now."

"Is that what you think?"

This is one of the reasons that I avoid this subject, because I feel very misunderstood when I discuss it with someone else. I can't explain why I don't feel anything about this situation; all I know is that I don't. I have many issues in my life, but this is not one of them. I'm sure the abuse impacted me as a child, but I believe it no longer does today. I sympathize with others who have been abused, but I need no one's sympathy, at least not about this. I think I just have an internal strength or coping ability that even I can't explain.

"Ann, listen, I am a married woman with a family today. I really don't feel anything about this matter anymore. I am a firm believer that time heals all wounds."

"Suzette, close your eyes for a moment."

"What? Why? You're not going to put me into some sort of trance or something?"

"No, Suzette. Just close your eyes for a moment."

I am beginning to be turned off with this session. I think she's trying to manipulate me into crying, and it's not going to work. I sincerely do not have any feelings about this issue anymore.

"Think of a ten-year-old little girl who you know. Let me know when you have an image of her in your mind."

"Okay, I have it."

"Who is she?"

"She is my ten-year-old goddaughter, Sierra."

"Do you have a good image of her?"

"Yes."

"What is she wearing and where is she?"

"She is in the American Girl store with Webb and me picking out a doll for her birthday."

Sierra looked so pretty on this day. She looked just like a ten-year-old girl should look. I am big on age-appropriateness, and how children should look their age. It warms my heart to see girls dressed as little girls and young ladies rather than as young women.

"Okay, so you've got a good image of her. Now, what is Tim's stature?"

I'll play along for now, but I can see where she is going with this.

"He's about six-two and over two hundred pounds."

"Now, imagine a man Tim's size hovering over and penetrating her little body. Think about her initial state of shock…how petrified she must be. Think about the knots of pain, anguish, and shame in her little stomach, and how she suffers in silence as she tries to make herself fall asleep that night. Imagine the Academy Award-winning actress she must become by morning, internalizing a secret that even an adult would be hard pressed to conceal. Her ten-year-old little mind concludes that her only option is to grin and bear it for the sake of her household."

I open my eyes, which are filled with tears.

"Ann, I see the point you're trying to make but—"

"Suzette, you have just shown me that you can feel emotion about Little Sierra, but you can't feel emotion about Little Suzette."

"Ann, please trust me when I tell you that I am over this. Drumming this up from the past makes me feel like I am going backwards."

This session is quickly going south. I am here to discuss my issues with Webb, not something that happened ages ago and that is no longer impacting my life. I did not come here for this and I will not be manipulated into feeling something that I genuinely do not feel. This is why I was suspicious about these types of practices in the first place.

"Suzette—"

"No, Ann! Please listen to me. I know it may be difficult for you to believe, but I really have forgiven Tim. I see him as a sick man. I put him in God's hands a long time ago, and I have moved on. I am interested in dealing with my current situation, and moving forward with my life. Please believe me when I say that I no longer feel anything about this situation."

While I may not always want to admit it, I know where I have issues in my life. I know that I am a people-pleaser. I know that I have self-esteem issues. I know that I am a perfectionist. Therefore, I would know if this abuse issue still plagued me in any way.

"Suzette, you don't have to convince me. I believe you when you say you have no feelings about this situation. You have no feelings because you turned them off a long time ago. This was part of your way of surviving the situation. But when that dam finally breaks…"

"You're telling me that even though I do not feel a bit of pain today, that the pain is still there?"

"Yes."

"So how is it that I have pain but I don't feel it?"

"We have ways of self-medicating our pain. For example, if I am stressed over a situation, I may go to my fridge around 10 o'clock at night and let Mr. Haagen-Dazs help me with my problems. We have all sorts of ways to self-medicate, whether it's through over-eating, drinking, shopping, gambling, or even sex. What do you use to self-medicate?"

"Well, if you put it in those terms, I drink alcohol. But, let me be clear that I am not an alcoholic."

"I understand. How much do you drink in a week?"

"I usually pour myself a glass of wine while I am cooking dinner, and I will have one more glass with my dinner."

"You do this every night?"

"I think it's fair to say that I do this at least three to four nights a week."

"Is wine your drink of choice?"

"No, I prefer Vodka martinis and gimlets, but I usually only drink these if I am out with girlfriends celebrating a special occasion."

I don't think she gets it. When I drink wine in the evenings, I am not medicating Tim, or anybody else for that matter. In fact, Tim is the farthest thing from my mind. Instead, I am decompressing from my day at the office. That's it!

"So, Suzette, it's like I said—when that dam finally breaks…"

"You said that earlier. What do you mean by that?"

"Suzette, you have old wounds that need to heal properly. Healing is a process. You can't leapfrog into forgiveness without first acknowledging and dealing with the rage and the hurt feelings that you have held inside for decades. So, when this dam of emotions finally breaks, you will be on your way to healing."

"Honestly, I can't help but feel 'if it ain't broke, don't fix it.'"

"Yes, but Suzette, it is broken."

She says that with such assurance—as if she may not know me but she knows my type. I am taking note of how she consistently pushes back towards me each time that I say that I am over this. Could it be that even though I don't feel anything, there could still be something there?

"Suzette, it looks like we're just about out of time for today."

"Ann, I must admit that I am disappointed that we are already out of time. I feel as though I am leaving this session without my primary issue being addressed. I came to discuss my situation about Webb, and we've hardly touched on that."

"Suzette, please don't be discouraged. We covered much-needed ground today even though it doesn't seem like we did. Please trust me on that. I am scheduled to leave the office early this Friday, but I will stay a little later just to meet with you for an additional hour. Can you meet this Friday at 2 p.m.?"

"Yes."

"We'll close out the discussion about Tim, and we'll move on. I promise."

"Okay, let's give it another shot for this Friday at 2 p.m."

Session #2 with Ann

At 2 p.m. on the nose, she pokes her head out of the door and signals me to come back to her office. Today, there are no formalities. I remove my coat, put my phone on vibrate, and our session begins:

"So, are you ready to resume our session from earlier this week?"

"Yes, let's go for it."

"Cathi shared with me what it was like growing up in the house with Tim. Did he ever physically abuse you, or your mother?"

"No. My mother wouldn't have it."

My mother always told me that if a man put his hands on you once he'll do it again. Samuel came home drunk and pushed my mother into the venetian blinds. That was enough for her. She put him out the next day.

"Although Tim never physically hit us, he would beat us emotionally on a regular basis. The slightest action or inaction on our part could set him off. Tim would often walk through the house looking for something to argue about. Once he started arguing, he wouldn't stop, sometimes until hours later. Just when you thought things were beginning to settle down, he would start all over again. We expended a lot of energy trying to avoid setting him off."

Like the typical abuser, he would always demonstrate some sense of remorse after one of his outbursts. He would always blame his actions on being a cop. That was his justification for everything. He would claim the streets were so crazy that sometimes they made him crazy, too.

Even as a young girl I viewed him as an authority figure who abused his authority over and over again. He had an unmarked car. He would put a siren on top of it and speed down our residential block just to show off when he was leaving the house.

"Ann, I guess the long and short of it is that I always felt like I was living on the edge of the next big blow-up when I lived with Tim. I dreaded to hear the garage door open."

"What would happen when the garage door opened?"

"When I heard that door open, no matter what I was doing at the time, I knew that I had to do whatever was necessary to *keep the peace*—whether that meant hanging up the telephone with my girlfriend or racing to the kitchen to pretend that I was cleaning it; I just couldn't be seen as goofing off."

"Suzette, just for clarification, you said the abuse with Tim stopped at age sixteen, right?"

"Yes."

"Did your mother and Tim split up when you were sixteen?"

"Yes. I vividly recall the day that relationship blew up just like the one with Samuel."

"What happened?"

"We were at the dinner table one evening and, just after the prayer, we began to put the food from the serving dishes onto our plates. I took one of the larger pork chops, and Tim accused me of taking *his* pork chop. In his rage, he overturned the entire kitchen table with dishes and food flying everywhere. My mother calmly got up from the table and walked to the bedroom. She called my uncles and asked if she could move back in temporarily, because she was leaving Tim."

That night, Tim begged my mother not to leave him. He apologized and cried profusely. It was too little, too late. My mother had finally reached her limit. She left Tim that day and never looked back. Although I felt like I had just been released from prison, and I was glad that I no longer had to live between two households, surprisingly I felt a little sorry for Tim. I knew my mother would never reunite with him.

After leaving Tim, a sense of normalcy was restored to our lives. Shortly after moving in with my uncles, my mother purchased a used car for my sixteenth birthday.

"Were your uncles surprised by your mother's decision to leave Tim?"

"I am not really sure. They knew there was tension at times between Tim and my mother, but I never confessed to them how bad things were."

"Why?"

"I feared hurting my mother."

"So, you chose to 'keep the peace' by sacrificing your own well-being on behalf of your mother's?"

"Yes, that is probably a fair statement. However, over the years, I have been able to keep the peace without sacrificing my well-being. On occasion, I have been known to cover for a family member by forging their signature to a birthday card when this person forgets one of the boys' birthdays."

There's a person in my family who has difficulty remembering birthdays. Over the years, this individual has forgotten both Julian's and Jonathan's birthday. Either boy would have been hurt if they knew this family member forgot his birthday. When this happens, I run out to Walgreen's, purchase a birthday card, put money in it, and sign the family member's name. I prevent the boys from having a painful childhood memory, and I prevent this family member from experiencing a great deal of regret.

Ann gives me a look and nods her head in disbelief. I try to reinforce my position. "Trust me, I hate being trapped in these situations. But, when they occur, I feel that I have no choice but to act on behalf of the greater good."

I didn't want my mother to partner with a guy like Tim. I don't want Webb to do the things that he does. I want my loved ones to remember the boys' birthdays. I am not inviting these situations into my life. However, when these things happen, I can't just idly sit by.

"Did you recently feel like you were in a similar place with Webb and the boys when you were contemplating divorce?"

"Yes, I definitely did."

"My dear, that's because you are. You have recreated a situation in your adult life that triggers you to 'keep the peace,' just as you did in your childhood. Suzette, although the circumstances are very different, the wound that you are revisiting is the same."

Hearing her say the words "the wound you are revisiting is the same" stung. I want to play it off, but I can't. I feel rattled because she took one situation and drew what appears to be a perfectly straight line from a dot in my past to a dot in my present. I have been functioning this way for nearly my entire life, and I had not made this correlation. If she so effortlessly connected this dot, how many more dots could she connect?

"So, now let me ask you: Wouldn't you like to be free of all of that?"

I can no longer resist the urge to let my tears flow. She has touched on something within me and there is no turning back. The guard is down whether I want it to be or not. I have nothing left in me to keep it up. I want to resolve matters, but even more so, I want to be free of it all. She instinctively knows this, and reaches for her box of tissues without taking her eyes off of me.

As I take my time to wipe my tears, my thoughts dip back to my childhood. As a child, I told myself that it was too risky to tell anyone that I was being abused. Telling someone meant risking ripping apart my entire family. As a child, I figured that my mother could lose custody of me, and my mother's relationship with my grandmother and uncles could be ruined forever. I reasoned that keeping the secret resulted in only one being hurt, and telling the secret could result in many being hurt. I felt trapped. This was a no-win scenario: hurt myself or hurt my family. I just told myself that I needed to be strong, and act on behalf of the greater good of my family. Similarly, when Webb and I are at odds, I also feel trapped in a no-win scenario. Do I divorce him and deprive the boys of growing up in the same household with him, or do I remain in this state of conflict?

As I try to gather myself, I want to believe that I have made some progress over the years from my days with Tim. I attempt to make another case:

"Ann, listen to me. Once I had a client who reminded me of Tim. He, too, got his jollies by watching everyone in his office fearfully jump to his every whim. When it was time to renew my contract with his organization, I decided not to. Would I have been able to do this if I was still being impacted by my childhood days with Tim?"

"Did you have other clients at the time you let this client go?"

"Yes."

"Maybe the stakes weren't high enough for you. However, you have shown that when the stakes are high enough you feel trapped between acting on behalf of yourself and the greater good. That's what we're dealing with here."

She is spot on. I only feel trapped when the stakes are high. This is when I weigh the greater good and me, and I always end up surrendering me. The more I think about it, there is an undeniable truth to her assessment, and I have been perpetually recreating a personal hell for myself.

"Do you know what I think, Suzette?"

"What?"

"I think God sees you as the greater good."

I have a perplexed look on my face, and I don't try to fix it.

"You look confused."

"I am somewhat. I thought God looks favorably upon us when we take a selfless approach to things. Isn't this what it means to be a good Christian—to sacrifice for others?"

"Suzette, it is obvious to me that you have a relationship with God. Personally, I love the Lord. He is the reason that I have my practice today. In fact, everything I have is because of Him, so I get it. But, do not confuse sacrificing for another with dishonoring yourself. I understand why you felt a need to respond to things the way you did as a child, but you are no longer a child, Suzette.

"Even when you purchased the birthday cards, your intentions were genuine but your actions lacked integrity. Acts like these dishonor you, because in this instance, you have to live with a lie. The God that I serve doesn't expect us to sneak around, forge signatures, and to lie all in an effort to prevent someone from getting their feelings hurt. I think the God that we both serve is capable of taking care of both us and them."

I think that she raises a few good points. I have always acted from the standpoint that "God knows my heart." Yes, forging another person's signature on a birthday card is wrong, but it was done to save another from having their feelings hurt. I guess I always assumed that God would overlook the dishonoring piece if my heart was in the right place when I did it.

"Ann, I see your point."

"So why don't you trust God enough to know that He will comfort Julian and Jonathan when that family member forgets his birthday?"

Sheepishly, I concede. "Good point."

"Suzette, another way to think about things is that sometimes we need to detach with love. When you attempt to take matters into your hands, and to intervene on others' behalf, or even on God's behalf, you are thinking and behaving in a grandiose way. This is all symptomatic of being a codependent."

"I'm sorry, did you say 'interdependent'?"

"No, the term is codependent. Suzette, we're nearly out of time, so I'll explain that term to you in greater detail during our next visit. For now, I'd like to circle back to our earlier discussion about your childhood, or family-of-origin issues."

We both do another time check. Before she continues with her feedback, she removes her glasses and leans towards me with both of her forearms rested on her thighs.

"Many times we will recreate in our adult life those situations that evoke the same emotional trauma from our childhood. When we do this, we typically respond to the situation using our child mindset rather than our adult one.

"In your situation, you feel trapped between doing what is right for Suzette and the greater good. When this happened to you as a child, the ten-year-old Suzette told you there were no choices. When the adult Suzette feels trapped, remind her that she definitely has choices. Pinch yourself if necessary. A feeling of entrapment means the ten-year-old Suzette is attempting to cope with matters, and not adult Suzette."

For the last few weeks, I have felt like my insides have been in knots. I ride in my car and feel the tension throughout my neck and back. I feel as if her feedback is zeroing in on my issues just like a good masseuse would zero in on my tissues.

"Next, Suzette, are you familiar with Al-Anon?"

"Yes, I am familiar with the organization. I have even attended a meeting or two before, but I don't think it's for me."

Al-Anon is derived from Alcoholics Anonymous, and it is the support arm for family and friends who are currently dealing with active alcoholism, or who may have a history of alcoholism in their family.

"Suzette, there is a history of alcoholism in your family. In your own time, you may want to revisit your assessment of the organization."

"Okay."

In my head, I am thinking, "Not hardly, but okay for now."

"Now, as it relates to your marriage, I get the sense that you are trying to manipulate Webb into doing what you want him to do. You can't control Webb. You don't have that kind of power. There is that grandiose thinking again. What you can choose to do is to give Webb the opportunity to respond to the change in you."

If I am honest with myself, I have been trying to manipulate Webb to do what I want him to do. Her point about me not having the power to change him is well made because I have tried everything, but to no avail.

"Finally, I want you to ask yourself this question: I have no doubt that God sees you as the greater good, but do you see yourself as the greater good?

"Give this some thought, and let's talk about it during our next visit. Shall we meet one week from next Tuesday, same time?"

"My phone is turned off now, so I can't see my calendar. Let's schedule it for now, and if there's a conflict, I'll notify you."

"Okay, it was good seeing you again, and don't hesitate to call me if you need to talk before our next appointment. I'll keep the Webbs in my prayers!"

"Thanks, and I appreciate it. Ann, I must admit that I feel much better about this session than I did our first one. Today's session has shed a lot of light on things for me."

"Yes, and we're just getting started. Suzette, becoming aware of and working with your core issues will touch every aspect of your life—your parenting, your relationships, how you lead your business, but mostly, it will help your relationship with you, which is the key. However, I won't lie to you by telling you this work is easy. In fact, a lot of it is painful and messy, but you will be all the better for it. That, my dear, I can promise you."

We both stand.

"Ann, thanks again and I'll see you in two weeks."

On my elevator ride down to the garage, the thought of generational madness crossed my mind—my grandmother did it, my mother did it, and now I'm doing it. Sometimes we can be fully aware of an unhealthy behavior pattern that repeats itself generation after generation, such that we make a personal commitment that this behavior pattern will stop with us; yet, we end up repeating it, too. The obvious question that was percolating in my mind was: "If I can repeat unhealthy behaviors of which I have been fully aware, isn't it possible that I could also be recreating unhealthy behavior patterns of which I am completely unaware?"

Coming Full Circle

Sometimes a loved one's issues will spill over into your life. You dread being pulled into a situation that you didn't ask for, but you also feel it your duty to save the day for those you love. You reason, "If not me, then who?" You ordain yourself as the *one* who knows what's best for everyone, so you proceed to take matters into your own hands. You have just moved into the realm of attempting to play God.

God longs for worshipers, not executive assistants. The next time you feel trapped between yourself and saving the day for them, pinch yourself and remember *Him*. A feeling of entrapment is not of God. He always gives us choice, and our first choice should be to seek His Will for the situation. You may find that your role is not to serve as the glue, but to do something new, like to detach with love. This time, it just may be His Will for things to fall apart. Sometimes it is in the tearing down of things that it is also in the building up of new things.

I choose to trust God to be God.

"…Only in returning to me and resting in me will you be saved. In quietness and confidence is your strength…"
(Isa. 30:15 NLT)

Chapter 26

Scratch

It's 11:02 a.m. and I'm on the elevator riding up to her office. Technically, I'm late because my appointment is for 11 a.m. In my head, the scolding begins as I promised myself that I would never arrive late to these sessions.

As soon as she hears me in the lobby area, she signals me to come back to her office. There isn't even time to grab a bottle of water beforehand.

I switch my phone to vibrate and our session begins:

"How are you doing today?"

"If you would have asked me that question three days ago, I would have said things are progressing along. Webb and I have started to make amends, which feels good."

"That's great news, Suzette. The last time we spoke, it sounded as if you guys may have been contemplating divorce."

"Yes, but that turned out to be an option that neither of us really wanted to pursue."

"So, what has happened in the last three days?"

"What has happened this week is all my stuff. This time, I can clearly pinpoint what's going on, but I consistently fail at changing my actions."

"Tell me exactly what you're talking about."

"Each year around this time I prepare a presentation deck for the team on how the company performed against last year's goals. I take the initial lead at offering insights into why we may have missed certain goals and what we need to do differently moving forward. I circulate the deck to the team for their feedback and additional comments. This is the moment my problem starts. Actually...I said that incorrectly. My problem starts with all that I take myself through before I send the email."

"What sort of things do you take yourself through?"

"In a nutshell, I take myself on a whirlwind anxiety trip before I allow myself to release this document."

Once I finish the deck, I comb through it continually, searching for any place to make the slightest improvement. I sleep on it. I wake up on it, only to discard the revisions that I made just the night before. I do this until I can finally muster up the courage to press the send button.

My real problem is that perfection, to me, is not a ten on a scale from one to ten; it's a twenty-six. Therefore, I invest a considerable amount of time (more than I am willing to confess) trying to produce sheer perfection. When it's time to be assessed, "good" doesn't do it for me. I need to feel that whatever I did was great, and I need to hear the words come out of my assessor's mouth.

"Is this the norm for you?"

"I am fully aware that I am a classic perfectionist. I realized this when I was in school. If I earned a 95% on a test, I would immediately want to know what question I missed rather than acknowledge myself for earning an A. I am also aware that perfection is an illusion and, ultimately, a trap."

Even in this moment, I pause because I am looking for her to nod her head, as if she is impressed with how self-aware I am. She does not.

"Go on, Suzette. I am listening to every word."

"This is where my frustration comes in. I know better but I don't do better. I promised myself this year would be different. Yet, here I am again, being held hostage by a single company email despite the fact that I am the founder and CEO of the company."

In business, I think you should always surround yourself with people who are smarter and more experienced than you. This part, I have done well. Consequently, I have had less success at feeling secure around them. For example, this document will be sent to Tanya. Tanya holds her bachelor's in engineering and dual-master degrees in engineering and business from Massachusetts Institute of Technology (MIT). That's three MIT degrees! This document will also go to Mike and Webb. Mike's last gig was overseeing a $600M division for a Corporate 100 firm, and Webb has so much experience from his early years on Wall Street to his most recent ones in private equity that I am convinced he's been cutting deals since he was eight.

"What happens after you send the document?"

"Good question. You would think that once I finally release the document that I would be *released*. Unfortunately, this is not the case. I am still on the hook, because I have solicited their feedback. So, this is only Round 2 for me. I loathe all of my perfectionism on the front end and wait with baited breath for someone's validation of me on the back end."

"Did you just hear yourself?"

"What?"

"You said 'validation of me'...not 'validation of my work.'"

"Did I? Well, I didn't mean to say that. I do know the difference between the two."

"Do you?"

"Yes. When I correct the boys, I am always careful to admonish their behavior and not them."

"You seem to be practicing what's right as a parent, but you're not treating yourself with the same care."

"I won't push back to that."

"So going back to your document, what types of responses have you received so far?"

"The day I emailed the document, I received zero responses. The next day, Webb chimed in with his recommendations, and it seemed like the team was off to the races with their responses back to him."

"Suzette, you sound bothered by the traction that Webb's email received compared to yours."

"I am, somewhat."

I think Webb felt slighted that I didn't collaborate with him on the document this year. Last year I worked with him on it, and that didn't go well for us. I felt like he didn't value my ideas, so this year I decided to go it alone. I'm sure he feels validated that his email was wellreceived by the team. I can read that 'Itoldyouso' look on his face even though he hasn't uttered a word. I'm also frustrated with the team, because it feels like they chose him over me. I can't show this, however, because I still need them to freely contribute their best ideas without fear of reprisal.

"Are you competing with Webb?"

"No, I don't think so. Webb and I will often agree that a problem exists; however, we can totally disagree on how to resolve it. This happens to us a lot in business. Webb has a more straight-no-chaser demeanor, while I have a softer side. I didn't say pushover, just softer. Webb doesn't value a soft side in business."

"And when you don't feel valued by Webb, you do what?"

"I take on the 'I'llshowyou' attitude. In my head I say, 'I can show you better than I can tell you!' This is where you might sense that I am competing with him. It is less about winning and more

198

about proving that my approach has value. If I sense a person doesn't value me, or doesn't believe in my abilities (like I feel with Webb and the team right now), I become adamant to prove them wrong."

"I could feel the pressure rising within you when you said those last words."

The tears begin to form in the crevices of my eyelids.

"Ann, sometimes I hate working with Webb. He has a way of making me feel small."

"Do you remember our last talk when I told you that you don't have the power to change Webb?"

"Yes."

"Well, the same applies here. No one else has the power to make you feel a certain way about yourself that you don't already feel. The only way you can even buy into the lie of you being small is if you believe some of that lie yourself."

There's a steady stream of tears flowing down my cheeks now. Although she hands me her box of tissue, I don't rush to wipe the tears this time. It feels good to let nearly a week's worth of pain and frustration just flow out of me.

"How old do you feel right now?"

"I'm sorry. Did you just ask my age?"

"No, I asked how old do you feel at this moment?"

"Well, you've said a lot, maybe more of the truth than I wanted to hear, so I'm probably behaving like an immature little girl."

"Give me an age, Suzette."

"I feel like I'm ten years old. Why do you ask?"

"Let's use this as a placeholder for now. I promise to answer this question and any others before we wrap up. I still would like to clarify a few additional points from your childhood. I'd also like to hear your response to my question about you seeing yourself as the greater good."

"Ann, the short answer to that question is 'no.' When I feel the way that I do about myself right now, I do not feel like I'm the greater good."

"I see. We'll come back to this, too. Okay, so far we've talked quite a bit about your mother and your relationship with Tim. We never talked about your father. Did you have any sort of relationship with your father growing up?"

"No."

"Did he live in New Orleans?"

"Yes. He, his wife, and three children lived less than five miles from me, but he never recognized me as his daughter."

"That must have hurt."

"I had the love of my uncles. They were like my father."

I never missed a beat growing up with my uncles, mishaps and all. Somehow I could never remember until late the night before that I had a class field trip the next day, and I needed a bag lunch. Hawee began his day at 4:30 a.m. each day, without fail, so that he could make a hot breakfast for everyone before he left for work. Because his day started so early, he usually went to bed around 9:30 or 10 p.m. Many times, I would tell him that I needed a lunch for the next day after he had already gone to bed. He would fuss for about thirty seconds, and then he would get out of bed, get dressed, and drive to a grocery store to buy the necessary items for my lunch. I went to school the next day with a wonderful lunch filled with my favorite goodies. I never missed a single heartbeat of love.

Another time that I will never forget is the Great Flood of May 3, 1978, in New Orleans. During this time, I still lived with my uncles most of the school week, because my mother worked evenings three days a week. Georgie always drove me to school, and Hawee picked me up, rain or shine. It was pouring the morning Georgie drove me to school. During the school day, the storm dumped about two inches of rain per hour for at least six straight hours.

My emotions shifted throughout the day. First, I was mesmerized by how fast the water continued to rise. I looked outside my classroom window and found a pole to gauge how high and how fast the water was rising. I was blown away every time the water surpassed my imaginary marker on the pole. Too young to understand the health risks, I wanted to get outside and wade in all of this water. It was exhilarating for me to live through my very first storm rather than hearing about it secondhand like the ones that occurred before I was born. My excitement continued when we learned schools would be closed for the next few days. However, by the end of the school day, my excitement had fizzled. Things were no longer fun. Only the rooftops of cars parked along the school's side street were visible. I began to worry about everyone's safety and how Hawee would make his way to me in such deep waters.

I peered out of the second floor window again and again, searching for any sign of him. My name had not been called on the school intercom to report to the office for a message. The later it got, the more worried I became. Hopelessly, I sauntered over to that same window again, and to my surprise, there was my Hawee coming down the street in a neighbor's small boat to pick me up! Whenever I recall this fond childhood memory, the lyrics "Ain't no mountain high enough…Ain't no river wide enough to keep me from you" pop into my head.

"Suzette, I understand that your uncles are irreplaceable. However, to have your own father choose to ignore you when you lived right under his nose for your entire childhood must have hurt you on some level, right?"

"Hawee came to my school once on Parent Night to meet with my teachers and to pick up my report card. A classmate was baffled by the notion of a student's uncle coming to Parent Night. The idea was foreign to her. She grilled me for the longest time about this. It was days like these that I wished my father were around to avoid having to explain my story."

"Explaining your story felt like what to you?"

"It felt awkward explaining my family dynamics to people who were not close to me. For starters, there were five different last names between the two households. Being in a family that has five different last names is tough to explain as a child."

"How did you feel around your friends?"

"I had about five girlfriends from school who were close to me. Each of them lived in one household with both parents and their siblings. There was no story to tell about their living situation. Some of my girlfriends and their parents knew my father and his wife. They were all Creoles (a mixed race of African, French, and Spanish people who were born in Louisiana) who had deep roots within New Orleans' 7th Ward. They also knew that my father had made a conscious decision not to acknowledge me as his daughter. When I saw the love my girlfriends received from their fathers, and the public rejection that I received from mine, I knew we were all friends who happened to live worlds apart."

Defined another way, Creoles are the social upper crust of black people who can sometimes be distinguished by their mulatto-like complexion, straight or wavy hair texture, and two- to three-syllable French or Spanish last name, which usually has an aristocratic ring to it as it rolls off your tongue. I never told anyone, but as a young girl, I used to fantasize about marrying a Creole one day just to have one of those beautiful last names. Creoles are typically clannish with a lineage that spans several generations. No chance of having five different last names in one of their households. They're also cliquish and tend to value more of the *who-you-know* mentality rather than what-you-know. From where I sat, if you were a Creole living in New Orleans when I grew up, you were *it*.

Conversely, I felt like a square peg trying to fit into a circle of Creoles. My mother is not Creole, therefore I am not Creole. Hybrids don't count. Either you are one of them or you're not. Most of my girlfriends' families were Catholic, Creole, and connected. On the other hand, I was Methodist, non-Creole, and disconnected. Outside of school, our family and social circles were worlds apart.

"Do you think you have any anger towards your father?"

"My feelings towards my father have changed over the years. I think as a young girl I felt some hurt and anger towards him for not acknowledging me as his daughter. By my teens, I felt two things: if he doesn't need me, then I certainly don't need him, and if there's any remote chance that I do need him, I would never give him the satisfaction of knowing that. However, as an adult I have moved on from all of that. I see now the story I was so reluctant to tell as a child is a very rich story, and his absence was central to the richness of my story. I have already shared with you how important forgiveness is to me. In this instance, I believe that God gave me two amazing uncles in place of my father, and for that I am eternally grateful. At the very least, I think God expects me to forgive my father so I did a long time ago. And, as I expressed in our previous session, I believe that if I choose not to forgive him, I am only hurting myself."

We both do a simultaneous time check before she chimes back in. "Suzette, you've shared a lot more about your story today. I just checked to be sure that we don't run out of time before I give you my feedback on a few matters. First, I want to explain codependency to you."

"Yes, you mentioned that before."

"Codependency is a pattern of painful dependency on compulsive behaviors and on approval from others in an attempt to find safety, self-worth, and identity."

"Can you please repeat that slowly?"

"I have a colleague who simplifies it even more. Think of it as being externally dependent. We are codependents when we become externally dependent on titles, material possessions, the validation of others…seeking anything external to give us a sense of safety, self-worth, and identity."

"That definition seems to fit me like a glove."

"Yes, it does, and this all stems from a deep desire to control."

"Control? How is this about control?"

"Let me first explain things more, and then put into context by using your relationship with Tim and your father, so it doesn't feel like I am oversimplifying things. As children, we cannot have our primary caregiver not be able to take care of us. Instinctively we need to attach to them, so we need to see them as good and capable people who can take care of us. We cannot see our caregivers as bad or wrong, even in an abusive environment. Therefore, as children we internalize a bad or abusive situation and see ourselves as the one who is damaged, not our caregiver.

"This reminds me of children who tell the most creative stories to explain their injuries after being physically abused. Even in their physical pain and trauma, they will tell as colorful a lie they can dream up to protect their parents or guardians.

"We tell ourselves that they wouldn't act this way if we weren't so damaged, or if we behaved differently. As children, we try to control the outcome of the situation by trying to fix ourselves. It is also important to understand that control, in this instance, is synonymous with shame. As the child attempts to take control of the situation by changing his or her behavior, the child also takes on a great deal of shame, because they see themselves as the one who is damaged and needs fixing.

"Suzette, you have done this with both Tim and your father. In terms of Tim, you did whatever you believed was necessary 'to keep the peace,' thinking this would make Tim a less abusive person and it did not. You applied this same line of reasoning with your father even though you had no relationship with him. You told yourself that he must have been ignoring you for a reason. In other words, he couldn't be ignoring you because he's just that type of man. No, you believed that he ignored you because you were worth ignoring.

"Suzette, my dear girl, your codependent nature was born out of all of this. As a child you saw yourself as damaged…someone who needed fixing, so your sense of self-worth was always poor. In essence, you saw yourself as a good person who was never enough. You're all grown up now but little has changed with the way you see yourself—good but still not enough."

Her words pierced my soul such that my facial muscles went limp. The tears streamed down my cheeks and my lips quivered uncontrollably.

"When you saw yourself as never being enough, you reached for things outside of yourself to give you a sense of safety, self-worth, and identity. Growing up, your number one priority was to fit in. When your story didn't align with the stories of your girlfriends or classmates, you felt like you didn't fit in. This is probably when you became very good at conforming to fit into whatever social circle you were pursuing at the time, or just being a good people-pleaser."

This gives even more color to the two personalities that I shifted between as I moved back and forth between my two households.

"Suzette, you didn't lose your voice as much as it was taken from you. Since you believed your authentic self was not good enough, you saw a lot of risk in presenting that to others for fear it wouldn't be accepted. So it's easier for you to conform to others' standards rather than to risk stepping forward with your own."

"This explains my closet meltdown."

"Your closet what?"

"A couple of years ago, I saw this show on television about color coordinating your closet. I had a free afternoon so I began to rearrange my closet by color. I quickly noticed the extent to which I had purchased so many dark and lifeless suits over the years. Someone told me that navy and gray suits worked best in corporate America and, of course, with my desire to fit in, I purchased a closet full of navy and charcoal-gray suits. I call this my closet meltdown, because when I realized that I had a closet full of work clothes that I didn't like, I couldn't answer the simple question of what I did like. It hit me like a ton of bricks that I was a grown woman who still didn't have her own sense of style. Even when I wore a high-end suit, sometimes it felt like the suit was wearing me."

"Suzette, your closet meltdown reinforces my next point about the 80/20 Rule, a concept from a colleague of mine. Most of the emotional pain that we experience today has 20% to do with the current situation and 80% to do with our past. Your closet meltdown is a case in point. You learned early on as a child how to conform. You never changed your messaging, so as an adult you still conformed, this time to some unwritten corporate standard. What can be so devastating about receiving certain messages in our childhood is that we continue to replay the abusive or negative messages to ourselves long after the abuser is out of our lives.

"Another example of the 80/20 Rule playing out in your life is through your perfectionism. As a student, you overlooked the opportunity to acknowledge yourself after you earned a 95% on a test, and went immediately to the one question you answered incorrectly. The student has now graduated to CEO of her own company, yet she struggles with releasing an internal memo to her own team, fearing that she might have one oversight."

She connects yet another dot.

"Suzette, even though this behavior brings you angst, you continue to recreate these unwanted situations in your adult life, because it feels normal to you and it's all you know."

She has really done an effective job in linking my childhood and adult behavior patterns. Although I have always known that I was a perfectionist and a people-pleaser, and I sought validation from others, I was never able to make this crystal clear link before now. It feels like she's doing a "before/after" exercise with me; the only problem is that my *after* looks a lot like my *before*.

"Ann, again, this has been a very enlightening session for me."

"I'm glad. However, there are still a couple more points that I'd like to make to you."

"Please continue."

"The 80/20 Rule also applies to Webb and the relationship with your father. Your 'I can show you better than I can tell you attitude' is more about your father than it is Webb. He chose to ignore you, Suzette. You want to show him, your father, better than you can tell him."

"Ann, this is where I disagree with you. I don't have a relationship with my father, so there is nothing to prove to him or to show him. I may have been angry as a child; however, as an adult, I am very appreciative that things turned out the way that they did. Maybe if my father had been in my life, my uncles would not have played such a dominant role in my life. As you know, my relationship with God and being able to forgive is very important to me. It is still my belief that I forgave this man a long time ago."

"Suzette, consider this scenario: If I roll over your foot with my SUV, I will likely break your foot. It doesn't matter whether I did it intentionally or if it was an accident. The point is that you have a broken foot, and it is okay to be angry and hurt, because your foot is broken. Your father made a conscious decision to ignore his little girl who lived less than five miles from him her entire childhood. It doesn't matter that you had loving uncles. I could care less that he married someone else and had a family. When a child is ignored by her own parent, it hurts. Forget the reason, Suzette, you need to deal with the hurt. But, before you can even go to the hurt, you need to deal with the rage you have towards him."

"I know what you said the last time, and I still say this must be a silent rage that I have buried deep within me."

"It is."

"How did you like the group experience with RMM?"

"I actually liked it, and connected with the group more than I thought I would."

"Perfect! I facilitate a small women's group that meets here weekly. A new six-month semester starts this month. Do you think you would be interested?"

"Yes, if you think it would help me."

I also think that I will really like being in an all-women's group, too.

"I would also suggest doing another RMM session when the time is right."

"Okay. Is there anything else?"

As these prescriptions begin to sink in, things are beginning to feel quite official. The verdict is in. I really do need therapy. The reality of all this begins to feel uneasy, which I'm sure is written all over my face.

"Suzette, I think that's it for now. You look worried. Don't be. Remember, I told you this work is not easy, and it can be messy, but you'll be all the better for it."

"Yes, I do recall you saying that."

"Good. Do you want to meet in two weeks, same time?"

"Sure."

Coming Full Circle

We often want to hide, and ignore, the ugliest and darkest parts of our lives. The shame and the hurt are things that we don't want to relive, and the vulnerability that we experience when we reminiscence on these things makes us uncomfortable. Ironically, our failures and our sorrows may be some of the greatest resources God has given us to learn and to grow. It's what didn't go right that often makes us different from everyone else. We get so focused on how we're not like everyone else that we don't realize that we're unique and special, and those things that make us unique and special are actually a gift. In order to heal, you have to acknowledge and make peace with the fact that your past had a purpose.

I choose to be honest about the pain
and complexity of my past.

"Three different times I begged the Lord to take it away. Each time He said, 'My gracious favor is all you need. My power works best in your weakness.' So now I am glad to boast about my weaknesses, so that the power of Christ may work through me. Since I know it is all for Christ's good, I am quite content with my weaknesses and with insults, hardships, persecutions, and calamities. For when I am weak, then I am strong."
(2 Cor. 12:8-10 NLT)

Chapter 27

Bag Lady

I AM JUST SITTING DOWN to complete the paperwork for another RMM workshop that Ann emailed me several weeks ago. The workshop starts tomorrow morning, and according to the office assistant, I am the only participant who has not submitted her paperwork.

I have put off completing this paperwork, and answering all the personal-history questions, for several weeks, and now I labor over it obsessively.

One hour, thirty-seven minutes, and two glasses of wine later, I press my email send button and release this paperwork. It is not thirty seconds later, and the berating commences. There's that voice in my head scolding me for submitting this form so late. The guilt starts to infiltrate my thoughts. I play back every negative message about me not being organized, and not being able to keep my word to myself, much less to someone else. I also fear that Ann will see me in a different light, and this will impact our relationship going forward.

Then, out of the blue, my thoughts shift again, but in the opposite direction. I tell myself, "Oh well, it is what it is." For whatever reason, I couldn't bring myself to complete the form any sooner than I did. The form is finished. I emailed it; end of story. I must admit, however, that working with her this past year has paid off. This isn't the first time that I have been able to catch myself midstream when an old behavior pattern has reared its ugly head. Ann's words of "progress, not perfection" come to mind. These days, I tend to speak my truth rather than only think it.

Ann and I talk a lot about me standing in my own truth. So, I ask myself again, "What is my truth as it relates to RMM?" First, I think my underlying reluctance comes from the fact that I dread revisiting the past. Sometimes I prefer to move forward, and to let sleeping dogs lie. Second, as shallow as it might sound, I really do want to write a bestseller, and I am willing to do another RMM workshop if this will help me to get there. Third, I have no desire to reconnect with my father at this stage in my life. I still believe that I have forgiven my father for everything. However, if I am wrong, I really want to forgive him, and move on with my life. Finally, I want to be free of all of this. I don't have a name for *this*, but whatever it is that is holding me back from being able to genuinely forgive this man, I want to be free of it.

It is the next morning and RMM is well underway. Cathi is facilitating again, and the meditation and the picture drawing exercise has just concluded. The guy sitting next to me, Mark, finished his picture first, and has already requested to discuss his picture. From what I can see, he is in a fishing boat with an older male figure who might be his father.

Mark begins his introduction by telling us that he grew up in a middle-class family in Minnesota, and he's the middle child of three siblings. He talks a bit about his relationship with his mother and siblings, and then he mentions his father. In an instant, his neck begins to turn red. He pauses for a moment, and he says that his father is the reason that he chose to do RMM.

Mark explains that his father has been recently diagnosed with cancer, and the prognosis doesn't look good. He says that his dad's position is that "he'll beat this thing," but the family is beginning to fear the worst. Mark's wife did the last RMM session, and suggested this session as a way to help him process his feelings about his father. Mark married within the last three years or so, and he and his wife do not have any children yet. He alludes to having some basic couple-related issues that he would like to work through too, but his father is his number one priority.

The same day that RMM ends, Mark is going on a family vacation. This may be the last family trip with his father, and Mark wants to say the right things to him. Cathi asks Mark, "Who can play your father?" He taps my knee as he says, "Suzette can."

I am completely taken off guard. I expected him to choose one of the guys. I see the seriousness in his eyes, and I want to be available to him, but I am unsure of myself in the moment. I've never done anything like this before, so I don't really know how to play his father even though I want to support him. I am also honored that he has selected me, so I definitely don't want to screw this up for him.

Cathi interjects again, "Mark, what do you need to do with your father?" He responds by saying that he wants to tell him what he's been feeling since he learned about his cancer.

Cathi looks to me and says, "Okay, Suzette, you got that?" As I give her an affirmative nod, she grabs a "Dad" name tag that her co-facilitator Nicole just made out for me. I pull back the adhesive, and stick this name tag to the front of my blouse. The name tags are done because in this moment, I am not Suzette, or rather I am Suzette playing the role of Mark's father.

Mark and I are seated in an Indian-style position facing each other. I am eagerly and compassionately gazing into his eyes. Although his sadness is palpable, he appears to be lost for his first words. I gently look away until he begins to speak. I can surely relate to being ready, and then when the moment comes, feeling not so ready. Cathi senses his struggle and fills the room again with music; the sound is faint. This time, she has chosen the instrumental version of Led Zeppelin's classic "Stairway to Heaven."

The words come up for Mark just seconds after the music begins. The first part starts as a ramble, but then he gets his footing. He says, "He's been walking around with all this stuff on his heart to say, but he hasn't brought it up, because he's been trying to remain strong." His tears start to flow as he reminisces on his upbringing, and recalls a few specific childhood memories. His recollection of childhood memories prompts me to reflect on Hawee and Georgie.

His tears become contagious, because I begin to cry with him. I want to wipe my tears, but I can't because he is still holding both of my hands. I nod my head several times at him. It is my way of trying to affirm for him that his father is receiving, and is appreciating, his words.

As Mark continues on with his passionate discourse, I can sense that a shift is occurring between us. I can sense it, but I can't stop it. Mark seems to be crying less, and I seem to be crying much more. The tears are coming from everywhere. He releases my hands so that I can grab the tissue that the person is handing me over my shoulder.

Cathi intercedes. "Suzette, what's coming up for you?"

I feel awful. The spotlight appears to be on me. I didn't intend for this to happen. This exercise is about Mark, not me.

"I really felt Mark's genuine love for his father and his anguish that he might lose him soon. I can definitely relate to this."

"Suzette, what else are you feeling?"

"Cathi, I don't know. I can't explain it. When he talked about his childhood, it reminded me of my uncles, who were both like a father to me. So, I guess I could really relate to Mark's pain."

She gives me a little more time to think, and there's a long pause. I start in again. "Cathi, all I can say is that I feel compassion for Mark, and I hope that he gets to say everything that he needs to say to his father before it's too late."

"I think what you're really saying, Suzette, is that you don't want Mark to experience what you had to experience."

There is dead silence in the room.

"Suzette, you didn't get a chance to say good-bye, did you?"

Embarrassingly, I am now crying through my eyes and nose. The tears and the mucus are just flowing out of me. I can't speak… all I can do is shake my head "no."

Mark has moved from in front of me to the side of me and is now rubbing my left shoulder.

Cathi interrupts. "Kevin, come over here, and lie down on your back. Please move quickly! Sarah, pull the folded white sheet from the basket on the bottom shelf, and cover Kevin from head to toe. Suzette, come say what you would like to say to Samuel."

She says his name, and I lose it. I feel like my head is going to burst. She remembers…. How does she remember about Samuel?

As I scoot over to this body that is covered in a white sheet, the Eric Clapton song "Tears in Heaven" starts to play. This is not the instrumental version, and the first two lines of this song—"*Would you know my name/If I saw you in Heaven*"—moves me to hang my head in shame just an inch or so above the body that is laying before me. I confess, "I'm so sorry…. I'm so, so sorry, Sam. I should have taken you skating with me that day. Can you please, somehow, forgive me?"

As the song plays more, I cry more. Mark and I have really swapped places, because I hear him crying behind me.

I didn't hear her come up behind me, but Cathi comes over and squats down next to me. She softly whispers, "Let it all out, my dear lady…that's it…let it all out."

She rubs my back in a circular motion and goes on to say, "The thirteen-year-old Suzette never had the chance to properly grieve the loss of her brother. In your paperwork, you mentioned that you wanted to be free. It seems like your path to being free included you going back to grieve the loss of your brother."

With my face buried in layers of tissue, I reply, "Yes, Cathi, but when I wrote about being free I was referring to my father."

"I get it, Suzette, but it seems like God had other plans."

I am lost for words.

"Before we wrap up this piece of your work, I want you to know that Samuel's death is not your fault. You were a kid who wanted to go skating. That's it. You were a kid who wanted to go skating. Suzette, I am not God, but I can promise you two things: Number one, Samuel is in Heaven."

"Yes, I believe that."

"Number two, you do not honor Samuel by harboring guilt or shame over his death. I think I can safely say that he wants you to be free of any guilt or shame as it relates to his passing. Understood?"

"Yes, understood."

I surrender to the fact that this was definitely a teacher-student exchange.

As I get up to return to my place in the room, my eyes catch this small picture frame with the words "Trust the Process," which just leapt out at me. I knew that recognizing this frame when I did was no coincidence. It had been there all morning, but I hadn't noticed it until the words made perfect sense to me. I would have never guessed in a million years that I still needed to grieve Sam's death. As a teenager, grieving to me was synonymous with crying. Because I definitely did my share of crying back then, I assumed that I had grieved. Now that I am a mother, I can certainly see how a teenager could have a lot of unprocessed grief around the loss of an immediate family member.

Cathi invites Mark or me to speak. I defer to him, and he defers to me. Just before I speak, Cathi points to the "Dad" name tag that I am still wearing, and tells me to de-role. I remove the name tag and say, "I am not Mark's dad; I am Suzette." Cathi mouths the word "perfect" to me from across the room. I continue:

"Mark, thanks for trusting me to play the role of your father. I apologize for doing some of my work on your time. Hopefully, I will have the chance to make that up to you."

In a genuinely supportive tone, Mark says, "Suzette, you don't owe me an apology. Trust me, I don't know if you heard me, but I got a lot out of your work, as well."

"Thanks, Mark."

I turn to Cathi and the group to say, "I want to keep up with the genuine spirit of truth that seems to be in the room. As the time grew closer, I grew more and more reluctant to do this RMM session. It felt like I forced myself to be here this morning such that I wasn't even sure if I could bring myself to staying for the full workshop." I turn to Cathi and say, "Cathi, I'm sorry to say, but if I didn't feel different by lunch, I was going to give you some lame excuse and bolt."

Everyone laughs.

"Obviously, I see things differently now. I would never have guessed in a million years that I still needed to grieve Sam's death. I have been carrying around this *bag* of pain and shame since his death, and I didn't even realize that it was there."

I hear Cathi mumble under her breath, "Does this mean you're staying?"

"Yes, I'm staying, because I want to know how many more bags I'm carrying!"

Coming Full Circle

You might be familiar with the common saying about "knowing." It goes something like this: I know what I know. For example, I know how to tie my shoes. I also know what I don't know. I don't know about quantum physics. However, I don't know what I don't know. This is where most of us get tripped up. Old wounds have a unique way of impacting you in ways that you never knew. Not to worry, however. You have an all-knowing Father. Will you choose to journey with Him into your unknown world, and release what could be hindering you?

I choose to release weight that was
never mine to carry in the first place.

"Therefore, since we are surrounded by such a huge crowd of witnesses to the life of faith, let us strip off every weight that slows us down, especially the sin that so easily hinders our progress. And let us run with endurance the race God has set before us."
(Heb. 12:1 NLT)

Chapter 28

Fewer Bags

It is still Day One of the RMM workshop and things are well underway. Several participants, including me, have discussed their pictures, and revealed some of their family-of-origin issues. Cathi has announced that she will discuss the final drawing, and then she'll break for lunch.

Amy gets up to retrieve her poster board from the wall. From what I can decipher from her drawing, Amy appears to be playing in a park with a woman who could be her mother or older sister. She slowly moves to the center of the floor, and puts her poster board squarely in front of her lap. She, too, appears to be bracing herself for her first words, as this has proven to be an emotional exercise for most.

While Amy is collecting her thoughts, she has the group's un-divided attention. After about ten seconds of silence, Amy begins to discuss her drawing. She explains that her mother got a huge job when she was just a baby, so her mother was hardly there due to her work-related travels. The lady that she is playing with in the park is Amber, her babysitter. She recalls being the closest to

Amber above anyone else, but she died before Amy started the third grade. A few tears trickle down her cheeks as she reminisces about Amber's passing. She opens up that after Amber died, she no longer felt like she was anyone's priority.

She admits that her adult life feels similar to her childhood. She constantly struggles to find her place, and she still doesn't feel that she's a genuine priority in another person's life. She felt invisible then, and she feels invisible today. Her low self-esteem has driven her to personally sabotage her health, her personal finances, and some key relationships. She is doing RMM to hopefully have some breakthroughs on how to love herself, and to lose some of her fear around abandonment. Cathi acknowledges Amy's work and reiterates her commitment to help her begin the journey to work through some of her family-of-origin issues.

For now, Cathi remains true to her word and breaks for lunch. The entire group has agreed to walk to one of the nearby eateries. I'm game as long as this place has good comfort food. At this very moment, I can go for a juicy burger, crispy fries, and an ice cold soda. I know in advance that I will have a sweet tooth following my feeding frenzy. In my head, I promise myself that I will put a dent in these calories by extending my date with Mr. Treadmill tomorrow morning. I feel so far that this work is good, but it's also intense, so I just need to decompress a bit.

As we walk toward the elevator, someone reminds the group that there's a Johnny Rockets just a few blocks away. This sounds like a plan to me! I can cure my appetite and handle my sweet tooth all in the same place. Visions of a creamy chocolate malt topped with whipped cream interrupt my thoughts. On the elevator ride down, I experience a throwback moment.

Treating myself to a chocolate malt reminds me of Hawee. When I was in elementary school, he would always treat me to chocolate malts on his paydays, which were every other Friday. After he deposited his check from the school board, he would take me to the K&B Drugstore that was directly across the street from the bank to get a chocolate malt. I used the leftover change to play the mini-jukebox that sat at the end of the counter. I used to play everyone from Rufus & Chaka Khan to Con Funk Shun to my absolute favorite, Earth, Wind & Fire. Hawee would sit on the stool and smoke his cigarette while I bobbed my head to the music, and fed myself this delicious malt with one of those cold, silver-plated, long-handled spoons. This became one of our special escapades to unwind from the week. In retrospect, I think I looked forward to his paydays just as much as he did.

At the end of lunch while we're having our desserts prepared, Sarah says that she has an observation that she would like to share with me, if I'm interested in hearing it. Of course, I say "sure," but I am torn. Part of me wants to hear her thoughts, and the other part of me just wants to remain thought-free while I wait for my malt.

She goes for it. "Suzette, first let me say that I don't profess to know you just because we spent a morning together at RMM. However, I must say that you remind me of a girlfriend, and I think that my feedback helped her, so maybe it can help you, too."

Now I'm intrigued. What have I done that gives her the impression that she can help me?

"Suzette, when you talked about your book, I could see how important this project is to you."

I perk up, because this is a topic that I can talk about all day. I thought she was going to get really heavy with me by psychoanalyzing something I said earlier. Any discussion about the book is all good.

"It feels like there's something else driving you to do this book."

"What do you mean?"

"It seems like your ultimate goal with your book is to prove something."

"Prove what, and to whom?"

"I don't know. Only you can answer that."

I spoke too soon. She is, in fact, trying to psychoanalyze me.

"Suzette, it just feels like your desire to prove something by becoming a bestselling author is fueling your project more than the actual purpose of your book."

There's a short pause, because I am really lost on how to respond to her in this moment.

"You look confused."

"I am."

"Suzette, you only shared a little when you mentioned the book earlier, but what I heard sounds like you have something very special to offer your readers. However, when you tie in your mission to become a bestselling author, it feels like more than a little ambition is at play here. You still look confused, which makes me feel like I'm really screwing this up."

My thoughts are beginning to roam in my head. Immediately, I try to recall my conversation with the group to pinpoint exactly where my conversation became less about the book and more about me proving something with the book. What exact words and tone did I use? Next, I'm wondering who else might have gotten the same impression. With all of this running through my head, I'm sure I have this dumbfounded look on my face.

"Sarah, you're not…"

She cuts me off again, and using some animation this time, she hurls this line of questioning at me:

"Suzette, who do you want to shut up with this book? Who… who do you want to thumb your nose at when your book becomes a bestseller? Who do you want to *show* that you could do this without them?"

She had me at the word "prove" in her earlier statement. But, after using the word "show" this time, I really can no longer dismiss or deny her feedback. It is a fact that my attitude of "*I can show you better than I can tell you*" is deeply ingrained within me. I just didn't realize it was surfacing when I talked about the book. I am conflicted, however, in confessing all of this to her, at least in this moment.

"Sarah, I..."

She cuts me off again. "Suzette, just write your book. Let the fact that you have a beautiful story to share fuel your engine, and not the fact that you want to use the book as a means to prove something to someone else."

"Sarah, you must admit that we all have naysayers from our past that we'd like to shut up on occasion, right?"

"It feels like your primary aim is to make your book a success, so that you can rub that success in your naysayers' faces. It is this negative energy of wanting to rub it in their faces that appears to be driving you, and if this is the case, this will tarnish your precious book, Suzette."

I nod my head to affirm her final pearl of wisdom as Mark politely interrupts our exchange to let us know that everyone is ready to walk back. I return to the table to get my coat, and as I am getting all buttoned up, I can sense that Sarah is hanging back, so she can talk to me more during our walk back. I am beginning to feel smothered in thought. She has just laid some pretty heavy stuff on me, and I don't know if I can handle more "feedback" at this time.

We enter the building and realize that someone is holding the elevator for us. On the ride up, I don't allow my mind to wander. I am present in the moment, and appreciative that we left as a group and we're returning as one.

Once in the room, everyone returns to their original places. Cathi does another very short meditation. She has a thing for the music element, so she fills the room with her spa music once again. This time, the music doesn't bother me. I am more preoccupied with my own feelings as I feel this overpowering sensation to cry. I feel like I've been carrying a heavy load, and I am exhausted from it all. So much truth has been shared and brought to the forefront in this room that to suppress it requires more energy than I think

I have. During the meditation, I find myself less focused on the breathing component and more focused on maintaining my composure. I realize that these feelings are bubbling up as a result of Sarah's comments, but I am not ready to get into all of that with the group at this moment.

After the meditation, Cathi asks everyone to do a brief "check in" on their RMM experience thus far. Each person reflects on their insights gained, and even a few "ah-ha" moments are shared. While I am not lost for words, I definitely have less to share than I did earlier. I don't want to be, but I feel somewhat withdrawn since my talk with Sarah.

Cathi, on the other hand, is just the opposite. She's energized about the next exercise. From her tone, it sounds like we're about to get to the *meat and potatoes* of this program. To start this next level of work, each group member will need to "sculpt" his or her own family to show their place or position within their family dynamic. We will pick an age between seven and ten years old, and we will sculpt a visual snapshot of what our family resembled at that age. Any family member or primary caretaker who was a dominant figure in our lives at the age of our family sculpt should be included. Group members will role play each other's family members. This sounds similar to how I played Mark's father, but this time his other family members will be present. This is what it looks like to "sculpt" your family of origin.

Cathi's co-facilitator, Nicole, intervenes to provide a few sculpting examples. If you were the youngest, maybe you were closest to your mother. This can easily be depicted as a person sitting on the floor in a child's position next to the person playing the role of the mother, who would be standing. If your parents were often disconnected and at odds, you can separate them by distance by having one person on one side of the room and the other on the other side. Another option is to put them in close proximity with their backs turned to each other.

This sculpting process will not only reveal our place within our family, it will expose those messages, both explicit and implicit, that we received as a child. Cathi and Nicole's task will be to connect the dots from childhood to adulthood. In other words, they will show how some negative messages that we received as a child are still playing out in our lives today.

Listening to Cathi and Nicole explain this exercise prompts another flashback of a story I heard from a professor several years ago.

Before this professor began her lecture to the group, she shared a very personal story that put her on a lifelong mission to prove to the world that she was not stupid. Her story began when she was around five or six years old. Her mother belonged to some sort of members-only club, and this day was her mother's turn to host the meeting at their home. She was an only child, and had learned several ways to amuse herself. As her way of having her own party, she went into the pantry and retrieved a pot and two wooden spoons. She cocked this pot on her head, and paraded through the house beating the pot with the two spoons as she sang to herself. When she marched into the room where her mother was holding the club meeting, her mother called out to her, "Hey, don't you look pretty stupid?" In an instant her grin and giggles were wiped clean from her face. She was mortified. She was equally ashamed when she removed the pot from her head and found the entire room laughing. As an adult she understands that no real harm was meant, but as a child she ran with the literal interpretation of her mother's words and, hence, became a professional student. She spent the next four decades of her life on a mission to disprove the notion that she resembled anything close to stupid. This is what led her to earning degree after degree even when she no longer desired to.

My mind comes back into the room, and I see Cathi squint her eyes as she scans the group for her first taker. I think to myself,

"I am not the one." I can already see that this particular exercise presents a challenge for me. The first challenge is that I lived between two households, so it's difficult to sculpt my family when they don't all live under the same roof. Second, my primary reason for doing RMM is to uncover, and to deal with those issues related to my father. How do I sculpt a person into my family picture who was never in the *picture* in the first place? This exercise just doesn't work for me.

Amy must have gained some steam from the first exercise, because she volunteers to go first for this one. Just as her hand goes up to volunteer, Kevin's hand goes up too, but he's signaling to go to the restroom. Cathi calls for a five-minute break for everyone which will also allow her time to prepare the room.

I am grateful for this break, because I need the time to regroup. That sensation to burst into tears is back. I can't let Cathi or Nicole detect my state, because they'll want to deal with things on the spot, and I'm not ready.

There are several small offices available for RMM participants to make calls, etc. I give the excuse that I need to make a business call, so that I can go into one of these rooms to gather myself. I cut through the kitchen, and my hand involuntarily grabs a bag of chips from the basket of treats on the counter.

By the time I reach the office, my urge to cry is gone. I have no idea where it went. Sarah's feedback has my feelings all over the place, and Cathi's new exercise only exacerbated them. Although, I am not complaining, I would much rather *not cry* than to cry. In fact, I feel a hint of relief and glee as I still have this shiny, unopened bag of chips to look forward to. I have no tears, but I have these chips that I will devour even though I am still stuffed from lunch. I gently tear open the bag, and chide myself for being both greedy and fickle.

The short break has ended, and we're all back together in the room. Hopefully, Amy's work will distract me from me. She begins to sculpt her family by assigning the various roles accordingly. Amy makes an odd request to have one of the boys who lived in her neighborhood present in her snapshot. Cathi has no problem with this. Amy chooses me to play this neighborhood boy. I give my consent, and move where Nicole is directing me, but I don't like this assignment. Inwardly I contemplate, "What have I done to give her the impression that I would be good at playing a neighborhood boy?" I'm sure my disdain for this role can be found somewhere on my face; unfortunately, I don't have the energy to alter it.

Amy's snapshot is complete. She steps back as if to study this sculpt of near-strangers who are role-playing her family. The physical distance among everyone, coupled with her mother's back to the family and the disinterested look on her father's face, tells a story.

The tears begin to well up in Amy's eyes, and they're beginning to well up in mine, too. I not only see her pain, but I feel it. Nicole asks Amy to share what she's feeling. Struggling with her own composure, Amy utters one word: "shame." I think, "Bingo!" This is exactly what I would feel, too. Telling you about my family dysfunction and showing you my family dysfunction are two different things.

Amy stares hard into her sea of truth, and I stare with her. Her mother is standing in one corner of the room with a briefcase in one hand, and an unplugged landline phone in the other hand, while her back is turned to the entire family. Her father appears aloof in the opposite corner of the room with his back partially turned away from the family. Her babysitter Amber is covered in a white sheet. Her teenage brother and sister appear to be in their own worlds, which seems pretty normal, and I am the neighborhood scoundrel standing near the door waiting to taunt her.

Cathi moves Amy's way, and invites her to explain her family sculpture when she is ready. Amy starts with her mother. She describes her as rarely being around, and hardly ever in touch with her daily needs and activities as a child. Next, she looks toward her father and describes him as living there in the house with her and her two older siblings, but he was never really *there*. She sort of dismisses her teenage brother and sister as having their own issues to deal with, so they never had much time for her. With a look of discomfort, she shifts towards the covered still body that represents Amber, and confesses that after her death things were never the same for her. She felt almost entirely alone. The one person who genuinely cared for her died, and she was left to fend for herself.

By her adolescence, she grew a tougher persona because she sometimes had to physically fight off sexual advances from some of the neighborhood boys. She claims this is when she became the *great pretender*. She began burying their crude remarks and acts inside of her, and pretending as if none of it affected her.

I think back to Ann's remarks to me about having to become an Academy Award®-winning actress overnight after my first encounter with Tim.

As she references one neighborhood boy in particular, she turns my way. Cathi asks her if she's ready to do a little anger work.

She screeches out an emotional, "Yes!"

Cathi responds by scooting this large black, cushion block directly in front of her, and hands her this paddle to strike the block. She puts her finger on the center of the block and instructs Amy not to hold back, to unleash everything she's got, and to tell him everything she's ever wanted to say to him!

Awkwardly, Amy grips the paddle with both hands and lifts it over her head, but she only mildly ends up striking the corner of the block. As the paddle makes its first landing on this block, her trembling voice yells out a few expletives.

Nicole steps in to give her a personal demonstration. "Amy, don't hit it like that…instead, hit it like *this*! And, when you speak to him, do so loudly, fearlessly, and from your diaphragm or your gut. Don't worry. You're doing just great, and we all have your back."

In unison, each person in the group shouts some words of encouragement to Amy. I can only think my words, because I am playing her perpetrator.

As Amy pounds this block more and more, she gains her footing and her voice with each subsequent strike. Cathi told me beforehand to wear this dismissive look on my face as if her words aren't affecting me at all. I assume this is to infuriate Amy further so that she releases as much of her anger as possible.

While Amy is wearing this block out, I retreat inside my head for a moment.

If someone would have told me a week ago that I would be engaged in this type of activity this week, my response would have been, "Not in a million years!" If one of my girlfriends would have told me this, I would have said, "What you talking 'bout, Willis?" and we both would have had a good laugh.

My assessment of this work up until this point is that it is bizarre yet effective. I am still blown away by the fact that I needed to grieve Sam's death after all of these years. If I get nothing else out of this workshop, that was a big deal for me.

However, all that said, I still don't see myself hitting this block. Even if I felt rage in the moment, by the time I assigned roles to everyone and got positioned in front of the block, my rage would have dissipated. It's similar to how I had the urge to cry before, and as soon as I got to the room, the urge was gone. I guess my feelings have learned how to master the game of *hide and seek* over the years.

My full attention turns back to Amy when I notice her slowing down. She signals to Cathi that she's done for now. Cathi quickly rescues her by taking the paddle from her hand, and giving a few pats to her right shoulder to affirm her work. Nicole scoots the block back to its place, and other group members move their plush pillows back to their place in the circle.

Cathi is seated back at the top of the circle to give Amy and the group some feedback. "First things first, everybody: de-role! Second, I hope you're beginning to understand the group model. It is safer and more practical for someone to process their pain by using these group techniques than it is to physically release this anger with the actual person who caused their pain years ago. In Amy's case, doing this type of work to heal her little girl and to reverse some of the childhood messages that she received can only enable her to have a more authentic, adult-like relationship with her mother and father one day, if she desires to do so.

"To that end, we'll wrap up Day One here, but not before I assign a little homework. Go home or back to your hotel room, and treat yourself to a nice hot bubble bath. If you don't have bubble bath because you're a shower person like most of us, stop at the drugstore and pick up some, along with candles, and whatever would enhance your bath experience. My final request is that you journal about your experience afterwards. That's it.

"Thanks, everyone, and I'll see you back here tomorrow morning at 9 a.m. sharp."

I am not happy about this assignment. This exercise is about more than taking a relaxing bath. I presume that Cathi hopes this bath experience will help to take us *there*. I am not in the mood to go *there*, but if I have to do this, I will need total privacy. This means that I need to go home and ask Webb for this privacy. I am reluctant to do this. Asking for privacy means that I have to explain why I need privacy, which may lead to a series of *whys*. Now, I understand the reason some people chose to stay at a hotel: to avoid the *whys*.

I am reminded of Ann's words to me that as an adult, I shouldn't shy away from asking for what I need. If I am struggling with this; maybe it is *little* Suzette who is attempting to ask, and not adult Suzette.

I am here. I made the water a little hotter so that I wouldn't have to move to warm it up again once I'm nestled into a particular spot. I stopped at the drugstore on my way home to buy bubble bath and bath salts. I thought I had these items, but I didn't want to risk having to go back out again, so I stopped on the way home. I also have one candle lit.

Asking Webb for privacy turned out to be a non-event. I think he thinks that I'm doing this workshop to deal with matters related to Tim, so he really didn't ask any questions. He just gave me my much-needed space, and I was grateful.

Sometimes I wish that my issues were straightforward, because there are times when I am very conflicted. Sometimes I see myself as defective, but I tell myself this is due to the abuse. In other words, it is true that I am defective, but for good reason. Conversely, there are other times when I feel things are the other way around: I was damaged long before the abuse in my life began. I also believe that my abuser knew this, which is why he targeted me. He knew that I was defective, and if he chose me, he could get away with it.

My weeping begins in silence. There is no sound coming from any part of my body, just salty tears streaming down my face. I never think deep thoughts like this. It's not because I don't really accept that they exist; it's that I don't know what to do with them. I don't know how to fix being damaged as a child.

This makes me think about my conversation with Sarah earlier. I want to write a book that genuinely helps other people. I also want to write a book that corrects this defect. Maybe what I think is that when you see a bestselling author, you won't see the defect. And, yes, it would be rewarding to show those who didn't believe in me, or who rejected me, that I could accomplish something great in spite of them.

As I notice the water beginning to cool, I also notice that I am really craving a glass of wine. When you sign the RMM contract, you commit that you will not drink alcohol, have sex, or use any other forms of medicators. I think I want the wine more because I know that I can't have it. For a fleeting moment, I think about having a glass anyway. It remains just a thought.

I briefly delve back into my thoughts for a moment, and then I remember that I am supposed to journal about this. Never... never, will I journal about this.

It is the next morning, and the sound of my phone buzzing on the nightstand wakes me up. It's just a bit after 5 a.m., and I am awake nearly thirty minutes before the alarm will sound, so I should take advantage of this and get an early start to the gym, but I think not. MSNBC's "Morning Joe" is already on, so I think that I will treat myself to watching a bit of Joe and Mika, ditching the gym this morning. This is one of my favorite shows that I like to jumpstart my morning with. I never miss this show. In fact, I have my DVR set to record it each morning. As soon as my eyes open, I feel for the remote control to flip on Joe. Somewhere between thirty-eight to forty minutes after the hour, the sports segment will start, and this is when I will get out of bed to start my day.

RMM is getting started and Cathi has just entered the room; she takes her seat on her pillow at the top of the circle. Like clock-work, she opens the session with a short meditation. I know that I should be appreciating these meditations more than I do, but they don't do a whole lot for me. Each time I am supposed to focus on my breathing along with these serene thoughts, my mind ends up drifting off somewhere else. I can handle it, though, since they're really short.

Following the meditation, I notice that there are definite-ly more smiles in the room. Cathi wants a brief check-in from each person. Each person will share what he or she got out of yesterday's session or last night's homework assignment. There is a Koosh (prickly rubber) ball that is passed among group members to indicate who will speak next. It also allows you to fiddle with something as you open up about your feelings.

The ball is thrown to me, and I talk about my experience with last night's homework. First, I confess that I really didn't want to do this bath exercise. I felt as though the exercise was designed to make the person "go there," and I really didn't want to do that. But I went to the drugstore and bought my bubble bath and bath salts, and I got with the program. I also realized that I am supposed to ask for what I need. I needed privacy to do this exercise, but I was reluctant to ask Webb for this. I rose to that occasion, too.

There's another moment that I'd like to rise to, and that is hitting that block. Cathi looks up and says, "Are you saying that you'd like to do some anger work, Suzette?"

"Well, yes and no. I think I need to hit that block, because I am trying to do what is right for me even when I don't feel like it. On the other hand, the block is for releasing anger, and from my perspective, it doesn't feel like I have any anger to release."

"Well, let's wrap up with check-in, and then let you stand in front of that block, and we'll see if you have anger or not. Sound good?"

"Yes."

Now, my nerves are back. I toss the rubber ball across to Sarah. There are only a few more check-ins, and then it will be my time to stand in front of that block. Kevin checks in last, and Cathi turns to me and says, "You're it, kiddo!"

Nicole walks over to Cathi and begins to whisper in her ear. I have no idea what she's telling Cathi, but I hear Cathi respond, "Good idea." The next thing I know, Cathi asks me to leave the room for a moment.

I don't really like the way this is going. No one has been asked to step outside of the room before. I thought the plan was to hammer the block, and maybe to shout out a few expletives at either Tim or my father. I don't understand why I need to leave the room.

Sarah peaks her head through the doorway and calls me back. I notice that she is wearing a matronly-looking shawl around her shoulders and a pocketbook that is hanging from the midway point on her arm. She is arm in arm with Kevin. As Cathi explains the setting, Kevin and Sarah are playing the role of my father and his wife.

Cathi positions the block in front of me and hands me the paddle. The role-playing commences.

My father and his wife appear to be walking down the street, and they stop to have an exchange right in front of me.

My father's wife says, "Isn't that the girl over there who claims to be your daughter?"

"I have no clue who that person is, but she's definitely not my daughter," he says.

"She couldn't be yours anyway, because she's not Creole."

I listen to this exchange, and it means nothing to me. If I am supposed to feel rage because of what Sarah and Kevin, or rather my father and his wife, are saying, I don't.

I lift the paddle over my head, and I whack the block hard and say, "Shut up! Shut your mouth!" I repeat this rant a few times, feeling virtually nothing.

I continue to pound the block, but this time I shout directly to my father, "You know that I am your daughter...why don't you just admit it! Everyone knows that I am your daughter!"

He makes perfect eye contact with me and sneers, "You are NOT my daughter! In fact, I don't know who you are!"

In a flash, Nicole rips the name tag off Sarah's chest and pastes it on hers and says, "You're NOT his daughter...you couldn't be... you're a LOSER!"

Instantly, I lose grip of the paddle and I fall to my knees as the word "loser" pierces my soul. My head is face down in my lap and the tears are rushing out of me.

Mark is standing near me, and I hear him say to the others, "I've never witnessed anything like that before. I thought she was about to kick some butt, and instead, she just melted. When Nicole said the word 'loser' she just melted to the ground. It reminded me of the scene from *The Wizard of Oz* when the Wicked Witch of the West dissolved to the ground after Dorothy poured the water on her."

Nicole steps over, and kneels on the ground parallel to me. We have no eye contact, but she whispers in my ear, "Suzette, this is where the heart of your work lies. You are not a loser, even on your worst day. You never forget that, young lady."

After the first break, we have a journaling exercise.

Dear Journal,

During Amy's work I felt like we were both free. She was free from having to pretend and I was free from having to also pretend as if my father's absence didn't hurt. I can be free from what is not true, pretending like it didn't hurt just to avoid giving him the satisfaction. Instead, I can embrace what is true, that I am hurting, but I am not alone. God is with me. I can be free of the fantasy, having a man to call Dad, a man who loved me and would protect me. Instead I surrender to the purposeful and divinely orchestrated life that God has designed just for me.

Dear Journal,

My desire is to be free, and I see now that I also have to let others be free to be who they are. It is now time to let go of the need to convince, to prove, and to win them over. Freedom comes from accepting them and loving them as they are, and not trying to change them.

Coming Full Circle

Carrying physical baggage for an extended period of time can weigh you down and wear you out. Carrying around unhealed wounds from your past can have a similar effect. This baggage, although invisible, can bring about a spiritual and an emotional fatigue, and will ultimately use your yesterday to rob your today. There is a way out, but it would require you to put down your bags. Putting down your bags also means that you are choosing to put down your other weights of shame, blame, anger, guilt, etc. Do you really want to be free so you can soar to new heights, or would you prefer to stay with what you know, and remain weighted down on the ground?

I choose not to cheapen my calling
by working to win the praise of man.

"Yet what we suffer now is nothing
compared to the glory He will reveal to us later."
(Rom. 8:18 NLT)

Chapter 29

Peter in the Boat

I AM WORKING FROM HOME TODAY, so I finally decide to open Ashley's email after dancing around it most of the morning. She sent it to me last night; however, fearing that it might be negative, I left it until this morning to read. Opening her emails feels like I am opening the envelope to my final semester grades.

Ashley is my book editor. Lately, her feedback has been mixed, which makes me feel as though my writing is falling off course. Her recent feedback seems centered around the basics. "I need to see more detail…feel more depth…sense more emotion." These are basic writing techniques that we covered three years ago when we first started working together. I could handle receiving this type of feedback back then, because I was a writer with no formal training who was just starting out. I saw myself less as a writer and more as a woman with a story to tell. However, this recent feedback feels like regress to me. I can't help but question whether I really have what it takes to write a book that is good enough to touch my readers, or to inspire someone else's life—especially since I am struggling with my own.

Before reading the actual edits, I anxiously scan through the pages just to see how much redlining Ashley has done. Let's just say these pages look like a Texas roadmap. This hurts. As much as I have come to know that her feedback is less about me and more about the material, in this very moment it feels like I need rewriting.

I pour another cup of coffee, suck it up, and face her edits. I need to read through them, because we have an editing session this evening. As I scroll through the pages, I have a flashback to a time when Ashley's feedback produced a breakthrough in my writing. Her note in the margin read, "You tend to tie a bow around certain parts of your story." She was accusing me of gift-wrapping the beautiful parts of my story and glossing over, or entirely withholding, the ugly parts. I will never forget the rest of her note, which read, "Suzette, there is beauty in the ugly."

Her feedback pushes me to have my own moment of truth. At that time, I find parts of my story shameful and difficult to share with anyone, even Ashley. I did not want to share the ugly truths of sexual abuse, and a father who denied my existence. I definitely did not want to make the reader a fly on the wall in my therapy sessions. Also, publishing these truths for perfect strangers to read made me want to get back into the bed and pull the covers over my head.

This is when I went back to examine my ultimate intentions. Notwithstanding my desire for personal ambition to hush certain naysayers, my desire to use my life's story to inspire another's life was stronger. Consequently, I reason if this is my ultimate goal, then I can no longer talk around the truth, but that I had to tell it and trust the process thereafter.

Flashing back to this revelation brings me back to the part with which I continue to struggle. There was a time in my life when I lacked financial discipline. I am the complete opposite today. Now that I value saving, it seems as though each time I get to a certain dollar amount saved, there comes another lemon to hit my account.

The same is true for my writing. There was a time when I skirted the ugly parts of my story. Today, I don't withhold the ugly. My assumption is that once I correct what is holding me back, I will progress and not regress. I assume wrong. It seems the harder I try, the harder the lemons fall, and the more distractions come to interrupt my flow. This causes me to question whether I am on the right path. Maybe, I am simply guilty of seeing what I want to see rather than what is?

Meeting with Ashley at Starbucks: "I read through all of your edits. I can't help but feel as though my work is regressing, and I don't know how to get things back on track."

I promised myself in the car that I would not cry, and here come the tears. "I am so sorry for these tears, Ashley. I guess I am just tired and frustrated."

"No need to apologize, Suzette. I completely understand."

"The way that I feel sometimes is that I have invested three years already into writing this book, and I am not even at the half-way mark. I feel like I am in the middle of the ocean. I am too far from the shore to turn back, and still very far from my goal. When I appear to give it my all, I am often hit with distractions that seem to come from everywhere. I can't help but think that maybe I am on the wrong track, because if I were on the right track, things would flow more smoothly."

"Suzette, do you recall the story of Peter's attempt to walk on water?"

"Yes, vaguely."

"Peter attempts to walk on water and the wind starts to blow. We think that when we have good intentions that the wind is not supposed to blow, but, in fact, the blowing wind is a positive sign. It means that you are choosing to step out of the boat and into your purpose. If you don't feel the wind blowing, that may mean you are playing it too safe. The point is to keep our eye on Christ, who ultimately can also control the wind."

My emotions take a 180-degree turn. All this time, I have interpreted the *wind blowing* as a sign that I was on the wrong track, or that something was wrong with me. Perhaps, the wind blowing means just the opposite.

Coming Full Circle

There are two types of events that can happen: the ones you cause to happen, and those that happen to you just because. No sooner than you find a way to recover from being hit by one lemon, another hits you. When this happens, don't let your pursuit of perfection trump your pursuit of purpose. In other words, don't wait for the circumstances in your life to become perfect before you pursue your life's work. Remember, a goal achieved under imperfect conditions underscores the character and the tenacity of the achiever.

I choose to stay committed even when the process gets messy.

"These trials will show that your faith is genuine. It is being tested as fire tests and purifies gold—though your faith is far more precious than mere gold. So when your faith remains strong through many trials, it will bring you much praise and glory and honor on the day when Jesus Christ is revealed to the whole world."
(1 Pet. 1:7 NLT)

Chapter 30

Mirror, Mirror

ALL THIS TIME, I have been thinking very introspectively about the impact my healing and recovery will have on my life, both personally and professionally. I have not been thinking about how my healing, or lack thereof, will directly impact my children.

I was recently in a session with Ann where I was reminded of the very simple fact that children typically do as you do. It isn't enough to ask that they make different choices without first choosing differently yourself. In other words, a child's actions are typically a reflection of the one who is parenting them.

This brief exchange sent me into a bit of a tailspin as I remembered those things that I constantly ask my boys to change about their lives—things I haven't yet fully committed to changing myself.

Coming Full Circle

One of the most difficult things about being a leader is the responsibility of leading by example. While it's comfortable to have the space to fail if you need to, it is uncomfortable acknowledging that every decision you make is 100% generated by you. Your actions and your choices are, in fact, controllable, and to be a servant of God means that you have to be willing to make different choices, especially when there are others following in your footsteps.

I choose to accept my role as God's servant.

"No one sews a patch of unshrunk cloth on an old garment, for the patch will pull away from the garment, making the tear worse. Neither do people pour new wine into old wineskins. If they do, the skins will burst; the wine will run out and the wineskins will be ruined. No, they pour new wine into new wineskins, and both are preserved."
(Matt. 9:16-17 NIV)

Part Four

Service

Overview

THE TIME HAS COME! The caterpillar was able to endure its transformation process, and now a beautiful adult butterfly is ready to show itself to the world. After reveling over its striking beauty, it's hard to imagine all that it underwent during its transformation.

Its first few attempts to fly may be failed ones, but the butterfly never gives up. Initially, its wings will be limp, because its new parts have been cramped inside its old casing. However, once a sufficient amount of blood is pumped into its wings, it will be ready to take flight and will eventually fly high. While the butterfly may instinctively find flying high thrilling, instinctively, it will know this is not its life's calling. To fulfill its life's purpose, sometimes it will have to endure inclement weather conditions, and protect itself against predators. Nevertheless, it will learn how to soar high above its life's circumstances so that it can mate, and ultimately bring more beauty into the world.

Just as the time has come for the butterfly, your season is finally here, too! You are reaping the fruits of your hard work from choosing to think and live differently, and sustaining the awesome change in your life in spite of your initial relapses. In fact, you even see those relapses as blessings because they enabled you to rebound stronger, wiser, and even more committed to your personal and spiritual transformation. You have learned to do this by continually choosing to renew your mind and spirit in Christ Jesus.

At long last, you and the butterfly transpire as beautiful creatures. You both have mastered the art of what it really means to look good in this life despite your past. You now know how to beautifully soar above the vicissitudes of life. Similar to the butterfly, you, too, may be proud as a peacock by all that your life reflects today, but a peacock you are not. Your higher self is learning that your Heavenly Father is glorified when you use what He has given you to be of service to others more so than yourself. God's plan for your life is much bigger than you and deeper than what you could have imagined on your own.

Chapter 31

Stripping Myself of the Whys

"Sue, you have little ships coming in everyday. The more gratitude you show for these little ships, your big Ship, as you call it, will arrive, but in God's time." These are my mother's parting words to me as we end our telephone call. I call her while I am walking to the Starbucks to meet with Ashley for another editing session. I confess to her that it feels like things are never going to turn around for me...like my ship is never going to come in no matter how much I stay on my knees, work my fingers to the bone, and sacrifice some of my today for tomorrow.

Editing Session at Starbucks with Ashley:

"Hey, Suzette, what's up?"

"Nothing much, just more of the same."

"You okay?"

"Not really. Another missed deadline for this book is finally beginning to take its toll on me. I promised myself this book would be finished by my birthday. It was supposed to be a memorable gift to myself. Given that my birthday is just around the corner, I think we both know that it's not going to happen."

"Don't worry, Suzette. The book will be finished when it is supposed to be finished."

"I must worry, Ashley. I am turning one year older and I still haven't achieved certain goals. I thought I would have been much farther along professionally by this stage in my life. I am feeling genuinely unaccomplished at the moment, and there's no way to sugarcoat my feelings."

More and more this book has become the center of my life. I have taken my eye off of so many other things to commit myself to this project, and I feel like the progress that I have made month by month is still marginal. Maybe things wouldn't feel so bad if I had other wins to celebrate, but I don't feel as though I even have that.

"Suzette, I hate to be the one to tell you this, but too much of this book still seems to be all about you."

I am so sick of hearing this! I set a goal for myself. It was a reasonable goal. I missed it. I am angry, frustrated, and sad as a result of missing it. Why do we have to go down this same path of this being too much about me?

"Ashley, of course, this book is about me. It's my life story, so who else would it be about?"

"Are you sure you're okay?"

"Sure, things are just fine…peachy keen in fact. Let's just get on with the editing."

Unfortunately, I am no longer in the mood to hear any editing feedback. I am angry and disappointed in myself, and frustrated with Ashley, too. And, if I am totally honest, I am even frustrated with God. There are times that I believe that God has me stuck in a process, because He is trying to teach me. However, it seems that I am never at a place of having learned enough for Him. As soon as I learn one lesson, He's on to the next. When is there ever a break? I am frustrated with God, because He could be doing more, but He is not.

"Okay, Suzette. We can delve into the last four chapters you gave me to review, but first let's address some general points on grammar and style:

"Avoid clichés.

"Stay away from terms like 'folks,' and phrases such as 'all over the place.' These don't translate universally.

"Avoid phrases like 'as it relates' and 'the fact of the matter is.'

"Also, shorten your sentences, so they are easier for the reader to process.

"Finally, you may want to pull out your E.B. stylebook."

She has just referred me to the timeless style and grammar book, *The Elements of Style* by E.B. White and William Strunk, Jr. Every good writer keeps a copy of this book on hand. By Ashley's referral back to this book, she confirms that my writing is regressing. She referred this book to me when we first started this project. Now, we're near the final section of the book, and she's referring it to me again? If I had any doubt that things are off track for me, I don't anymore.

"Suzette, do you have anything to add, or any questions before I give you my feedback on the chapters?"

"Ashley, you can probably tell that this editing session is not going well for me."

"Yes, I can sense that. So, what's really going on with you?"

I give a longer than normal pause, and there it is. There is that one simple question that prompts the trickle of tears down my cheeks.

"I think your direction back to a style and grammar book that you referred me to at the beginning of this project tipped me over the edge. I want so desperately for this book to be finished, and it is not. In fact, this book is nowhere near being finished.

"Well, I don't necessarily agree with that."

Yes, Ashley, but I feel it's true. What's worse is that while I am confused on how to turn things around, I am even more confused on whether things are worth turning around. Sometimes I think that I should just cut my losses now.

"Suzette, do you know what I think?"

"What?"

"Sometimes when we find ourselves in the place that you are in at this very moment, we need to strip ourselves of the *whys*."

"What do you mean?"

"What we may want to do in the name of God may be good, but then we need to get to why we want to do it. For example, a pastor may want a ten thousand-member church. That's a good thing, but why does he want it? Does he want it so that he can say he is the pastor of a mega-church, and live well off of the church? Or, does he want it to save ten thousand souls?"

Her example of the proverbial pastor grabs me. I know this type of pastor. I can smell him a mile away. He claims that his work is about serving the Lord, when he's all about serving himself. Maybe I am guilty, too, because I want both. I want to do something that is pleasing to God, and I want it to be good *for me,* too.

"Ashley, I cannot lie to you. My truth as it relates to the book is a bit of both. First and foremost, I want to write a book that is pleasing to the Lord. My prayer is that after people read *Blues to Blessings,* they will become inspired to either turn to, or turn back to, God. I think that's one of the reasons the book is taking me so long to finish, because I want it to be just perfect for Him.

"That said, I also desire to be a bestselling author. I desire this so much that I have a copy of a *New York Times* bestseller list framed on my desk, so that I can envision the achievement of my goal daily."

I have always heard about the importance of practicing visualization, and how it can be another method to move you closer to actualizing your goal. About two years ago I was reading the Sunday edition of the *New York Times* when I got the bright idea to create a visualization of my goal to become a bestselling author. I cut out the bestseller list from the paper and replaced the title that was in the #1 spot with *Blues to Blessings*. I even inserted the number of weeks that I desired the book to remain at the #1 spot. Afterwards, I framed it and put it on my desk.

Recalling the visual image of that frame sitting on my desk, reminds me of the other frames on my desk. The frame of the *New York Times* bestseller list sits right next to my picture with the boys, and a picture of Sam. I have a multi-picture frame of myself and the boys when we were all seven years old. After RMM, I was inspired to add a picture of Sam at age six that was taken just before his death. It is something about the innocence of our souls at this age that warms my heart.

"Ashley, I guess the best way to describe it is that I am seeking a 'doublewin' scenario. It is a win for God, because I am doing something positive for Him, and it's a win for me, because I am fulfilling one of my personal ambitions."

I have always thought about the book as a double-win scenario, but I have never said "doublewin" aloud to myself before. Consequently, as soon as "doublewin" rolls off my tongue, there is a feeling of wrongness that comes over me. I can also sense by the look on Ashley's face that these words did not settle well with her, either.

"Suzette, it's better not to do anything than to do something for God on the terms of your own vain ambitions."

"I see your point, and I am not pushing back to it. My feelings seem difficult to articulate, but let me try. Up until this point, I have always felt that if I knew in advance that *Blues to Blessings* would only sell 100 copies, I would still write the book and give it the same valiant effort, because I genuinely feel that God has given me this assignment. However, it is also important for me to show that my life has value and purpose to it. Writing a book that becomes ranked #1 on the *New York Times* bestseller list is confirmation that my life has purpose and meaning to it."

As I pause for a moment, a deeper thought dawns on me. Another way to explain this is that I am trying to *confirm* that I am not a loser. I cannot believe that I am back here at this same place again! After all of these years, I am still wrestling the *self-worth* beast. This is the conversation with Sarah from RMM all over again. Her question to me was, "What are you trying to prove?" The truth is that I am still, consciously and unconsciously, trying to prove that I am not a loser. Becoming a bestselling author is living proof that I am no one's loser. It feels so unfortunate that after all of my efforts to grow and to become more self-aware, all I can claim is that I can spot this beast quicker, and even see through its many disguises, but I still struggle to slay it once and for all.

"Suzette, let's look at this from another angle. How many copies of *Blues to Blessings* do you need to sell for it to be ranked # 1 on the *New York Times* bestseller list?"

"I have no idea. I have always wondered about this, but I have yet to research this."

"Okay, let's pick a number. Let's say that you will need to sell 250,000 copies of *Blues to Blessings* for it to become a *New York Times* bestseller.

"I am not sure where you are going with this, but okay, let's go with 250,000 copies."

"Don't move your frame of the *New York Times* bestseller list. Next to it, also have a saying that 'You're helping to turn 250,000 souls to God.' I heard you say that you want to inspire your readers to turn to God, or turn back to Him. This is your purpose, Suzette."

Immediately, this feels right. I am still processing her words, but the vibe that I feel is good.

"Ashley, I never thought about it from this perspective."

"Suzette, your idea of a 'doublewin' has a stain on it, and maybe God is trying to remove this stain."

It has never been my intention in life to just make money. I always wanted to make my money by doing something both purposeful and great. In this way, I could checkmark two boxes. I could fulfill God's purpose for my life, and I could make those who ignored or dismissed me as ever being able to accomplish greatness regret they ever did. Your naysayers can't ignore you when you make it to the "greatness stratosphere," not even if they want to. This is the origin of my "doublewin" mindset.

This is why I have been vacillating back and forth between writing a book that is pleasing to God and scoring huge recognition from writing a bestseller. Sometimes I am seeking to live the life that God created me to live, and other times I am seeking to have the last laugh. My conflict arises when I do the latter but call it the former. To make matters worse, I am using God's work to shut certain people up, and I'm still calling it God's work.

This "doublewin" mindset will always produce a conflict between what I call my divine assignment and my personal ambitions. However, seeing my purpose the way that Ashley describes it dissolves this conflict.

"Suzette, I'll leave you with one more thought before we wrap up."

"Please, continue, Ashley. I am gaining so much from your thoughts thus far. By all means, please continue."

"When we focus too much on doing, and achieving that end goal, we're like a fish swimming upstream. Instead, we should live each day *being* who God created us to be. This will keep us in flow with the river. Even our smallest vain ambitions place us swimming against it."

"I understand that now. Ashley, although we didn't edit actual chapters today, something far greater happened: my mindset received a beautiful editing. I cannot thank you enough."

"No worries, Suzette. Well, I do have to go now, but we'll reconnect soon. Until then, keep writing."

"Yes, I will."

As I begin to pack up my things, I think more about the difference between *doing* and *being*. I have always thought that my life's purpose or calling meant I had to do something big. This is why most of my adult life I have been trying to answer the question "Why am I here?" I have prayed to God and asked Him countless times, "Father, what is my life's purpose?" I see now that I have been searching for the answer in the things that I do, rather than in the woman He created me to be.

If I believe that my life's calling is to inspire people to turn to, or to turn back to, God, then each time I do that—whether it's writing a book or talking with a homeless person—I am fulfilling my life's calling. I don't need to wait until a book that I author reaches bestseller status before I can claim that my light is shining. Inspiring a multitude of readers to deepen their relationship with God, or to turn to Him for the first time, is a far greater purpose than the personal validation from being named on some bestseller list. I can clearly see that letting my light shine doesn't necessarily mean seeing my name in bright lights. This is a big "ah-ha" moment for me!

On my walk back to my car, I have to cross the Chicago River over the Michigan Avenue Bridge. As I cross the bridge, I look down and I visualize my soul as one of those smiley faces with the sunglasses floating on a raft in the river. I envision that my smiley face comes in contact with another smiley face. This is my opportunity to Be Suzette. Sometimes this may not involve an exchange in words. It could be in the form of a warm smile or affirming eye contact. Behaving like this keeps me in flow with the river. Maybe this is why I love the youthful pictures of the boys, Sam, and me on my desk. At this age, there's no agenda. We're just cute, innocent little beings.

Conversely, I am swimming upstream when I use my energy as a means to a vain end. I think back to the complaining that I did with my mother earlier about my ship never coming in. She is correct. Each day is an opportunity to show gratitude for all of the little ships that are coming into my life. I will try to live each day as *being* the woman God created me to be, and trust that the universe will respond accordingly.

Coming Full Circle

If a loved one came to you today and asked for $50,000, your first question would likely be, "Why do you want it?" If they wanted to spend it on something illegal, you wouldn't give it to them. However, if you had it, and they wanted to spend $50,000 on doing something that would both improve your life and theirs, you might consider it. God's logic is fair and simple. What motivates us is equally important as what we're motivated toward. If you seek to do God's work or if you seek an opportunity, it's very important that you don't bring your own vain ambitions into what is meant to be pure. It's important that you keep your intentions pure; otherwise, the result itself will be tainted. If your intentions represent a seed that will grow into a result, and your intentions are split in half, this will only manifest in results that are also split in half. The potency of your results is often directly correlated to the purity of your intentions.

Regarding the church, service is often equated with what ministry you join and the things that you do to help build the church. However, God's greatest desire is that we have a direct and personal relationship with Him such that we are inclined to execute those tasks that don't necessarily fall into an official capacity. In other words, if He has your hands but not your heart, your work is pointless.

I will serve one God.

"I know you well—you are neither hot nor cold; I wish you were one or the other! But since you are merely lukewarm, I will spit you out of my mouth! You say, 'I am rich, with everything I want; I don't need a thing!' And you don't realize that spiritually you are wretched and miserable and poor and blind and naked."
(Rev. 3:15-17 TLB)

Chapter 32

Relapse

It has only been two days since my meeting with Ashley at Starbucks, and my spirits are already in relapse mode. I left her on such a high note, thinking that I had everything figured out. I was wrong...dead wrong.

My frustration and sadness continue to pour out of me, because I feel as though I am not getting a break from anywhere. I sacrificed my entire summer to finish the book. That didn't work out, so I have come to accept that the book will be finished in its own divine time. I look to business for a break there. Business was slow at the beginning of the summer, and is even slower today. We are limping into the fourth quarter. During all of this, I even feel like my parenting is starting to slip, so I feel guilty about that. I have been trying my hardest to practice gratitude for my "little ships" or blessings coming in each day, but it is difficult to remain in a genuine state of gratitude when the things that you really desire are just not showing up.

To lift myself out of this rut, I figure I need to sacrifice more and press forward with a relentless focus. For starters, earlier this year, I got the *feeling* that God wanted me to refrain from drinking even an occasional glass of wine as long as I am writing the book. To respond obediently, I have not taken one sip of wine since. In terms of my finances, I tithe when business is thriving and even when it is not. I don't know the actual Bible verses, but somewhere in either Deuteronomy or Numbers it talks about the importance of being a faithful tither. I am that. The scriptures also say ask and you shall receive. I have been asking so much that I feel all *asked* out. Through it all, God remains silent.

I am at a place where I no longer know what is true anymore. Maybe, am I living in a bubble, seeing what I want to see rather than what is? I feel like I am getting a keyhole view of what a person goes through before they commit suicide. I would never take my own life for a host of reasons; however, these thoughts creep into my mind, and I have a relationship with God. I can only imagine the darkness and despair the person feels who has no relationship with Him. When I feel as if I am in a state of delirium, and I can't trust my own thinking, I turn to those whom I trust the most.

Telephone call to Ashley —

"Hi, Suzette."

I am mustering up my composure, so she can decipher my words.

"Suzette, are you there?"

"Yeah…and it's not a good morning for me."

"Oh my goodness, Suzette, you're crying. What happened? Are the boys okay? Webb?"

"I need to talk. Can you meet?"

"Yes, sure."

"Where are you?"

"Sitting in my car in front of the Newberry Library."

The library is open today from 9 a.m. to 1 p.m., and this has become one of the most productive places for me to write. However, as soon as I drive up, everything comes down on me at once. The tears start to flow and they haven't stopped.

"How about the Starbucks on North Avenue in thirty minutes?"

"I'll be there."

I'm sure the way I was crying to her on the phone this morning, she probably thinks somebody died.

"Suzette, I came as quickly as I could."

"I really appreciate you coming."

I am talking to her with this really weird pair of sunglasses on. I don't have my good pair with me, and these were the only shades in the glove compartment. I am not in the mood to expose my distress to the Starbucks *aficionados*.

"Suzette, what is going on?"

"It's just everything, Ashley. My unraveling began yesterday when Webb mentioned my upcoming birthday. The thoughts of not feeling accomplished started to creep in again. For the first time ever, I dread my coming birthday. I thought I would have put more points on my *scoreboard* by now, and I am really hurting that I haven't."

"Suzette, I think you're being way too hard on yourself."

"Those feelings open up a can of worms: the book! Honestly, I thought I was over this issue and I guess I wasn't. Graphically speaking, it feels like when you think you've hurled for the last time until you realize that you haven't."

It's tough to reconcile the fact that I invested my entire summer in this effort and I'm still not done. I would write early mornings, late nights, and weekends. I even worked on the Fourth of July, and passed up a few *girls only* outings to keep my focus. Not to mention that I have not had a glass of my favorite red wine for almost the entire year. This is a real sacrifice for me.

"Suzette, think about it in these terms: the length of time that you're investing to write this book is a testament that you are writing a great book. If it wasn't, you would have finished a long time ago. Great books can often take a considerable amount of time to write."

I really needed to hear this. When I am drowning in my sorrows, this is when I appreciate that I have people like Ashley to turn to.

"Okay, Suzette, what else is wrong? So far, I heard you mention your birthday and the book."

"Business is still slow, so there's a lot of financial uncertainty, at least for the short term."

I can go on and on about the number of business opportunities that we advance to the five-yard line but that fall apart at the one-yard line. It happens so frequently, it is starting to feel like a real conspiracy. Even though we're living through the Great Recession, I never thought things would turn this dismal.

"Ashley, this is another area of grave disappointment. I am a faithful tither, so I never expected this would happen to me. Even when I overspent in other areas, I always paid my tithes first. I express my dismay to Ann, and she surmises that I am thinking about the blessings that can flow from tithes and offerings too narrowly."

I recall Ann's specific feedback. "You gave monetarily, so you are expecting God's blessings to flow back to you in monetary form. The God that I serve doesn't operate that narrowly. Instead, look for God's blessings to come in a myriad of ways."

"Suzette, I would have to agree with Ann."

"Yes, her feedback made sense. It was almost as if God was speaking through her to me."

My stomach is starting to growl. "Ashley, have you eaten yet?"

"No, I haven't."

"I think the restaurant next door serves brunch on the weekends. Do you want me to see if I can get us a table?"

"Sure, I'm game."

As we leave Starbucks, I slip my hideous shades into my purse. I think the puffiness around my eyes has gone down.

We step next door and we're in luck; there's no wait to be seated. Once at the table, I resume our discussion. "Ashley, as I was saying, things are in disarray, and my hard work and sacrifice haven't paid off yet. However, I went to Pastor Sean's class this week, and he spoke about how we can miss the larger picture that God is conveying to us when we focus only on raw obedience. He made the point that Jesus is less interested in our raw obedience, and is more interested in our being more self-reflective about our actions. In other words, Jesus doesn't just focus on my doing the right thing, but rather He focuses on those barriers such as egoism, self-righteousness, and bitterness that keep me from doing what is right."

While in Pastor Sean's class, I reflected on my personal raw obedience to tithe, and to refrain from drinking wine. I realize that similar to the way that I am trying to prove myself in the natural world, I am also trying to prove myself, or to earn my blessings in the spiritual realm with God.

"Pastor Sean's class sounds like it was an interesting one."

"Yes, it was."

"Ashley, but after all of that, I still find myself waiting on the Lord. I often compare my waiting on the Lord to waiting at the same bus stop. After waiting so long, I wonder if God is trying to tell me to move on, and I am just not hearing Him."

I often use a bus stop analogy to describe what it feels like to wait on the Lord. I start out eager to wait for Him at this particular stop, because I feel as though He led me here. I am not waiting alone as there are several others waiting with me to get to the same destination. As time passes, I observe that many who are waiting with me choose other options. Some decide to take cabs. Some pile into cars with others. Some get creative and walk down another street to take a different bus route. Sooner or later, I see that some of the same people who started out waiting with me have already made it to their destination. I often wonder how long I should wait before deciding to take another route, like the others.

"Ashley, I am at a point where I no longer know what is true. I know my bus stop analogy sounds silly, but it captures how I can sometimes feel overlooked and abandoned by God. When I feel this way, I can only conclude that I am being punished. I cannot seem to get over our *stripping myself of the whys* conversation. Maybe God is punishing me for my 'doublewin' mindset?"

"Suzette, God loves you and cares for you more than your little mind can comprehend. I can assure you that God is not punishing you."

I am relieved to hear her say this with such conviction. I thought the idea of being punished was a far reach, but I couldn't rule it out.

"Suzette, I have a good sense of where you are, and I would like to make a few points to you. First, are you reading your Bible? Do you fast?"

I am going to trust those are rhetorical questions.

"Suzette, imagine that you're fighting on the battlefield, and you're terribly wounded. He's not calling you off the battlefield because you're not a good fighter, and leaving others on because they're great fighters. Instead, He's calling you off because you're wounded and He wants to care for you. When you're healed, He'll put you back. You'll be even more prepared to deal with what's coming your way, but you can't continue to fight effectively the way you are now. Hence, the reason for my initial question about your reading the Bible and fasting."

"Second, God is more interested or invested in the change in you rather than your circumstances. When you begin to change, your circumstances will change too."

This part I already know. The work that I have done with Ann over the last few years has caused me to change in lots of ways.

"Third, God will sometimes remove so many things in our lives, because He wants us to turn to Him. I do agree that God will sometimes speak to us through other people, but there is no replacement for going to Him directly. You need to be fed by God's Word. I think if you get on a regular system of doing that, you'll begin to see things very differently. In fact, your writing may even change. Suzette, do you hear what I am saying to you?"

"Yes, Ashley. I am listening."

"Suzette, God wants you to turn to Him…not to me…not to Webb…not to Ann…not to Pastor Sean, but to Him."

Coming Full Circle

As much as another person's assessment of your situation can be spot-on, and their feedback might even be of God, there is no substitute for turning to God. While there's nothing wrong with having a confidant, and maybe it's one that God Himself placed in our lives, this confidant should not be a replacement for your communion with God.

I will serve God through my direct relationship with Him.

"But let all who take refuge in you be glad; let them ever sing for joy. Spread your protection over them, that those who love your name may rejoice in you."
(Ps. 5:11 NIV)

Chapter 33

His Divine Order Serves His Divine Purpose

"For I know the plans that I have for you."
(Jer. 29:11 NLT)

THIS IS THE VERSE that I have been pondering since I flipped to it in my Bible earlier this morning. Jeremiah 29 deals with how God decides to leave the Israelites in Babylon for seventy years. When I read this I think to myself, "Whew, that's a long time!" However, after this duration, God will restore their lives and fulfill His promises to them. The other part of this morning's reading that I've been reflecting on is how God is telling them to do what is right while they're in Babylon. In other words, don't wait for things to get better before you change your ways. Start changing your ways now.

I started reading the Bible a few weeks after meeting with Ashley when she made the point that I should begin to turn less to others for counsel, and more to God's Word. Initially, her advice sounded good, but ill-suited for me. I am not a Bible-reading person. I have always found the one or two Bible verses that the pastor predicates his sermon on each week sufficient.

After telling Ashley that I would give it a try, it took me nearly a week before I actually picked up the Bible. First, I needed to define for myself what *turning to the Bible* looked like for me. Would I pick it up daily, weekly, or whenever I felt inspired? Would I challenge myself to read it from cover to cover? I also had to honestly admit a couple of things to myself. First, I remember from my childhood the term "holy roller" was used to describe the extremely religious. I didn't want to start something that would lead to me becoming an "extreme" anything. Second, I had an underlying feeling of intimidation about reading the Bible. All of this prompted me to explore my feelings more.

For starters, I have never viewed reading the Bible as necessary to developing my relationship with God. Just believing what's in there has always been enough for me. I have it on hand, so that I can refer to it if someone points me to a particular passage. It is also the sacred writ that adorns most Christian households, and my household is no different. Growing up, the Bibles always sat on the nightstands next to the beds. Today, I have a Bible on my nightstand, and Webb has one on his. I have grown to feel safer just knowing there's one in the house with me. That's it.

Two weeks ago, I started mulling these thoughts over in my head. A few more days passed, and I still had not picked up the Bible. I would glance at it and tell myself that I would come back to it, but I never did. Finally, this morning I couldn't take it anymore. Instead of me staring at it, I felt as though it was staring at me. I walked over to my nightstand, picked it up, closed my eyes, and trusted that whatever page I flipped to was the page that God led me to.

I flipped to page 862 in my *Daily Walk Bible* (New Living Translation). Webb gave me this Bible a few years ago, and I have only referred to it a few times. I actually find it easier to understand than my traditional King James Version. The first sentence that I read in the Overview Section is "It's always darkest before dawn, and Jeremiah's prophecy is no exception." This particular passage deals with Jeremiah's trials and his faith. He purchases a piece of land that he knows will be conquered by the Babylonians, but he purchases it anyway as a reaffirmation of God's promise that in the end everything would be restored. The moment I read this first sentence I can't help but wonder if this is the message that God is trying to convey to me: "It's always darkest before dawn."

After reading this piece on Jeremiah, I am intrigued enough to read the next day. After the second and third days of reading, I decide that I would read at least a page of the Bible each day, for the time being. Next, I needed to figure out how I would fit this into my already hectic schedule. I wake up around 5 a.m. each day. Once I get out of bed, it's off to the races. There is little time in my day that is not allotted to doing something. Currently, I do about a thirty-second prayer each morning. That's it. Making a commitment to read and to digest a page of the Bible each day can be more than a notion, especially if I flip to a page in the Old Testament. The only way I see making this work is getting up even earlier than 5 a.m., and that is not an option for me. If I tried to do this on the back end of my day, I would likely fall asleep after reading the second verse.

Somehow, my grandmother and mother always find the time to begin their day with God. However, I would argue that my days are far more hectic than theirs. My mother meditates each morning, and my grandmother reads the Bible every morning without fail. When I say that my grandmother reads daily "without fail,"

I mean it. I have seen her practice this before she retired as a first grade schoolteacher, after she retired, and on holiday mornings. She even read the morning we buried my grandfather.

She always rises before everyone else, starts her coffeepot, and sits at the kitchen table to do her reading while the coffee is brewing. If you happen to be up with her around the same time, she will engage in minimal conversation with you until she has finished her reading. Today, she is in her nineties, and she's still following her same morning routine.

Needless to say, my mornings start differently. As I've mentioned before, my favorite morning television show is *Morning Joe*. I watch *Joe* religiously. This is what I do *without fail*. It is my one-stop shop for politics, news, and friendly banter. Just before I turn the television on, I get on my knees in the bed and I say a quick, thirty-second prayer. Then I reach for the remote control with one hand and my phone with the other.

The second day I read the Bible I do not turn on *Morning Joe*. I decide to practice (at least for this morning) what I have watched my mother and grandmother do for years. I put on a small pot of coffee and sit at the kitchen table to read while the coffee is brewing.

This morning, I decide to do more than just flip to a random page. I choose to journal a bit before I pick up the Bible this time. My intention is to capture my feelings prior to randomly turning to a page. I want to see if there will be any alignment between my feelings and where I feel I am being led.

A girlfriend recently cautioned me about the risk of *flipping* through the scriptures and misinterpreting them. At this time, I trust that God leads me to a specific page in my Bible, and supplies my understanding because it works for me.

As I have flipped through the Bible for a week, I am finding that these readings are not so bad after all. I think my underlying fear was that I would turn to something in the Bible that would either make me feel worse, or I would find it irrelevant to my current circumstances. I also made the assumption that what was most relevant in the Bible was all in the New Testament, so why even bother with the Old Testament? I feel differently about that now.

The book of Jeremiah is in the Old Testament, yet he is a person to whom I can definitely relate. Jeremiah declares, "Lord, you always give me justice when I bring a case before you. Now let me bring you this complaint: Why are the wicked so prosperous? Why are evil people so happy? You have planted them, and they have taken root and prospered. Your name is on their lips, but in their hearts they give you no credit at all. But as for me, Lord, you know my heart." (Jer. 12:1-3 NLT)

After reading this, all I could think was, "Yes, Jeremiah, yes! I understand your point exactly, especially the part about the Lord knowing your heart." He continues, "How long must this land weep?" (Jer. 12:4 NLT) My mind immediately goes to my bus stop analogy: "How long must I wait, Father?" While my own personal weariness pales in comparison to what Jeremiah faced, I can still relate to his anguish.

I can relate today, especially. My friend and former colleague Cynthia passed away. Cynthia was a loving and vibrant woman who lost her battle with a lung disease. Her memorial service is this evening. Cynthia's life was her husband and their children. We worked in the same department for years, and I would always admire how her family photos would grace her desk and credenza. She loved the Lord. She was an active member in her church. She was a working mother who never missed a beat in any of her kids' extra-curricular activities, yet she's gone. I had not seen Cynthia in the last few years, but miraculously our paths crossed one final time about a month ago. When a good person like Cynthia dies, my questions always outnumber my answers.

I walk into Cynthia's service late. I really hate it when I do this. The program just started, so I am not late in that regard. I am, however, too late to have secured a seat that would allow me to make an early exit. My intentions were to arrive early to pay my respects to Cynthia's family, see former colleagues, and stay for most of the service. That is now out of the question. The church is packed. There are only middle seats near the front and the mid-section of the church left to choose from. There will be no slipping out the nearest exit tonight.

Quite honestly, I am not in the mood for hearing a long-winded preacher tonight. I know that sounds awful, but it's just the truth.

After a few songs and remarks from relatives and colleagues, the pastor makes his way to the podium. He wastes no time getting right to the point.

He starts with "How many of you folks' faith have been shaken because you've been praying for Cynthia's healing and God chose not to heal her; yet, He chose to heal the drunk who has not been serving Him at all?"

I walked into this building ready to bolt for the door. Instead, I am refreshed and amazed by the timeliness of his topic. I feel like I've been praying to God, but I feel constantly overlooked by Him. I have no answers for why I am struggling so much.

"First," he says, "let me remind you all that we serve a sovereign God who can heal whomever He chooses to heal. Second, we can't confine God to a prayer request. He answers our prayers on a much larger scale and in His own time. In other words, because He didn't answer one prayer request doesn't mean that He doesn't have a greater plan on a larger scale that will come to pass in His own time."

Immediately, I think back to my reading from this morning: "For I know the plans that I have for you."

This small-town pastor's message is resonating with my soul. I am definitely guilty of confining God to prayer requests. When the deadline for my prayer request has come and gone and things only appear worse, or when my prayer isn't answered the way that I prayed for it to be answered, I can easily feel forsaken. This is especially true when I feel like I've done everything in my power to do my part. I just need God to do His, but He remains silent.

Tonight, I am reminded that He is always with me even when it feels like He's not. If I had arrived just a few moments earlier, chances are that I would be seated near an exit and would have ducked out before hearing a message that was written for me. My smallness and judgmental ways almost prevented me from hearing what I needed to hear when I needed to hear it. I feel so comforted when I experience God's Hand up close and personal like this. It makes me feel like He really does have me in His care.

The service is concluding and I feel my emotions surfacing. The finality is beginning to sink in. The phase of new beginnings feels already underway. From this moment forward, everyone's life in this church begins anew without the prospects of creating future memories with Cynthia. This somber thought triggers feelings of loss of other loved ones. As the church still plays her songs, my tears become even harder to resist.

I use gratitude to pull myself out of the moment. I am grateful that God allowed our paths to cross one final time. I am grateful that I had transportation to get to the services. I am grateful that I had something nice to wear to the services. I am grateful the boys are safe. I redirect my thoughts, and hold back my tears for now.

I feel more comfortable walking to the rear of the church to greet Cynthia's family, and to see my former colleagues. It is important for me to share with her children my genuine experience of their mother, and how much I learned from her over the years. Her children catch me off guard. I see no tears in their eyes when I step up to greet them. They possess a quiet strength about themselves. This, by the way, was Cynthia's demeanor. They seem confident that their mother is with God. In an odd way, I walk over to reassure them and, instead, they reassure me.

After saying my final good-byes, I walk down the street to my car in deep thought. Usually, I would already be on my cell phone before the church doors closed behind me. Not tonight. While I am moved by the pastor's message, I am moved more by God's orchestration of things.

It feels like I am seeing His Hand more and more. I flipped to a page in the Bible that speaks directly to my current circumstances. I caught one or two additional traffic lights, leaving me perfectly placed to hear a message that I otherwise would have missed. After years of absence, but for the grace of God, I reconnected with my dear friend Cynthia just weeks before her passing. All I can say is a subtle "wow."

If I ever felt disconnected from God, I surely don't anymore.

As I reach to turn on the engine, I softly utter "wow" again to myself. I've been sitting here for a few moments just processing things. It does something to you when you feel that intimate connection to God. It can be the smallest thing that no one else would even pick up on, but you know it is Him and only Him that caused things to unfold in the manner they did.

After buckling my seat belt, my hand reaches for the knob to the CD player. I decide not to turn it on just yet. I am still appreciating the solitude. Once I enter the expressway, I notice that I am still riding music-free. This is so abnormal for me. It's fine, though, because there are some leftover thoughts still ruminating in my head from the pastor's message tonight.

I begin to see a relation between the expectations that I place upon myself and the expectations that I place upon God. Take for instance how I set goals for myself. Just as I am so goal-oriented that I prefer to avoid the process and just push for the end, so do I also look for God to operate in the same way when answering my prayers. In other words, my faith is ultimately tied to the prayer request just like my value is tied to whether I achieve the goal or not. Similar to how I disregard progress and only value the end goal, so do I become fixated on God answering a specific prayer request that I discount all of the ways that He could be answering my prayers and working out so many other situations in my life. This realization is huge for me.

Once again, I am reminded of the Bible verse Jer. 29:11 NLT that I read this morning: "For I know the plans that I have for you." I also recall the Israelites being instructed not to wait for their situation to change before they changed their ways.

Coming Full Circle

God doesn't always give us what we want. Why does the thug get saved and the loving mother lose her life? Life isn't fair. So when we hold on so tight trying everything in our power to create our desired outcome, we can sometimes use our energy unnecessarily; what will be will be. The unrelenting focus to yield a certain outcome eats up a part of us that keeps us from being fully engaged in the moment. This is another form of "quitting and staying." We stay fixated on a certain outcome and quit living life on life's terms. When we do this, we forego the opportunity to grow and evolve spiritually.

I will serve God by trusting His Will rather than expecting Him to accommodate mine.

"In every thing give thanks: for this is the will of God in Christ Jesus concerning you."
(1 Thess. 5:18 KJV)

Chapter 34

Daily Bread

THIS IS MY THIRD WEEK of getting up around 5 a.m. to read the Bible and to meditate. The meditating has been a real challenge, so I usually spend more time reading. I've mostly cut *Morning Joe* out in the mornings. I record it and watch it a bit in the evenings. I can't believe it. It's an election year, and I'm missing *Joe*. I am also still journaling before I flip to that *random* page in the Bible to which I trust God has led me. Before wrapping up, I usually journal once more to reflect on what I just read.

Sometimes I reread what I've written to see if there's a pattern in the messages that I am receiving. I look over the last four days of journal notes, and there is a definite theme here. The message seems to start when I flip to a page in the Bible, and it is then reinforced in my daily life.

Here's what happened over the last four days:

Day One

I feel like God nudges me at 4:10 a.m., and about two to three minutes later I spring up from bed. I am not tired or dragging when I do so. This amazes me. Jonathan has to be at school early this morning, and I have found that waking up early when the entire house is still asleep works best for me. I say my prayers, get dressed for the gym, and make my way down to the kitchen table, where it all happens.

This morning I turn to the Book of Ezra, a book I know nothing about. The part of Ezra that I flip to deals with Zerubbabel, who has the task of completing a temple project. I learn from the reading that Zerubbabel and his builders endure a number of obstacles such as dissent from local citizens and a fifteen-year construction delay. In other words, even though Zerubbabel's assignment is purposeful and noble, his path to finishing his task is not easy and straightforward. My book and business immediately come to mind. I read on to learn that Zerubbabel perseveres, never giving up his faith, and he and his builders end up finishing the temple project.

Day Two

Whatever allowed me to spring up from bed yesterday morning is not allowing me to do the same this morning. I am dragging and sleepy, possibly from getting up so early yesterday. Nevertheless, I continue to press forward to have my morning prayer before going downstairs to journal, and to read the Bible.

While I am on my knees praying, I can't seem to help that some financial matters are running through my mind at the same time. I am preoccupied with some of our month-end financial obligations. Actually, I am a bit anxious about things. Due to the federal budget cuts largely as a result of what is commonly known as "sequestration," LOM's business has slowed considerably. Webb's private equity business is steady but lumpy, as the deal business can often be. Webb is currently financing his business, some of LOM's overhead expenses, and an overwhelming majority of household expenses.

After journaling just a paragraph or so, I pick up my Bible and flip to 2 Kings, chapters 18 and 19. These chapters deal with Hezekiah's reign as king. In his early years, Hezekiah is characterized as a man who prayed to God no matter the circumstance. Whether it was something as significant as praying for help to fight the Assyrian army or something in his personal life, Hezekiah sought God's divine intervention.

This morning I felt guilty about not being able to control my financial anxiety during my morning prayer. In other words, I should not be worrying when I should be worshipping. I see that Hezekiah put his prayer requests before the Lord, no matter what. I have always prayed to God no matter what too, but I felt as though this special morning time was supposed to be more about me worshipping and meditating, and less about prayer requests.

I see that differently now. If I need to shift into prayer-request mode, that seems to be just fine with God. This is a perfect example of how I am surrounded by the divine Presence of God. Even when I am questioning whether I am using my time with Him the way that I should be, He sends me to a passage like this one.

Just as I am closing the Bible, my fingers flip to the Book of Psalms, chapters 7 through 9. I take a few extra moments to read these chapters, because I think it is possible that I am being led to this section of the Bible, too. There appears to be a method to David's communication with the Lord. More often than not, he appears to praise God first before he petitions him in prayer for anything. This is evident in verse after verse. If I am looking for a solution to dealing with my financial anxiety, I think that I just read it!

Day Three

I am still in need of God's help with handling our financial matters. I continue to worry about several looming financial deadlines as business remains slow. This morning I flip to the Book of Psalms, and the top of the page reads, "I am exhausted from crying for help; my throat is parched and dry. My eyes are swollen with weeping, waiting for my God to help me." (Ps. 69:3 NLT) I am still in awe as to how I am able to randomly turn to a passage that captures (to a degree) what I am feeling in the moment.

Later this day, I receive a call from my grandmother Millie. She is calling me to share some good news. Millie is a spry ninety-three-year-old. She still lives alone, drives, cooks for herself, and exercises every morning. She exercises by either riding her stationary bike or doing a few basic yoga exercises.

However, lately, her arthritis has prevented her from exercising. It is also causing her to slump over and to walk with a cane, all of which she dreads. She began praying to God to heal her pain, but the more she prayed, the worse her pain became.

Her point to me was that she never stopped praying. She continued to pray and to thank God even when her pain was nearly unbearable. Immediately I recall Psalm 9. Her telephone call was to share the good news that she had just finished her yoga exercises.

Day Four

After hearing Pastor Joel Osteen's sermon today, I am convinced that God is sending me the same message, but from different sources. First, I randomly flip to Psalm 9 and read about David's method of praising God, which is by thanking him first. Second, Millie calls me to report that she's back to exercising again after she never stopped praying and thanking God for his healing. Third, I listen to Joel's message today and it is literally entitled *"Thanking God in Advance."*

I have actually practiced thanking God in advance many times before. However, after what I consider a long period of seeing nothing, I would begin to doubt. I see now that the message is to stay with it. Do not change course. Keep on praising Him no matter what. Keep thanking Him in advance.

Millie's birthday is coming up next month, and I really want to do something special for her. My dear friend Ila creates one-of-a-kind commemorative birthday greeting books. I presented Webb with one for his 50th birthday. He claims it as his best birthday gift ever. Essentially it is a compilation of birthday greetings from people across various walks of a person's life. If you're visualizing a scrapbook, kick it up about ten notches. The layout alone is exquisite, and the specialty papers and the tasteful embellishments she uses to capture each motif make it all picture perfect. All that said, the average price of this book is about $1,200.

Ila knew that I wanted to give this book to Millie, but I couldn't afford a $1,200 price tag at the time. I will never forget her words to me: "Let's not worry about the price. Let's just get to the store to pick out Miss Millie's favorite colors, so I can begin work immediately to have this piece done in time for her birthday." She couldn't see my eyes over the phone, but they were filled with tears when she told me this.

This situation reminds me of my conversation with Ann about my tithes working for me, but just not in the way that I expected. The other thing that I realize is that if my tithes would have flowed back to me as easy as 1-2-3, there would be no trials and no opportunity to see the Hand of God. With the fruit of my tithes coming back to me in a multitude of ways, I am really blessed because each one of those *special ways* that I receive gifts and blessings has God's Hands all over it.

To sum matters up, I have three key takeaways from this experience. The first one is simple. I was measuring richness in terms of dollars and cents, and that was wrong. Second, even though things may not flow back to me in an orderly way, but somehow I am still being kept, I am getting my *daily bread*. Everything is so synchronized that I have what I need when I need it. It is almost mind-blowing. I may not have the desires of my heart, but I am being sustained. When I comprehend that only God is sustaining me, my relationship with him is deepened. Finally, I also see that trusting in the unseen, or rather God's Hand, is becoming more powerful and reliable than even what I see. What I see carries a risk of changing, but what comes from God ain't changing…it's solid!

It is now the end of the following week, and God's message is still being reinforced. This time, it is by way of a Pastor Sean sermon, which is predicated upon Luke 24. This particular chapter deals with the Resurrection of Christ, and how Mary and Mary Magdalene brought spices to Jesus' tomb when they knew he was already dead.

Part of his sermon addresses how frustrated we can become when things are not working out according to our timeline. I listened as I personally reflected on how abandoned, hurt, and disappointed I felt on my birthday. Things had not worked out in all of this time, so I just assumed that things were not going to work out. Maybe I was on the wrong track and had been for some time. God was sending me signal after signal, but I just couldn't figure it out. Things were this way in my life because of something I did, or didn't do, and I didn't know what next right action to take.

The pastor's response to all of that was simple: "You think you're not where you're supposed to be, but you're exactly where God wants you to be, so enjoy the process. God will always give you what you need when you need it." My job is to hold on until I get there. Keep bringing the spices, without fail, even though Christ appears to be dead; Mike always says, "Live to fight another day;" Millie says, "Keep praying even though it feels like the pain is getting worse;" my Uncle Georgie says, "Press on."

Coming Full Circle

You may find yourself in a season where only your needs are being met. You are getting your *daily bread*, but not much else. You begin to lose hope when things don't materialize according to your plan and timeline. Instead, be encouraged that all seasons are purposeful, even the ones that seem difficult to endure. God may be answering your prayers, but just not in the way that you envisioned.

Sometimes our prayers can be one-dimensional. "Father, please make a way for this month's rent, or tuition, to be paid," or "Please heal me." We must remind ourselves that we are praying to a Sovereign God who has the power to respond to our one-dimensional prayer request in a multi-dimensional way. This is when less is more. You should feel heartened for two reasons. First, even when you're only getting your daily bread, rest here because you know that it is only God sustaining you. Second, in addition to answering your prayer request (of course, in God's own way and time), He can use your current season to teach you, to strengthen you, to prepare you (for the next season), or to bring you closer to Him. In the end, you're all the better for it. Remember, we have a tendency to focus on our prayer requests, and God instead will focus on us.

I will serve despite season or harvest.

"I am not saying this because I am in need, for I have learned to be content whatever the circumstances." (Phil. 4:11 NIV)

Chapter 35

Look! No Hands

I STILL REFLECT on Pastor Sean's comments: "We think we're not where we're supposed to be, but we're exactly where God wants us to be (so enjoy the process)!" While I've heard some version of this counsel many times before, it is resonating with me at a deeper level this morning. I have a history of chasing one goal after the next while never being fully content with the notion that I was exactly where I was supposed to be in life. There was always something more to do...more to accomplish...more to prove.

I could only enjoy the process when a situation was on the course that I had envisioned. When things seemed to go off course, joy or contentment was the least of my experience. The irony is that I always end up grateful that my situation unfolded the way it did even though I couldn't see or appreciate this when things were in the *process* of unfolding. This is the point from the sermon: God's way will ultimately prevail, so why not enjoy the *ride*?

A good example of where I have realized the benefit of enduring the process is with writing *Blues to Blessings*. My vision was to write a motivational book for women that would have been released years ago. God's vision was for me to write a book about faith for everyone that would take me years to write, and that would aid in my personal and spiritual transformation, as well. When I started writing this book several years ago, I had no idea it would unfold into four beautiful phases (Awareness, Preparation, Transformation, and Service) where each phase deals with my growth in each area. I never knew that I would end up sharing some of the most intimate details of my life, and find peace with my decision.

As cliché as it sounds, it is clear to me that this was all a part of the process. Therefore, rather than spinning my wheels trying to resist it, I should practice embracing it. I see now that trying to leap over the process to race toward some end goal means that I may miss the witnessing of God's fingerprints throughout the process.

I am learning to practice a little less grit and a little more ebb and flow. One specific example was how I ended up selecting the forty Bible verses that would end each chapter. My idea was to muscle the process over one weekend. I would revisit the theme for each chapter, and perform keyword searches by using my Bible's concordance to identify the Bible verses. That's it. In one weekend, I would select and finalize all forty Bible verses for the book. God had a different plan. He would ultimately lead me to all forty Bible verses over the course of two years either from my daily readings or from a third party that I knew *only* came from Him. As much as I wanted to believe the fantasy that I was actually in the driver's seat, the reality was that I was really just going along for the ride.

I learned from the work that I did with Ann that this innate desire to be in control is rooted in my childhood. I recall her saying something to the effect that instinctively, as children, we need to attach to our caregivers and see them as people who are capable of taking care of us. Even in situations of abuse, we cannot see them as bad people. Therefore, as children, we internalize a bad or abusive situation and see ourselves as the one who is damaged, and not our caregiver.

Ultimately, as children, we try to control the outcome of our situation by trying to fix ourselves. This is likely when our affair with control begins. In my situation, I did what was necessary to *keep the peace* living in the house with Tim, thinking this would make him a less abusive person and it did not. I used this same mindset with my father even though I had no relationship with him. I reasoned that my father ignored me, because I must have been worth ignoring—hence, the birth of the invincible *supergirl* persona who tries to carry the weight of a dysfunctional household on her ten-year-old back while attempting to prove to the world that she shouldn't be ignored.

Because I saw myself as someone who needed fixing, my sense of self-worth was always low. When I saw myself as "less than," I reached for things outside of myself to find a sense of safety, self-worth, and identity. Most often, my self-worth fluctuated based upon what I had or didn't have at the time, or what I had most recently accomplished (enter my codependent nature).

I guess it's fair to say that I have been wired by codependency and this doer mentality for as long as I can remember. This is why doing and controlling feel so normal to me. On a grander scale, I chased one pinnacle goal after the other. At a more granular level, I busied myself with a myriad of to-do lists. I would even get a short-term fix from controlling minor tasks when the major areas of my life felt like they were spiraling out of my reach. I have spent most of my life either trying to fix myself or to manipulate others into doing what I thought was best for them, or acting on behalf of the greater good (even when the greater good wasn't so good). The *supergirl* has grown into one exasperated *superwoman*.

Running around like the Energizer bunny did two things for me. It helped to anesthetize my pain, and to perpetuate the false hope that all my doing and fixing meant that I was actually in control. What I know for sure is that in the real scheme of things, I am not in control. God is in control. While my invincible persona may have served its purpose by comforting the little girl in me to survive certain things, the little girl is all grown up now. Thus, the time has come for me to let go, and let God.

I understand that having less to do means I will have less to control, as doing involves much more control than *being*. I also accept that this behavioral shift will not occur overnight but will be a process for me, mostly in unchartered waters. Using Ashley's analogy, I will see myself as being in flow with the river rather than swimming upstream. If I ever feel like I am stuck, I will remind myself this is where God does his best work. Just being feels like things are finally in order...divine order.

Finally, studying the Word sheds more light on my life experiences than I could have ever imagined. Nothing else has such rich context that can put matters into the proper perspective like the Bible.

I am reminded of the recent passage that I read about Lazarus' death. This passage reinforces two key points for me. First, that things are timed perfectly even when they do not feel like they are. Second, sometimes what appears to be a problem (in this instance Lazarus' death) is actually serving a higher purpose.

When Lazarus died and was buried for four days, those who knew about his death thought it was the end for Lazarus. The assumption was that Jesus did not arrive in sufficient time to save him. However, Martha's astounding faith enabled her to see matters differently. "...Lord, if only you had been here, my brother would not have died. But even now I know that God will give you whatever you ask." (John 11:21-22 NLT) This simply amazes me, because death was seen as the ultimate end during this time. No one up until this point had ever been brought back from the dead. The word spread throughout the town of Bethany and beyond, that Lazarus had been brought back to life by Jesus after being buried for four days. Jesus had to let Lazarus die to further show the people that He is the Son of God. Lazarus' death was for the glory (or purpose) of God.

The Lazarus story teaches me that when I let go and let God, I release of my own timetable associated with my desires. I stop petitioning God to act outside of His Divine Order. Letting go feels like when I was a young girl riding my bike up GentillyBoulevard (the one that I wasn't supposed to be riding on), and showing off to anyone who happened to be watching me, "Look! No hands!" As a child, I released my hands from the handlebars and rode freely, trusting that the rest of my body would guide and sustain me. As adult Suzette, I must let go and trust God that He's got me, always.

Coming Full Circle

Losing the need to control is real freedom. Everything in the natural world may require some form or degree of control. In the spiritual world, there is no need for it. Sometimes we come to the spiritual world with our natural-world hat on. This is the hat that has controlling, directing, orchestrating our affairs written all over it. In the spiritual world, this hat is not needed. We should take it off at the door, but sometimes we forget to. Once we reach the understanding that God is God and we are not and that our sense of control is limited, we can be free to Be. Our capacity to love and to understand, to forgive and to be compassionate, increases.

I will serve on God's terms knowing that my reward will come from unforeseen places.

"So we fix our eyes not on what is seen, but on what is unseen, since what is seen is temporary, but what is unseen is eternal."
(2 Cor. 4:18 NIV)

Chapter 36

Be Still and Know that I Am God

THIS MORNING I FEEL as if I have relapsed spiritually. I am questioning God once again, and doing things that I thought I moved past. The last several days have been tough. My core issue seems to be the financial uncertainty that continues to hover over my household and business. I feel angry, because from where I sit, it feels like God is being silent.

My spiral started the other morning after flipping to 1 Corinthians, and becoming fixated on two verses in particular. If I'm going to believe that God is leading me to those scriptures that inspire and comfort me, I also must believe that He is leading me to those scriptures that warn or chastise me. I believe this to be the case when I read, "Dear brothers and sisters, when I was with you I couldn't talk to you as I would to mature Christians. I had to talk as though you belonged to this world or as though you were infants in the Christian life. I had to feed you with milk and not with solid food, because you couldn't handle anything stronger..." (1 Cor. 3:1-2 NLT)

Immediately, I see turning to this passage as no coincidence. This is God communicating His disappointment with me. Reading this makes me feel like I am not being given credit for of my efforts to deepen my relationship with Him. I continue to worship God under all of these circumstances, even through His silence, yet I am still considered "an infant in the Christian life...as drinking milk and not able to handle solid foods."

After this reading, I stir around in the kitchen for a little, but I cannot shake my feelings. Finally, I rest my purple-gloved forearms on the sink, and enter into my own monologue with the Lord.

"I am angry, Father, and there is no need to deny it, because You already know that. I feel ashamed of my anger. You have done marvelous things in my life, so I'm sure many would ask, 'How is it possible that I could feel anger?' On the one hand, I feel like a spoiled brat, because I am not getting my way. On the other hand, I feel sheer exhaustion from having to endure this constant struggle with things. It feels like the needle is not moving on anything that I am praying to You about."

All that said, each time I go through a rocky point on my journey, I later appreciate how I prosper from it, and am even able to write about it. My current thought is, "What shall I tell the reader whose dark season seems never ending?" I feel unworthy to even address this, given my own relapse.

I think the short answer is that you keep the faith, and continue to do more of the same. However, it is tough to continue practicing the same when there is a continuous onslaught of negative events that seem to come from every angle. These feelings are compounded when God appears silent. This is what can weaken the human spirit over time. This is when you need to feel a win. Even if it's not the win that you've been praying for, it's a win nonetheless.

Pastor Sean has relocated to California, and I've started attending Ashley's church where the Pastor John Hannah presides.

I find him to be a wonderful pastor who is very passionate about teaching God's Word. Pastor Hannah said on Sunday, "Even Jesus asked if there was a way for the Father to be glorified, so He would not have to suffer *in the way* that He did." Is a win what God gives to freshman believers while seasoned believers have to go without?

This is why I need to offer my reader more than just "keep the faith." I need to go to a much deeper place and wordsmith my feelings from that place. I could even put these pearls of spiritual wisdom into a nice acronym to increase the reader's retention and applicability of it.

"So, here is what I ask of You, God: What do I tell the person who has come a long way on their spiritual walk, but still has farther to go? In other words, they are drinking spiritual milk, but they haven't moved on to solid foods. How do we keep our hearts from becoming bitter in the process?"

Yesterday, I had a very important discussion with each member of my household. I asked for the next thirty days to focus on the book. I told them if I had thirty days to focus solely on writing that I could likely finish the book, or come very close to it. They all said they would support me in this endeavor. Webb really threw his support behind me. He reminded me that his friend Bob recently took a job out of state, but he still has his condo near downtown.

Webb calls Bob, and I have the keys to his place for the next two weeks!

Today is my first evening at Bob's place and I feel absolutely wonderful! I am so grateful to have a place as beautiful and as centrally located as this to come to write and to be with the Lord. This is the happiest that I have been in the last several days.

I am also in a better mood, because I had a good talk with Ann earlier. As I always do, I just pour my heart out to her. After listening to me, her first observation is that God has not moved away from me, but rather I have let things come between me and God.

I allow things such as our finances, the fate of LOM, and finishing the book to all stand in between me and the Lord. I realize that even with me trying to get into a daily routine of putting God first, I still let other things dominate. A person who is advanced in their walk doesn't allow that to happen. A spiritually mature person will let go, and let God handle their problems and will really do it. I mean they won't just talk the talk. A less spiritually mature person (which is where I guess I've been lately) won't "let go and let God." Instead we will try to *play* God in a sense by taking matters into our own hands. Sometimes when we behave this way, we're not even aware that we're doing anything out of order, because this is the way that we've always behaved.

Ann thinks the time away at Bob's place is much needed. She cautions me not to jump right into writing the book. Her words to me are, "Suzette, spend some time with the Lord, and become renewed with Him. He will give you the words to say." Once again, I feel as if God is speaking through her. Finally she recommends that I read the book the *Battlefield of the Mind* by Joyce Meyer. I figure the first day or so, I will study the Bible and read this book. Then, if it is God's will, I will resume my writing. She also asks me how was I going to tell others what to do in this area, when I was not doing well in this area myself. This is the question that I've been revisiting daily.

The biggest message for me is that no matter how tough and hectic things become, I cannot let that come between me and God. Specifically, I cannot let anything come between me and my intimacy with the Lord.

The first couple of days at Bob's have gone smoothly, but this morning is not off to a good start. Just as I was making the bed, and getting ready to do my daily readings and to journal, the phone rings. It is my mother, who is disturbed with me. Jonathan needs a pair of khakis for a dress rehearsal at his school this evening. Jonathan calls her to take him to the store, because he doesn't want to disturb me. This child continues to show his support of me even in the slightest of ways. My mother, on the other hand, has no problem disturbing me. She calls to assure me that Jonathan will have everything he needs for his dress rehearsal this evening, but she is not happy that she has to reschedule her appointment this afternoon. I thank her, and apologize for her being inconvenienced.

I call Webb next to let him know that we need to reimburse her, and while I'm on the subject, I remind him of a few other bills that are coming due at the end of the week. Money discussions are never one-way discussions with Webb these days. He always dovetails right back to me getting a job. To say the least, our call doesn't end well.

Two phone calls and ten minutes later, I end up in another tailspin. In ten short minutes it seems that everything has shifted. The energy in the room feels different. My spirit is in a different place. The eagerness that motivated me just moments ago to journal, to do my daily reading, and walk to an Al-Anon meeting is all gone. (Ann suggested to me when I first met her that I should start attending Al-Anon meetings, and I've just recently begun to go.)

My thoughts are swirling in a cloud of confusion. I cannot ignore the fact that their arguments have merit. I revert back to wondering if this is really what God wants me to do or if this is more about me. I ask myself, "What sense does it make to stay at Bob's for another week when the book will obviously not be finished, and we need to pay bills today?"

I call Ma to ask her thoughts on whether she thinks I should continue to stay at Bob's or if I should return home. She starts with, "Well, Suzette, I don't want to tell you what to do."

Then, she politely proceeds to tell me what she thinks I ought to do.

"Suzette, you and I come from two different generations. I need to know for certain that things are covered, and not *hope* they are covered. I could not be in another place writing a book while I had financial and family obligations that need my attention today. I agree with Webb. The family supported you to go to graduate school, and now your family needs your support, but you're off writing a book. If it were me, my children would come first. You can write the book after Jonathan graduates from high school. I have to run. Remember, I had to reschedule an appointment so that I can take Jonathan shopping for his pants this afternoon. Good-bye!"

I thank her for her time and thoughts, but I don't think she even hears me before she hangs up the phone. I get off the phone with her feeling worse. I start to cry. I cannot counter Webb's argument, nor my mother's. While financial uncertainty looms over my household, I choose to be in someone else's home reading one book and trying to write another.

At this point, I am both frustrated and confused. I am frustrated because God has the power to change my circumstances and He has not. I am confused, because He is not giving me any guidance on whether I should stay at Bob's to spiritually renew myself and to write or immediately begin packing my things to return home. And, once back home, should I sincerely look for a job? In a strange sense, it feels like I already have a job. I have been called to work for the Lord, but I just have no proof of employment. I feel so alone and misunderstood, especially by those closest to me.

I am sitting on the couch, and I sort of swivel my body to get down on my knees to pray. Just as my knees touch the floor, I hear, "Be still and know that I am God."

Given all the thoughts roaming backwards and forwards in my head, these words come through crystal clear. I only wish that God is telling me to "Be still." If this were true, I could breathe a sigh of relief. Conversely, this could also be a way for me to avoid taking personal responsibility for my own plight.

The tears continue to flow. Because I am all alone, I feel at liberty to wail on a little louder and harder. If I need to cry, let me take all liberties to have a good, hard cry to get these feelings out of my system once and for all.

During all of my wailing, my phone rings. It's Karen. I pick up the phone only to quickly put it back down. I am a blubbering mess. I don't want to explain to anyone why I am so torn apart. The phone continues to ring. Just as I am about to hit the "ignore" button, I spontaneously decide to accept the call. Karen has heard me cry many times before, and she knows much of the story already so I won't have much explaining to do with her.

I answer and she immediately hears my agony. She gasps, and inquires as to what's going on with me. I give her the gist of my conversations with both Webb and my mother. She responds, "You've got five minutes to cry, and to let it all out, then you must get back to moving forward." I tell her that I am back at the place of feeling that God has turned radio silent again. She says, "Sue, you just have to be still."

Instantly, I realize that it was God who spoke to me earlier, and not me. It *was* God who first told me, "Be still and know that I am God." No sooner do I process these words than doubt creeps in to tell me that God didn't say that to me. To reinforce His words, He just had Karen call me to say "be still." This is my confirmation.

Feeling a little better, I decide to go to the nearby Al-Anon meeting after all. I convince myself that the walk will be good exercise. I arrive and the lead speaker discusses his 4As for God. I honestly can't recall the first three, but I take note of the last one. His last "A" stands for "allow" God.

As soon as the floor opens for participants to share, one man talks about his unfortunate rage. He says that he lives with so much rage, it's like he puts a cloud over the sun, only letting a fraction of sunlight in. Another man chimes in, "Even if the clouds are covering the sun, I still feel the sunrays. In other words, even though I don't see the sun, I still know it is there." Even though I do not see God, I still believe that God is here.

I lie in bed a little longer this morning. I am not asleep, but I am meditating about how I feel I have a deeper, spiritual understanding of things this morning. I am still a participant in Ann's small women's group, and last night was our weekly group meeting. Ann gave me extra time to share with the group what's been going on with me lately. After our meeting, Jamie, Ann's co-facilitator, emailed me this scripture:

The Wise and Foolish Builders

"Therefore everyone who hears these words and puts them into practice is like a wise man who built his house on the rock. The rain came down, the streams rose, and the winds blew and beat against that house; yet it did not fall, because it had its foundation on the rock. But everyone who hears these words of mine and does not put them into practice is like a foolish man who built his house on sand. The rain came down, the streams rose, and the winds blew and beat against that house, and it fell with a great crash." (Matt. 7:24-27 NIV)

Reading this scripture crystallizes everything for me. Two weeks ago I crashed. This is the reason that I believe that God made Bob's place available for me. When I first break down, I reach out to Millie. She tells me God will sometimes take us through trials to strengthen us. She also talks about the importance of examining our attitude while we wait on the Lord.

My attitude has not been good lately. I still want things on my timeline rather than God's. I was telling myself that I was accepting God's timeline, because I knew that's what He expected of me, but my heart had not changed. A perfect example would be coming over to Bob's place to write. Even though I said many times before that this book would get done in God's time, I still had not fully surrendered to this point. I came to Bob's place with the sole intention of finishing the book.

After Ann suggests that I read Joyce Meyer's *Battlefield of the Mind,* I go out the next morning to buy the book with the hope that if I read the book from cover to cover, I would have some epiphany, and then I could immediately resume my writing. It has always been a means-to-an-end mentality for me.

With all of the reading and studying, I begin to think that my time at Bob's place will not be as fruitful as I had hoped, because I was not writing actual chapters. What I realize is that I am writing. I am writing the material that will go into those chapters. Even more so, I am having some profound experiences and spiritual revelations that will only add substance to my writing.

Initially, Millie's counsel to me falls on deaf ears, but is confirmed after hearing these.

- God says, "Be still and know that I am God (which requires real strength)."
- Karen reiterates, "Be still."
- Millie says, "He's trying to strengthen you."
- The lead Al-Anon speaker says, "Allow God."
- An Al-Anon participant says, "Even when it's overcast and I cannot see the sun, I can feel the sunrays."
- Hearing Bishop T.D. Jakes' sermon *"Sit on Me."* He preached that God will ride you through to your destiny if you can trust Him until the time is right for Him to fulfill His promises.

- Reading the *Battlefield of the Mind* and the example of how Jesus dealt with suffering and the attitude He upheld.
- Reading Matt. 7:24-27 NLT, which puts an exclamation point on everything for me.

Two weeks ago I crashed, because I was succumbing to all of the various situations around me. My spiritual foundation at this time was built on sand. God was saying to me that if you are going to work for Me, your spiritual house must be built on a rock, a solid foundation. I cannot be unstable and move this way and that way each time the wind blows. The wind will definitely blow from this direction and from that direction and possibly from multiple directions at once. The question remains, will I continue to be blown over every time, or will I situate myself on the solid rock of Christ and know that He supports me and the wind? As I'm typing this passage, I recall the chorus of one of Millie's favorite hymns, "On Christ, the solid rock, I stand...all other ground is sinking sand."

I believe that God is saying to me, "Be still in everything at this time":

- Be still in your finances and know that I am God.
- Be still in your business affairs and know that I am God.
- Be still in the book and know that I am God.
- Be still in the boys' college tuition and know that I am God.

I started out earlier last week searching for the right words to say to the seasoned worshipper who has become weary on her journey. I see now that I was looking for the right words to say rather than the right way to behave. When your spiritual foundation is weak you will feel you're being hit from every angle, and will likely focus on the greatest problem of the hour. So the fix in this instance is not about creating a clever catch phrase or acronym that the reader can remember to say each time a problem arises. This may help in the moment and only for a moment. The key is getting to a place where your spiritual foundation is rooted in the Word, and you know that God is greater than your greatest problem or sorrow ever could be.

Coming Full Circle

Surrendering is a three-legged stool. We've addressed surrendering to God's will and to His divine timing. This, however, is about surrendering to God's approach.

Those two voices are here again. Where do these two voices come from? They are opposite sides of ourselves. One understands that we are not in control and the other is so fearful of not being in control. This is when the wrestling match begins. This is overwhelming, and when we are overwhelmed we instinctively attempt to control. The catch-22 is that the more we attempt to control, the more out of control we actually are. In fact, the more dangerous our potential outcome becomes. Thus, it is only by complete surrender to the God who actually controls all of it that we can be assured of an outcome that glorifies God. What we can control is our choice to surrender.

The irony is that when we are in a place of servitude, our desire and God's desire for outcomes may mirror each other, except for the clash of wills over the approach. As a servant, you may seek the completion of a project, which results in an outcome that glorifies God. However, God anticipates His glory by completing you. God has not moved away from you as much as you may have allowed things to come between you and God. The very thing that you are doing in the name of God, or doing to glorify God, may become an idol and hinder your relationship with Him. While you may see the work as a priority, God sees you as the priority. Your assignment may be your project, but You are God's project.

I will serve God by fully surrendering to His approach which will involve the refining of my character.

"I am the vine; you are the branches. If you remain in me and I in you, you will bear much fruit; apart from me you can do nothing."
(John 15:5 NIV)

Chapter 37

Going Through It

I FEEL AS THOUGH GOD may be preparing me for something difficult, given the recent scriptures that I've been turning to lately. My theory feels confirmed after this morning's reading, which focused on how both Paul and Jeremiah learned to endure and live their lives about their struggles. Paul professes, "I have learned how to get along happily whether I have much or little." (Phil. 4:11 NLT) This makes me wonder if God is trying to prepare me for living with little.

This is a trying time for us. We are both entrepreneurs who face the uncertainty of making payroll and paying vendors while subordinating our self-interest each month. Webb says, "You've never been in business until you've had to make payroll," and now I am a firm believer. Today, we are anticipating a response from the bank on our recent proposal to restructure a loan that is secured by our home. This is being done with tighter banking regulations and a weak real estate market caused by a national mortgage crisis. I don't even want to think about what might lie ahead for us if the bank rejects our proposal. I believe that God is teaching me how *to be still and to know that He is God.* For me, being still means to be calm. I am trying with every fiber in my body to remain faithful and focused on Him. I can comprehend the concept; now I am just trying to hold on by practicing it.

However, I was comforted by Pastor Hannah's sermon this morning, which was based on Acts 12, Peter's time in jail. What he claims to know for sure is that no matter whether the circumstance is great or difficult, God will get the glory. Here's a recap of my sermon notes:

- Peter is jailed and surrounded by multiple guards during his imprisonment. His obvious goal is to escape, but he must make it past twelve guards and through the gate to cross over to freedom.
- Peter's chances to escape seem impossible. There is a man chained to his left, and another chained to his right side. The king told the guards that any one of them would be killed if they were caught sleeping or doing anything but keeping an eye on Peter. They decided to stand guard in groups of four, and rotated shifts just to watch Peter.
- An angel appears to Peter in the middle of the night. The angel instructs Peter to "Get up!" This is important because the angel appears, and neither lifts Peter up nor carries Peter. In other words, the angel is there to help Peter, but not to do for Peter what Peter can do for himself. Pastor Hannah emphasizes this point.
- Peter made it past the guards and through the gate, the final place before he's free and on the other side. If he had panicked, he could have awakened the guards and risked everything. Peter pressed forward and made it past the gate. Here is where Pastor Hannah underscored the importance to begin preparing oneself for God's promises.

- Sometimes we may feel the "heat" from a situation. We must remember that the heat is not to destroy, but it is there to make us stronger. Do not let what is intended for evil prevent us from giving God the glory. He said sometimes you are farther along than you think. Keep pressing toward that *gate* until you cross over.

In closing his sermon, Pastor Hannah reminds us that getting to the gate is a pivotal moment for Peter. Something happens to us when we're in fearful situations, and our natural inclination is to panic. If we look with our "natural" eye, the situation will look very ugly, so we must not forget to use our *spiritual eye.*

Fear grips me as soon as I open my eyes this morning. Even though I know that God's divine wisdom and intelligence is ordering my steps despite what I see, the thoughts of financial hardship and loss continue to run rapid through my mind. More and more I realize that this period of financial crisis is something that I must endure. I stay on my knees praying to God for nearly thirty minutes thanking Him, and trying to release my fear.

I had a morning like this one last week. I couldn't settle my mind down such that I ended up praying twice, because I couldn't recall if I had prayed already or not. I should never experience preoccupation when I am praying to God, given all that He has done for me and shown me.

When this happened last week, God gave me a nice reminder. He led me to the Book of Micah, a book that I had not read from before. The verse that leaps out at me is: "As for me, I look to the Lord for his help. I wait confidently for God to save me, and my God will certainly hear me." (Mic. 7:7 NLT) Mentally, I underscore the word "confidently." As soon as I read this, I acknowledge that my confidence could be stronger. I do not chide myself like I would have done previously. Instead, I pledge to myself that I will continue to grow in strength.

My efforts, today in particular, will be geared toward surrendering. If I have to "go through it," I am asking God to show me how this is genuinely done. The word that comes to me is "process." I vow to myself right here and now to take this process on. I reach for my Bible, asking God to lead me to whatever passage He has for me this morning. As God would have it, He leads me to the passage that deals with Him having to "go through it!" He leads me to John chapters 13 through 15. I especially take note of "Now Jesus was in great anguish of spirit, and he exclaimed, 'The truth is, one of you will betray me!'" (John 13:21 NLT)

The moment I read John 13:21, I feel God's Presence. I am in anguish, and I am led to a scripture where even Christ experienced anguish. This is no one but God. My eyes, of course, well up with a few tears. These chapters go on to tell about the Holy Spirit, and how Jesus never leaves those who follow Him. There is so much here that I am sure once I reread these chapters I will uncover even more. In fact, that's exactly what I am going to do. I will place my bookmark here and I will reread these chapters once I get to the office, because I believe there is more for me to see.

I decide to call Millie on my walk to the gym to share my experience. We end up talking for nearly an hour, thus I miss the gym. Her words are always so encouraging, and her spirit uplifting. After our talk, I walk upstairs to get ready for the office when I realize that I have not walked or fed Logan yet. Logan is our newest member of the family. He is part cocker spaniel and part English setter; we adopted him last year as a birthday gift for Jonathan. While I'm walking Logan, out of the blue, I blurt out, "The Lord is my shepherd." I realize that I am parroting my Uncle Hawee. This is what Hawee often said when something was going on with him.

After walking Logan, I decide that I want to be able to recite this scripture in its entirety for myself. If I were reciting it along with someone else, I would be able to remember the words. It's similar to if I were singing along to a song playing on the radio.

However, I can't recite these words verbatim on my own, and I really want to. I also know it's in the Book of Psalms, but I can't recall the chapter, and I don't have the time to look it up. I lob a quick call to Millie. She responds, "It's the 23rd Psalm, Suzette," in a tone that implies, "You should know this."

Instead of referring to my Bible, which is the New Living Translation (NLT), I prefer to read the King James Version (KJV). This is the version that I am most familiar with. I quickly pull up Psalm 23 on my laptop. I read it at least three times. On the last read, my eyes catch a glimpse of the time on the microwave. I see that I am late, and that I really need to get to the office.

After reading the scripture, the words that tend to stay with me are "He leadeth me." As a way to assure myself that things are in order, and that all is well, I continuously repeat these words under my breath. I go to my closet and scan my suits. I have the perfect outfit picked out in a nanosecond, and it doesn't need to be steamed. I say, "He leadeth me." I go to the train station, and as soon as my feet hit the platform the train arrives. I say, "He leadeth me." I feel that if the tiniest things are in order, there is a good chance that the greater issues are also in order. This may sound silly, but it's working for me this morning.

I walk into the office, and all of my compartmentalized to-do lists begin to flood my thoughts. Actually, I'm doing a lot better in this area, because in the past, I would easily have double the lists and double the tasks. I am reminded of the Al-Anon slogan, *"Progress, not perfection."* Anyhow, I have a to-do list for the house that has its own sub-categories: kids, payment of household bills, and household tasks. I have a to-do list for LOM. I have one for the book. I have another for trying to close our financial gap, which entails looking for interim consulting opportunities. In an effort to keep all doors open, because I never know which one God will come through, I even have one for dreadful tasks such as securing job leads.

It's not that I dread working. I dread working for someone else. I am already an employee of LOM, although no one would know that, given the fraction of a salary that's stated on my W-2 form from last year. LOM is nearly a decade old, and I know that if I take a job, this will ultimately lead to LOM closing its doors. This is what's so tough for me. I know where LOM was born. It was born at the edge of my tub where I was on my knees telling God that I was finally ready to take the leap of faith to start my own company. I was going to let this little Light of Mine shine, and He would be the Chairman of LOM's board. I would never enter into any serious business dealings without praying and seeking His Counsel first. Now, I have to experience the thought of not only losing my business but maybe our home, too. I just can't believe this is happening. I am a good person, a faithful tither, and a loving mother and wife. Intuitively, I know that I must quickly divert my thoughts before I end up down this familiar rabbit hole again.

After going back and forth between staring at all of my lists and staring off into the abyss, I decide to keep my word to myself. I remain obedient to my promise from this morning to reread John chapters 13 to 15. I even read up to John 17. There are several verses in these chapters that stand out to me, so I decide to take a few notes. One passage in particular reads, "As soon as Judas left the room, Jesus said, 'The time has come for me, the Son of Man, to enter into my glory, and God will receive glory because of all that happens to me. And God will bring me into my glory very soon.'" (John 13:31-32 NLT)

I used to wonder why things didn't happen when I wanted them to happen. I learned that things happen in God's divine time, so that He can get the glory. The story of Lazarus is a perfect example of this. Now, I am experiencing "glory" on another level. My grandfather used to say, "To God be the glory." As a child, and even as an adult, I never fully grasped what he meant by that until now. I understand now that God also gets the glory when a person surrenders. There are those things in life that we must face whether it is a situation like the one about possibly losing our home or a more serious matter like the one author Steven Pressfield shared on "*Super Soul Sunday*" regarding his trials with cancer.

Sometimes we are confronted with life, and we must deal on life's terms. As much as we want to avoid reality by escaping it, self-medicating it, denying it, or putting up that valiant fight to ignore it, we learn that we can't. We can't sidestep things, so we must step into them. Stepping into it, or having to go through an experience that is unknown (you really don't know if or how you're going to come out on the other side) is terribly frightening. Jesus knew how His situation was going to end, and He still anguished over having to go through it. I am learning that "going through it" does the following for us:

It can bring us closer to God
It strengthens us
It teaches us
It allows for God to get the glory

When we go through a situation, we also *grow* through that situation. When we make it to the other side, we're stronger, spiritually wiser, more in relation with God, and more in a position to teach and to lead by example for others. This is how service ties into glory. When you serve others, you are serving God. "Now I am giving you a new commandment: Love each other. Just as I have loved you, you should love each other. Your love for one another will prove to the world that you are my disciples." (John 13:34-35 NLT)

As soon as I finish studying and writing, my phone rings. It's a request to schedule a phone interview for a job. I talk briefly with the manager, and we schedule the interview for 10 a.m. tomorrow morning. I hang up the phone completely surprised that I actually received a follow-up call, because I submitted my resume without a referral nearly a month ago.

One month ago:

I am standing in my kitchen and I had just finished pouring my protein smoothie before leaving the house to do my morning exercises when something strange happens. Just as I am placing the container part of the blender back on its base, I hear the words, "Call them." My first thought is, "Call who?" Is God telling me to call the company that makes my blender? Those words come through crystal clear in the same voice that they always do, so I know they are from Him. I just need to understand what I should do with them.

It's now mid-afternoon, and my mind drifts back to what I heard in my kitchen this morning. I tell my-self, "It's time to face God's words to me earlier. He could only be telling me one thing, which is to call the manufacturer of my blender for a job." I reason with myself that while I am not sure where this is all going, I am certain these are His instructions; I cannot dismiss them. Of course, I have the "if-then" scenarios playing in my head, too. If God is telling me to seek employ-ment, then He must also be telling me that LOM will ultimately close its doors. The self-talk goes on and on. Nevertheless, I choose to release all of that and take the next step, which is to follow up with the blender com-pany.

Instead of placing a cold call, I decide to browse the company's website first. I click on the "Careers" tab, and

I see they are hiring sales representatives to conduct live demonstrations of their machines in the Midwest. If I look on the bright side of things, I've always said that if I had to work for another company that I would prefer it to be a company whose product I believe in. I use this product daily, so that would definitely be the case here. I browse their website for a few moments longer, and decide to upload my resume with a short cover note. After I click the "submit" button, I feel like not only did I just submit a resume, but I *submit* myself to God's instructions, too.

After scheduling the interview, I even feel inspired to text Webb. He'll be happy to know that there's some activity on the job front for me, even if it's not the six-figure corporate job that he always envisions me returning to.

It's about two hours later and I look up from all my to-do lists, and acknowledge that the day is mostly a productive one. There's a part of me that wants to stay to tackle the remaining tasks while I am still in the mood and on a good roll. However, I promised one of the Al-Anon members that I would meet her at tonight's meeting. I decide to keep my commitment and go to the Al-Anon meeting instead.

I walk through the door of the meeting and learn that tonight's topic is about losing fear. As I make my way across the room to sit down, I feel so loved and comforted by God. I say in my heart, "He leadeth me."

After the lead speaker shares her struggle with losing fear, the floor is open for anyone to share. The first lady who shares makes a point that causes the entire room to nod in agreement. She says, "We either fear that we're going to lose what we have or we fear we're not going to get what we want." Immediately, I do a self-check. I am precisely in that place tonight. I do not want to lose what I have.

Toward the end of the meeting, a soldier shares his story. He is that tough, fearless, one-word-answer military type. He's the guy you want on your side. He tells us how he has lived a pretty normal life, and there's not anything that has come across his path that he hasn't been able to handle. Thus, he has never seen himself as a fearful person. However, finally, he believes that he has met his match: addiction. After years of trying to manipulate his son toward sobriety, he is finally surrendering to the fact that he is powerless over whether his son will ever choose to live a sober life.

On my drive home from the Al-Anon meeting, I visualize a continuum where fear is at one end and faith is at the other end. There has to be a point where I begin to gain momentum in either direction. I am trying to pinpoint when that shift occurs. When I choose to surrender, to let go and let God, and cling to Him for understanding and direction, I become less fearful and more faithful. When I can appreciate the facts of a situation but still allow the Truth of His Word to order my steps, I become less fearful and more faithful. I think another dimension of moving along this spectrum is when I hear God's Whispers and see His Fingerprints. It is at this moment where He gives us choice. Will we *quit* hearing His voice and *stay* where we are because it's what we know, or will we press forward (sometimes against all logic) into the unknown, trusting in a power greater than ourselves to carry us over to the other side? When you choose the *whispers* and *fingerprints*, you are in this world, but no longer of it. This is the shift.

The closer I move toward faith, the more worry and anxiety begin to dissolve. I even feel more present, which has always been a challenge for me. When I am not weighted down with as much worry and anxiety, I am freer. When you have enough faith-filled experiences to pull from, you not only fly like a butterfly, you soar as one. That said, you can never really soar as a butterfly unless you surrender, and choose to go through it.

Remember that Peter makes it through the gate. Paul is let out of jail. Jesus is resurrected! The impossible becomes very possible when your Father is a Father of the impossible.

Coming Full Circle

Everything up until this point has been about understanding what you have to do. Now, it's time to execute. This is your Nike moment.

We ultimately fear going through the storms of life. Our human or natural inclination is to ask God to remove the storm, or at least to postpone it. When He doesn't remove it, you may try dealing with matters from multiple angles on your own until you finally surrender. This is exactly where God wants you to be. While He has the power to calm both you and the storm, He is much more invested in your transformation.

Being calm in the storm is the ultimate test of faith. Faith requires energy, and each time you choose to invest your energy in fear—control, anger, impatience, manipulation, deflection—you are depleting the very energy that your faith needs to complete your divine assignment.

The moment you surrender yourself into a realm of peace and stillness, God begins to get the glory—first, from you; second, from who you will become; third, from the new fruit that your life will bear; and fourth, by the number of people who will be touched by your testimony. This is the process unfolding in a major way, with God getting the glory at each juncture. This is the process; there are no shortcuts. Control withers on this vine.

My faith will serve as my fuel,
and I will not allow fear to empty my tank.

"Blessed is the man who remains steadfast under trial, for
when he has stood the test he will receive the crown of life,
which God has promised to those who love Him."
(James 1:12 ESV)

Chapter 38

No Paul or Jeremiah

I AM FEELING GOOD THIS MORNING, but I am preoccupied, too. Yesterday, I received a job offer from the blender company. It was extended to me at the end of my second interview. To avoid losing the opportunity, I accepted the offer as soon as it was given.

My normal morning routine involves making a healthy smoothie for the entire house after journaling and reading a passage in the Bible. One of my life's guiding principles has become to put God first, myself second, and everyone and everything else third. When I serve God first, and take care of myself next, I am better positioned to be of service to others.

What I absolutely love about my blender is the quality of its blend. This allows me to go heavier on the vegetables that I can add to the smoothies, and still get Webb and the boys to drink it. This morning, I blended blueberries, one half banana with kale, beets, yellow squash, red cabbage, carrots, flax seeds, and protein powder with one cup of chocolate almond milk. While Webb and the boys know their smoothies contain something *green*, they have no idea they're drinking beets and squash, too. I guess it's fair to say that I have come a long way from starting the day with Pop Tarts and juice boxes.

I've already begun training for my new position, and here are a few journal entries to show how things are going so far:

Day 2

Today is my second day on the job. It is a little harder than I expected. Yesterday was harder, because it involved setting up the booth. I will do my best today in meeting and greeting people. I will try hard to learn and to familiarize myself with the process, and will do an honest day's work.

Day 3

This morning I prayed for physical strength and stamina. Standing at this sales booth for such long hours is so tiring, and my body just feels achy. I believe something positive will be born out of this experience, and this is just a part of the process. I bring a welcoming spirit to the booth, and I thank God for this opportunity. I am especially grateful, because given all of this work I am still very connected to the current chapter that I am writing.

Day 11

It's been days since I have written in my journal, or opened my Bible. I am currently attending a regional sales meeting this morning, so I am up early trying to squeeze in a reading before my day starts. Working such long hours makes me want to stay in bed until the absolute last minute. I feel like I have so much going on, but I can't allow these things to sidetrack me from what I have learned to practice over the last fifteen months.

I also continue to pray to God that I am on the right track. I feel I've bet so much on this one vision and if I'm wrong, then what next? I can feel shame start to creep in at my low points, and I don't like that. I am not treading in tumultuous waters, they're just unknown. Both create different levels of anxiety. I know I am heading down the wrong path when I revert back to comparing myself to others.

Webb made a good point the other day when he said those activities that feed me each week are currently nonexistent. I haven't read any scriptures, or attended church in weeks. Ann's weekly group no longer meets. I also haven't been to an Al-Anon meeting in a long time. I am lacking what I need to replenish me.

Two days ago, I finished the LP Roadshow, a ten-day event versus the standard seven-day show. I made it through seventeen consecutive days of working twelve-hour days. I did not sell this show out as I had hoped for, but my sales were far better than average. The company was surprised that I was able to generate these sales figures being fresh out of training, and given the bad weather that kept many shoppers home for several days.

On a personal note, working so many weekends also meant that I wasn't able to attend church like I am accustomed to. On the last day of the show I felt hungry for a good sermon. I decided to attend Pastor Hannah's 7:30 a.m. service even though I knew I wouldn't be able to stay for the entire service. I am handed a church bulletin upon entering the sanctuary. I notice in the bulletin that the sermon topic is *Endurance*. Instantly, I know this is what God has been teaching me. The first scripture that Pastor Hannah uses in his sermon deals with Peter in the boat. I see this as no coincidence. I reflected on this same passage during the first week of the LP Roadshow when I escaped to the bathroom to have a short prayer.

Well, the LP Roadshow is over, and I'm trying to get back on track with my daily journaling. Yesterday was actually my first day off, but the only thing I reached for was my remote control. This morning, I am trying to connect the dots on what God is teaching me about *endurance*, and I have just turned to Chapters 8 and 9 in the *Book of Mark*.

After reading these two chapters, I am confident that God is teaching me, because some of the passages tie perfectly into my recent experiences. I ask God for three things: the strength to endure whatever is necessary for his name to be glorified, the grace to handle this part of my *walk* in a way that is pleasing to Him, and I also pray for understanding.

Reading Mark 8 prompts me to recall my lowest point while working the LP Roadshow.

LP Roadshow (Day 12 or 13)

On this particular day, the store was so empty the Chicago Blackhawks could have played hockey in there. Meanwhile, I am in the middle of the store demonstrating a $500 blender to the thin air. My mind begins to roam. First, since this is a commission-only job, my first thoughts are that lackluster sales will mean a lackluster paycheck. Next, I begin pining over the fate of our loan. There still has been no word from the bank on whether they will agree to our proposal. I move on from there thinking this is no way to monetize the hefty sum invested towards my education. The next level of spiraling leads to a question, "What kind of example am I setting for the boys?" My thoughts finally wander back to that morning in my kitchen when I heard the words "Call them," and I start wondering why, or if, God even directed me this way.

In Mark 8, Jesus is telling his disciples about his imminent suffering, but Peter, in essence, tells Jesus not to say this. Jesus responds, "…Get away from me, Satan! You are seeing things merely from a human point of view, not God's." (Mark 8:33 NLT)

This verse rings loud and clear to me. This is what's been going on with me lately. Whether I was grappling with the learning curve of a new job, juggling the other facets of my life outside of work, or just suffering from sheer exhaustion, I had stopped spending time with God. I was going unfed in a very important way. When I did this, I allowed the "human point of view" to creep in. The human perspective can be powerful in its own right. First, it will always factor in those things that we live our lives by, such as logic, fairness, what we've rightfully earned, etc. Second, the human perspective can easily permeate our thoughts, because we're so surrounded by it.

This is what happened to Peter when he began walking on water. As long as he remained focused on Christ, he was able to walk on water. The moment he began to process his experience from a human perspective, he began to lose his balance, and ultimately sink. I lost my way during the LP Roadshow, because I allowed other priorities to come before my time with the Lord.

Endurance means being able to stay focused on Christ (or the Word), and being able to block out all others, or at least to put it into the proper perspective. It also means having the ability to endure the test, or the suffering knowing there will be a shift, but in God's time.

My work has always been in this area. I have never had an issue with believing in God's power to deliver. My challenge sometimes comes with not knowing *when* He will deliver. Faith is not based on seeing and knowing the details in advance. Faith is based on standing on His promises even when it seems as though a promise doesn't exist. I am learning that being able to endure difficult times produces character in a person.

During the LP Roadshow, God sends me an unexpected message from an unexpected source. I didn't catch its relevancy until now. My friend Sheila, whom I have not spoken to in a while, but who used to email me Bible verses from her daily meditations, forwarded this one to me out of the blue: "More than that, we rejoice in our sufferings, knowing that suffering produces endurance, and endurance produces character, and character produces hope, and hope does not put us to shame, because God's love has been poured into our hearts through the Holy Spirit who has been given to us." (Rom. 5:3-5 ESV)

Having an *enduring* faith is being able to sustain a spiritual perspective for the duration. It means that you never let the human perspective trump God's Word. It is being able to walk on water without looking down. In Mark 9, a father brings his possessed son to Jesus for healing. Jesus asked his disciples to heal the child, but they couldn't. "Jesus said to them, 'You faithless people! How long must I be with you until you believe?'" (Mark 9:19 NLT) The father responds, "…I do believe, but help me not to doubt." (Mark 9:24) Believing is only the beginning. The real question becomes, "Can you keep the doubt out?" This is where a faithful person's work lies.

Coming Full Circle

Sometimes we become so inundated with life that we prioritize life over the Giver of Life. We allow that daily grind to come between us and our relationship with God. When things go awry, the human perspective dominates our thoughts. Because we're so accustomed to it, we lean on this surface level view for an in-depth understanding of matters. We allow what we see and hear in the natural world to govern our actions, and to inform our fate while we neglect to seek and understand God's purpose for our lives. We are not only in the natural world, we have also become *of* it.

When the turbulent winds of life blow our way, especially the ones we didn't see coming, we feel less prepared to deal with them, because our spiritual foundation is weak. Sometimes when the chaos and turbulence hit, we wish we could fly above it all, similar to how a pilot flies above the choppy air that is causing the turbulence. While our objective may be similar to the pilot's, our methods differ. The pilot will steadily climb to a higher altitude until he finds smoother air. Conversely, we will first need to go deeper before we can fly higher.

We will need to seek a deeper spiritual understanding of our *turbulence* before we can live above it. Going deeper insulates us from the flying debris (human perspective) thrown off by the turbulent winds. The apostle Paul and the prophet Jeremiah were masters at going deeper in order to go higher. Amidst all the chaos they knew how to go deeper spiritually to find that peace that transcends all understanding.

The first step in building spiritual depth is to incorporate God into your daily routine. For some, this may be reading and studying the Bible daily. For others, this may be daily prayer or meditation, or even keeping a daily gratitude journal. Whatever your path for worship, make it your daily practice. Avoid falling into a habit of daily rituals done out of duty, but instead, yearn to go to an even deeper place with Him. Buckle up, because you will go Higher than you ever imagined.

I will serve God patiently and indefinitely, and endure the test even when I don't have all the answers.

"Let us not become weary in doing good, for at the proper time we will reap a harvest if we do not give up."
(Gal. 6:9 NIV)

Chapter 39

Send Me

I'VE BEEN ON THE JOB for several months already, so I've become clearer about my likes and dislikes. I get along well with my colleagues, I still appreciate the flexibility in scheduling, and I still enjoy talking to customers about eating healthy. In hindsight, it is probably fairer to say that I have "pet peeves" about the job rather than dislikes. And, these pet peeves tend to be more customer-related.

My job is to demonstrate the blender in order to sell it. I demonstrate it by blending up a few different recipes such as smoothies, sorbets, and hot soups to better showcase the blender's full range of capabilities. Sometimes just as I begin to prepare a recipe (let's say it's a smoothie) a customer will approach the booth and begin fiddling with my display blender, and asking specific questions as if they are interested in purchasing a machine. However, no sooner than I begin pouring the smoothie into the sample cups, the customer grabs one or two samples and politely walks off. They were obviously more interested in what I was pouring out of the machine than in the machine itself. That's fine. What unnerves me is not that they weren't interested, but that they pretended to be.

The time I spend answering their fake questions could have been spent courting another customer.

My other pet peeve involves discourteous customers. In this scenario, I am talking to an interested group of customers when a passerby will rudely interrupt my presentation to ask me these three little words: "What's in it?" They are, of course, asking me what's in the last recipe that I prepared. This is a fair question given the various food allergies. For example, some customers prefer their smoothies not contain any dairy products. Before they drink my sample smoothie, they want to be sure it doesn't contain any dairy. My issue is not with the question; it is with how the customer rudely cuts into my presentation to ask the question. This matters to me, especially, when I am in the middle of making a sale.

Pet peeves aside, my sales have dropped over time, and so has my morale, especially at the end of a particularly disappointing Sunday performance. Mentally, I have checked out, and have begun to make my smoothies robotically. I am really more preoccupied with how I will explain to management that I underperformed at a prime Chicago retailer. Just when I think matters couldn't get any worse, I look up and see Ashley coming down the escalator.

Ashley has never bought into the idea of me selling blenders as a real job. While she recognizes it as a job to help me meet some short-term financial obligations, she really sees it more as an assignment that is preparing me for something greater.

Our eyes meet as she spots the booth on her ride down the escalator. I check the time and realize that I have about forty-five minutes before closing. I figure that I can make my voice smile for the next forty-five minutes, so she can get a firsthand look at how I conduct my demonstrations. After she stops by to greet me, we both agree to debrief over a bite to eat once I close the booth down—hence, the reason she came toward the end.

In no time, my sales demonstrations are in high gear once

again. As I'm demonstrating, I tune into myself on the PA system (sometimes I will tune out my repetitive sales pitch after talking for so many hours) and I like what I hear. I look up a few times to locate Ashley. I finally spot her toward the back, blended in among the other customers.

After blending my last recipe, I quickly shift into breaking-down-the-booth mode. As I store the produce and wipe down the counters, the possible explanations that I can offer management for such a drab roadshow begin to flood my brain. I think my real concern is that I will be asked to address why my sales for the last several roadshows have sunk below my normal sales average.

I have intimated to management that the reason for my low sales streak is due to the retailers' customer base. I meet customers all the time who love this blender, but who lack the disposable income to spend $500 on the spot. Instead, it has to be more of a planned purchase for them, thus they don't buy a blender from me during that current roadshow. However, the FW retailer is located in one of the most affluent neighborhoods in Chicago. The average female shopper in this store could afford to purchase this blender for herself and her girlfriend if she desired. This is why I am baffled as to why I didn't achieve higher sales.

The only other obvious factor in this equation is me. I am the reason for these sales, but it seems as though I am doing today what I have always done since I've been on the job. I would even argue that I am doing it better, because my skills would only improve over time.

I walk over to the food court in the store, and Ashley is already seated at a table. Now that I am no longer behind the booth, I am able to give her a hug, and to thank her again for coming. Before I sit down, she tells me that she has to leave sooner than she expected, so she won't be able to dine with me. I am hungry, but I am also eager to hear her thoughts.

"So what did you think?"

"I absolutely love that sorbet you make. You have to give me the recipe."

"I'm glad you like the sorbet. But what did you think about my demonstration?"

"Well."

I can't believe it. She seems very unimpressed with my show. Her comment catches me off guard, and I'm sure it's written all over my face.

"Ashley, I'm not sure what you were expecting."

She interrupts me.

"Okay, let me further explain. Your show wasn't bad. I was just expecting to see more from you."

Defensively, I respond, "I'm not sure what *more* you were expecting to see. I demonstrate a blender. I prepare four different recipes. I do this repeatedly for roughly ten consecutive hours. It is not easy standing on your feet for ten straight hours repeating the same sales pitch over and over, and still maintain good delivery."

"Suzette, I'm sure. I will give you that. Your delivery is very strong. That is definitely your strength. You sound great."

"So what didn't you like?"

"Even though your sales pitch was eloquent, it didn't pull me in. Your voice carries well over the microphone, but I didn't feel a connection to you."

I am still feeling somewhat defensive, and less willing to concede my own position. Next, I delve into my customer pet peeves with her. I explain how some customers insult my intelligence when they pretend to be interested in the blender only to get a sample, and how others will rudely interrupt my demonstration. I acknowledge that this may all sound petty to her but I make clear how challenging it is to tolerate all of this while enduring the long hours and the physical demands of this job. She listens attentively before she chimes back in, this time using a more sympathetic tone. "Suzette, I think you are forgetting something very important. This is less about a job, and more about an *assignment* for you. Today you are standing behind the booth selling blenders, and tomorrow you will be standing behind a booth selling *Blues to Blessings*. I can assure you that you will encounter the same type of people who will try to insult your intelligence, or who may rudely interrupt you when you're selling your book. The question is how will you treat them?"

In my head, I acquiesce to her point. When I look up to respond to her, she softly talks over me to finish making her points.

"Suzette, if your intention is to help someone and you sense they may be trying to fool you, you help them anyway. You could be wrong. You never know why they are in front of you. To give you an example, I know a pastor who had a recent encounter with this homeless family. He didn't know the family personally, but he felt an urge to let this family stay temporarily at the church's only vacant parsonage. When he met with the family, he detected a few inconsistencies in their story. Maybe there were moments when he felt like this family was attempting to insult his intelligence. However, he didn't let that stop him from fulfilling his original intention, which was to give a homeless family temporary housing."

This resonates with me, because I have always dismissed the person who tried to play me for a fool. I always feel a compelling desire to convey, albeit slyly, that any efforts to play me didn't work. Kindness is an act that I rarely consider during these times.

"Suzette, my thoughts are that you should make your shows less about your sales results, and more about your customers. I think you did this in the beginning, but you stopped somewhere along the way. Second, you may need to get out of your own comfort zone to reengage your customers. Use this booth as a training ground for your greater work. Get to the place where working the booth becomes *wax on, wax off* for you. Finally, please have some fun while you're up there. If you have to stand behind a booth for so many hours make it fun!"

Whew, this girl knows how to hit me in my gut! She is absolutely correct on all fronts. I have, in fact, placed more emphasis on my sales results than my customers. As passionate as I am about talking shop with customers on making healthy concoctions, I've nearly abandoned this aspect of my role. I do have a reservation about getting out of my comfort zone for the risk of looking silly. Finally, I am also guilty as charged from disengaging from customers who come off as discourteous to me.

As she makes her last statement to me, her purse straps are already on her shoulders. This works for me because she has to go, and I have to eat.

"Ashley, thanks so much for coming. As always, you've given me so much to noodle on here, but the only noodle I can think of right now is the one that I am about to put into my mouth."

She giggles a bit as we both hug and say our good-byes. I turn and walk in the opposite direction back towards the eatery within the food court where I have decided to place my order.

As I sit back down at the table devouring large quantities of food in single bites, my thoughts revert back to Ashley's insights. As usual, her comments are worth noting, especially one in particular. She reminded me of the conversation we had the day I told her that I took this job. We both believed that this job was less about becoming a pro at selling blenders, and more about God using this role to prepare me for something else. This is why we concluded that the job was simply an assignment. Becoming so caught up in the day-to-day workings of the job, I lost sight of the "assignment" part.

In fact, the more I think about it, this whole notion of being on assignment for the Lord is a big deal. One could argue that each day of our life is assigned by God. It's not that I disagree with that, but I do believe that God will put certain assignments on our path to either prepare or to test us. I think as much as God wants us to trust Him, he also wants to know that He can trust us.

One clear example for me is that I have truly made this assignment all about the number of machines I sell. While I recognize this is the way that I am compensated, it shouldn't consume me, yet it has. As passionate as I am about helping others to eat healthy, the number of machines I sell has even begun to trump that. The healthy eating aspect was the magnet that attracted me to the job in the first place.

First things first, I need to begin making my experience at the booth more about the customer. My colleague Maria exemplifies this. She is always armed with a wealth of information to benefit her customers. While I know the basics about the machine, I have never invested the additional time to learn more because I've always seen my role as temporary. That was the wrong way to look at things. If I sincerely believe that God has assigned me the job of standing behind a booth all day greeting hundreds of people to sell blenders (no matter how peculiar selling blenders at this stage in my career sounds), then I must give it my all. When you're on assignment for the Lord, you give it your all whether it's for one year or one hour.

My state of deep thought continues on my drive home. I often create analogies for myself to simplify things. This may sound silly but it works for me. Let's say that God created me to be a "helper" in this life. Thus, my life's purpose is to help others. Therefore, if someone crosses my path and their intention is to fool me into helping them, I shouldn't quickly dismiss them because their intentions seem bad. Instead, I should help them just the same. By using my energy to help this person instead of judging their intentions, I accomplish two things. First, I continue to fulfill my life's purpose. Second, my encounter with this person might encourage them to help someone else. Not only do I remain true to being a helper, but my life is bearing fruit when my actions inspire others to become helpers, too. To the contrary, if I dismiss the person upfront based on their initial actions, I forgo an opportunity to fulfill my *helper* role. I should never allow someone to adversely influence me away from who God has called me to be.

I have another FW Roadshow coming up in less than a week across town. I need to make some real changes to my show before then. In the words of my mother, "I need to get my act together."

It is the day before my second FW Roadshow, and it is a family affair. Webb and Jonathan have just finished setting up the booth. They must have my booth setup down to a science, because they did it in record time tonight. My mother and my mother-in-law Myrna are here to help me, too. Myrna is what I call the Queen Administrator. She is my go-to person for anything administrative. She records all inventory for me before the show starts to make tracking inventory easier during the show. My mother, on the other hand, is very particular about the booth's appearance. She dedicates her time to making the booth look picture-perfect. For her, the skirting for the tables must hang just right, the machines must be optimally displayed, and my fruits and veggies must be fresh and nicely situated in their baskets.

I stand back a few feet away from the booth admiring the final setup. I will rest well tonight knowing that everything is in order. I am especially grateful to my family, who all sacrificed a part of their evening to give me that peace of mind tonight. With everyone's help, the booth has been set up in sufficient time, allowing me to join the weekly sales conference call, which begins in about an hour.

I make it back home to dial into the sales call a moment or two before it starts. Most of the call is uneventful until the end. We typically close the call with a joke or a motivational quote. One of the sales representatives volunteers to close our call like this: "In memory of the late Maya Angelou (who died earlier that day). I would like to leave everyone with one of her quotes. 'I've learned that people will forget what you said, people will forget what you did, but people will never forget how you made them feel.'"

I am both impressed and moved as a few tears fill the corners of my eyes. I was not expecting the call to end this way. I will take it one step further. This quote will be the tenor of my next roadshow, which begins tomorrow. Rather than having the attitude of what I can get or how much money I can make, I will have the attitude of what I have to offer. This offer will be for everyone, and not just those who look like prospective customers. I hope that all who visit my booth will leave feeling just a little better.

There is a spiritual high that has come over me the last several weeks. It feels like my modus operandi has been rewired. I presume this is what it feels like when you finally get out of the way of yourself. You feel this way when you open your heart to others, and know that God is in control. I believe God is teaching me that working from my heart is a requirement if I am going to work for Him.

This shift in me started to happen during the second FW Roadshow. My central focus was to make anyone who approached my booth feel welcomed. My measure of success would be based on the number of positive interactions I had with people rather than the number of machines I sold. I started to feel a difference the first day after selling only one machine. I felt it more on the second day after employing the same approach, but selling only three machines. However, the third and fourth days of the show felt reminiscent of that Sunday during the LP Roadshow when I sold those sixteen machines. I had been trying for the longest time to find that same groove that I experienced that Sunday, but I could never find it. I found it during the second FW Roadshow. I ended up with a sold-out show, which was a first for me. I dismissed the end results, and just poured my heart into whatever I was doing, with a knowing that God would handle everything else.

I thanked God profusely at the end of the show for this shift, but it was almost as if I valued the shift in me more than I did the shift in my sales. I have grown so much in this role since Ashley came to observe my show, and it's only been a few weeks. I surely have grown in leaps and bounds since several years ago when I took that software sales position kicking and screaming. So, I guess this is what I am calling a spiritual high when I can marvel at the ways I have changed.

I felt this same way about Peter when I flipped to a passage in the Book of Acts last week. Peter says, "Aeneas, Jesus Christ heals you! Get up and make your bed! And he was healed instantly. Then the whole population of Lydda and Sharon turned to the Lord when they saw Aeneas walking around." (Acts 9:34-35 NLT) He continues, "…Get up, Tabitha. And she opened her eyes! When she saw Peter, she sat up!" (Acts 9:40 NLT) Tabitha had died. My initial reaction after reading these Bible verses was that Peter has really come a long way since his attempts to walk on water, and even his denial of Christ. While I am certainly not Peter, I will acknowledge that I have come a long way, too. God is teaching me and changing me each step of the way.

If ever I need to inspire myself, I reflect for a few moments on Peter's transformation. That's what I had to do at a roadshow last week when I relapsed. In this instance, I had just prepared a smoothie, and I was about to prepare a sorbet when this lady walked up and began touching and squeezing my produce. I can appreciate that the produce looks appetizing, but I had to politely ask her not to touch it.

Instantly, she called me a name. In a nanosecond, I fired back calling her the same name. I couldn't believe it. Everything happened so fast. My button was pushed, and in a heartbeat my goodwill went out of the window. Moments later I felt awful. I wanted to apologize to her. My response may have been characteristic of the woman I was twenty years ago, but it is does not reflect the woman I am today. But, the truth is that it did. We can all have moments of relapse. The key is to learn from those events and to be armed differently the next time around. Later that night, I asked for God's forgiveness, and I thanked Him for sending the lady my way. She taught me an excellent lesson on another way that I can dim my own light.

I think God receives glory when I learn from my experiences. Paul reminds us that even when we are weak we are strong. I especially had to learn an important lesson when it came to all of the uncertainty with a commission-based job. You can easily fall into the trap of "Will I sell enough?" and "Will I make enough money?" I have learned that it is when I can still have some of that fear ruminating in the background of my thoughts, and I can still offer a random act of kindness, or still make someone feel better when they leave my presence, and look radiant and not defeated while I'm doing it, I am being. This is my Butterfly moment. When I can do this enough times knowing that my Father has me, this is the *wax on, wax off.* Getting to that higher place where I am not focused on the reality of widgetselling or whatever my earthly experience may be at the time, but I am free to be because my Father tells me, "Look at the birds of the air, they do not sow or reap or store away in barns, and yet your heavenly Father feeds them. Are you not much more valuable than they?" (Matt. 6:26 NIV)

Coming Full Circle

Mary is an exemplary portrayal of what it means to be a faithful servant of the Lord. Notwithstanding all the uncertainty this young virgin must have felt about her future after the angel Gabriel told her that she would give birth to a son and she was to call him Jesus, her response is still a faithful one: "I am the Lord's servant. May your word to me be fulfilled." (Luke 1:38 NIV) Her true character is revealed in this moment. She loves God more than she loves herself. She prioritizes His call for service over serving her own ego, or image. This is why Mary remains in a class all her own when it comes to being a true servant of the Lord, but we can still learn from her actions.

Mary teaches us three key steps to being a faithful servant of the Lord. The first step is obedience. Sometimes being obedient will require us to desert our own plans of how we see our future unfolding, and to trust God's plans for our future. This is precisely what Mary did. She deserted her stronghold for tradition such as a festive wedding, marriage, and children, and she embraced the Lord's request for her service instead. Second, Mary used this situation to demonstrate her devotion to the Lord. Not only in that moment did she desert her own life's agenda, but she did it without hesitation or question. This second step is where many of us stumble. Sometimes we can force ourselves into obedience, but not with the best attitude. We are not of good cheer, because we don't have all the answers. Mary had instructions, but no answers, yet her attitude brought glory to God. Third, Mary served at the Lord's disposal. No matter how peculiar or foreign an assignment from God may seem, we will have to put aside our ego, trust Him and be willing to serve at His disposal. Mary served with her being. She was a vessel. Are you willing to serve at God's *disposal* today with a *devoted* heart even if it means that you have to *desert* your own plans and embrace His?

I will serve wherever God sends me,
and to whomever He sends me.

"But Jesus called them together and said, "You know that the rulers in this world lord it over their people, and officials flaunt their authority over those under them. But among you it will be different. Whoever wants to be a leader among you must be your servant, and whoever wants to be first among you must become your slave. For even the Son of Man came not to be served but to serve others and to give his life as a ransom for many."
(Matt. 20:25-28 NLT)

Chapter 40

8 Suzettes Ago

I LOOK AT A PICTURE OF MYSELF that was taken nearly twenty years ago. I am wearing both a dark suit and a pretty smile, although what I am drawn to most are my eyes in this photo. Depending on the occasion, I may have been using my smile as my armor, but my eyes can tell no lies. My eyes reveal a sense of fragileness, and even somberness. I put the picture aside but I can still feel the tears welling up, because the Suzette today feels somewhat accosted by the Suzette then. Recognizing that familiar pain in her eyes makes me want to weep for who this young woman was some twenty years ago. This time, I feel no shame for her, only compassion. I pick the picture up again and resist the urge to weep for her, and instead, choose to write to her.

My Dearest Suzette,

I have just come across a picture of you that must be at least twenty years old. You're wearing your signature Cover Girl smile, but the look in your eyes tells a different story. They seem riddled with pain and self-doubt. If my memory serves me, this is a period in your life where your questions outnumber your answers. Well, I'd like to pen a heartfelt letter to you, imparting those things that you'll need to become aware of, prepared for, some changes you'll need to make, and ultimately, how your relationship with God will continually evolve.

However, first, I'd like to give you some assurances. Your life has purpose even if what you're currently going through tells you otherwise. Second, while your journey will not be without its share of bumps, turns, and even foxholes, you will end up exactly where you are supposed to be.

At the time of this letter, you and Webb will have been married for nearly twenty years, and are still living in the same home that Webb believes God led him to more than ten years ago. More importantly, your three sons, Josh, Julian, and Jonathan II, are all thriving. Josh is a senior in college, and his dream to play soccer came true when he started as a freshman in the NCAA tournament. Julian is a junior majoring in physics and mechanical engineering, and is now a Dean's List student. Jonathan is a sophomore in high school, and an honor student while he plays varsity football and lacrosse.

Things work out on the business front too. One of your greatest fears is that your business, Light of Mine (LOM), which you named one night while on your knees at your tub, would have to close its doors due to a slowing economy. LOM remains open as you're on your way to celebrating your tenth year in business.

You should also know that you have a resiliency about yourself that enables you to rise stronger and wiser after each fall. In fact, your ability to transform your thoughts and actions reminds me of none other than the miracle that is the incomparable butterfly. Just as the butterfly has four phases to its life cycle, your life seems to have four phases too. It's like you must first become Aware in order for you to Transform, because you are ultimately being Prepared to Serve.

Finally, in order for you to appreciate and to be capable of tending to the territory you'll be given, you're going to have to undergo some changes. Here's what you will need to know.

First, here are some things that you will need to be aware about:

Your greatest work will involve those issues related to your self-worth. For as long as I can remember, you have always needed to be seen as someone good and worthy. You thought if you could overwhelm everyone with all of your goodness, chances are they wouldn't see what you considered as your damaged goods underneath. Your idea of being damaged goods is born out of the time when you were compromised as a young girl. You were compromised, and not knowing any better, you began to compromise yourself. Even though this mindset was set by a child, it would follow you long into your adult years.

Next, you have an innate desire to control. You will need to be conscious of this behavior and the false premise that it is predicated upon. As a child, you attempted to control the outcome of your abusive situation by trying to fix yourself. You took on such behaviors as being a people-pleaser, a perfectionist, and a high achiever to accomplish this. Of course, the fallacy is that you could never control the outcome of your situation by fixing you, because your situation was marred, not you. Gaining this core understanding is important to you shifting your core beliefs about your value.

Finally, you will need to become aware that your old wounds need healing.

Here are some things you will need to be prepared for.

First and foremost, don't worry about where the resources or wisdom will come from. God will send the right people to help you just at the right time. For instance, when you finally reach the point when you are ready to journey through life searching for its meaning with someone who doesn't profess to have all the answers either, but who is willing to take that *ride* too, God will send your husband, Webb. When you choose to take the first step toward healing your old wounds, God will send you Ann, who is a trained professional in healing and recovery work in those areas where you need it most. He will even send someone whose only job may be to teach you to seek His voice directly. Enter Ashley. She is the editor of your spiritual autobiography, and she will remind you that while it's good to have confidants, there is no greater confidant than God Himself.

You should prepare yourself that your definition of success will continue to evolve. Your *modus operandi* most of your adult life is to become a success. This is a must for you, because you are on a mission to prove to all the naysayers who didn't believe in you that you would make something of yourself. Your mind has always been wired to think in this order: you must first *do it* in order to *make it*, so that you can finally *be it*. Over the next few years, you will experience firsthand that you're already *it*. You are a child of the Living God, and there is no higher *it* factor than that, but during the time when you are experiencing angst about your life's accomplishments or lack thereof, you have little appreciation for this truth.

Here are some ways that you will need to change.

Your first order of business will be to adopt the mindset that God sees you as the greater good. Initially, you will feel conflicted about this truth. In one respect, your mind associates achievement with something that is earned. Thus, one doesn't just end up being seen as the greater good by God, or obtain the privilege to rest in His good graces without earning the right to be there. In another respect, you accept the Christian belief that the price has already been paid for you (with the Resurrection of Christ), but you struggle with its practical application to your everyday life. Theoretically, you accept this Truth, but you find it difficult to walk in It.

Next, you will need to recognize that *adult* Suzette has choices. As a child you reasoned that serving the greater good meant suffering in silence, so you always felt trapped between acting on behalf of the greater good of others while neglecting the innermost desires of Suzette. You also fear that if you no longer act on behalf of the greater good, the greater good will end up in great disarray. You will need to learn how to love and honor certain relationships without dishonoring yourself, and how to detach with love from others.

You will need to accept that the prerequisite to changing one's behavior begins with making different choices. For real transformation to occur, your new *"ah-ha"* moments must translate into new action. In the beginning, changing certain behaviors will seem easier said than done. The most difficult behaviors to change will be the ones that feel like second nature to you, such as perfectionism and people-pleasing, or those you have grown to depend on like using alcohol and food to self-medicate.

You will need to embrace and trust your life's process more. Transformation does not occur overnight. You will have many failed attempts at trying to take on new behaviors while trying to release old ones. Sometimes it will feel like you are realizing tangible benefits from your efforts, and other times it will feel like your efforts are all in vain. At times, you will pout, cry, and dread it all, even to the point where you will want to abandon some processes altogether, such as the healing process. You will be encouraged at each turn, showing you that as messy as the work becomes it is all a part of the process, so begin to trust it. This is when your sense of resiliency will benefit you greatly.

Finally, your interaction with God will change. As you desire a more intimate relationship with Him during some difficult periods, you will seek Him beyond your church-going Sundays.

Here is how service will lead to your success.

You will first make the conscious choice to serve one God. It will become evident to you that that you cannot claim to do something for God on your terms. Your eyes will begin to open to the fact that serving your personal ambitions can be like serving another God. When you finally release the grip on your ambitions, God reveals to you that your life's purpose is so much greater than you could have ever imagined.

As you continue to seek God's purpose for your life, you begin to read and eventually study the Bible once you get beyond the stereotypes you associate with it. I believe this is when a gradual but steady shift begins to take place within you.

When I contemplate the woman you have become by this point, and I contrast her against the woman in the photo, it seems as though this photo was taken some eight Suzettes ago. Your mind and spirit are continually being renewed. For instance, you no longer feel a desire to search for inner peace in a great glass of wine. You now go directly to the Winemaker.

That said, just because you have identified the only Source for true peace, this is not to imply that your life will always be peaceful. The storms of life will continue to rage on in all sizes and degrees of intensity. Some storms you will be able to anticipate, and thus escape. Others will come with the sole purpose to teach, strengthen, and to prepare you for the ones that are inescapable, and will require you to meet them eye-to-eye.

You have learned from firsthand experience that an enduring faith is what's needed to endure life's most difficult storms. This is when you can practice a peace and stillness within, and know that God is God in spite of the raging storm going on around you.

All that said, you are not perfect, so knowing better doesn't always lead to you doing better. Sometimes, doubt will creep in and your faith will struggle to endure. On occasion, you will allow life itself to come between you and God. Be encouraged and take great comfort, because where your faith doesn't endure, His Love for you always will.

Experiencing the Greatest Love firsthand inspires you to shift your priorities yet again. As a young woman your idea of what it meant to "make it" in life was always synonymous with reaching some material height like earning a degree, bearing a title, or realizing financial gains. As you grew older your idea of "making it" expands to incorporate the concept of prosperity. You will define prosperous living as being in good health, fulfilling your life's purpose, and having good wealth.

Prosperity becomes your new pinnacle.

However, once you begin reading and studying the Word, this definition no longer settles with you either because it still feels like something is missing, or is at least out of order.

Your notion of success has always been centered on the gift. You could finally rest or be content once you achieved the end goal, or obtained the gift. You are learning that true prosperity and contentment can only be found in the Gift Giver, not the gifts. Therefore, your definition of what it means to ultimately make it in this life is being able to appreciate whatever blessings God showers your way, while also being able to dwell in the presence of God and be content and fulfilled there, even when there are no gifts...when there is only your *daily bread* to give thanks for. This epitomizes prosperous living.

Your greatest revelation about your life's meaning will be when you understand that your divine purpose in this life is less about serving you and more about bringing glory to God by being of service to others. Your Heavenly Father is glorified not only when your ways are transformed, but when your life is a walking testament and inspiration for others to transform. This is likely why He has always been more interested in changing you more than your circumstances. Learning all of this gives you the courage to tell your story exactly as it is, ugly parts and all. Your understanding of what it means to serve the greater good goes to another level.

One day while you're doing your morning reading, you will flip to the passage about Peter healing the lame man at the Beautiful Gate. You've read this passage several times before, and have always identified more with Peter than the lame man. However, this particular morning you identify more with the lame man. This man has been begging outside the Beautiful Gate for many years of his life. For the first time, you see yourself in the lame man. You, too, in a sense have been begging your Heavenly Father to let your life have meaning, so that you can become a success. On the day he begs Peter for alms, Peter chooses to heal him instead. Not only is the lame man healed, but so many other lives are touched by his healing.

You have been broken, shattered, tired, and worn. You have needed healing and God has been just to give you exactly what you needed when you needed it. Success for you becomes a natural byproduct of God's hand on your soul. The story and testimony that you will live to tell, that God has provided, is not your own, but has been at work since your birth to heal the lives of those you may never meet. Your story—your life—is a beacon of God's glory. That is success.

Love & Light,
Suzette

I will serve through my sacrifice,
and not through the compromising of who
God has created me to be.

"You didn't choose me. I chose you. I appointed you to go and produce fruit that will last, so that the Father will give you whatever you ask for, using my name."
(John 15:16 NLT)

Endnotes

Chapter 36. Be Still and Know that I am God

Mote, Edward, *My Hope is Built on Nothing Less* (Recorded by Bradbury, W. B.). On *The golden censer: a musical offering to the Sabbath schools, of Children's hosannas to the Son of David*. New York, NY: W.B. Bradbury, 1864.

Chapter 39. Send Me

Maya Angelou, BrainyQuote.com. Retrieved Nov. 17, 2014, from Brainy Quote.com Web site: http://www.brainyquote.com/quotes/authors/m/maya_angelou.html

Bibliography

"The Butterfly Life Cycle." Thebutterflysite.com, September 10, 2009.

English Standard Version. Biblegateway.com, 1993

"Life Cycle of a Butterfly." Indianchild.com, September 6, 2009.

Wilkinson, Bruce H., ed. *The Daily Walk Bible: With 365 Devotional Helps to Guide You Through the Bible in One Year.* Atlanta: Walk Thru the Bible Ministries, Inc., 1997.

About the Author

Suzette Webb lives in Chicago with her husband and children. She is also the author of *Moments of Truth* and CEO of The LOM Group. However, at her core she sees herself as a product of God's grace and a woman who desires for God to receive the glory for her life's story. Visit her at www.bluestoblessings.com.

Order More Copies of
Blues to Blessings

To ORDER ADDITIONAL COPIES OF *BLUES TO BLESSINGS* at bulk prices (ten copies or more), please contact The LOM Group with the following information. We'll respond to you promptly.

- *Name*
- *Address*
- *Phone Number*
- *Fax (if applicable)*
- *Email address*

- *Quantity Required*
- *Shipping Address (if different)*

Payment can be accepted by check or credit card.

THE LOM GROUP, LLC
401 N. Michigan Avenue
Suite 1200
Chicago, IL 60611

customerservice@thelomgroup.com

312.276.4972 FAX